OUR DIVERSE SOCIETY

RACE AND ETHNICITY— IMPLICATIONS FOR 21ST CENTURY AMERICAN SOCIETY

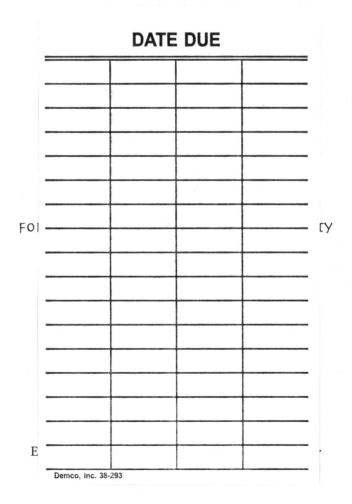

DATE DUE

FOI ʀʏ

E

Demco, Inc. 38-293

Cheryl Y. Bradley, *Publisher*
Schandale Kornegay, *Manager, Publications*
Marcia D. Roman, *Managing Editor, Journals and Books*
Brooke Graves, Marcia D. Roman, *Copy Editors*
Rebecca Tippets, *Proofreader*
Bernice Eisen, *Indexer*

Interior design by Bill Cathey, NASW Press, Washington, DC
Cover design by Britt Engen, Metadog Design, Washington, DC
Printed by Port City Press, Baltimore, MD

Library of Congress Cataloging-in-Publication Data
Our diverse society: race and ethnicity—implications for 21st century American society/David W. Engstrom, Lissette M. Piedra, editors—2nd ed.

    p.cm.
    Includes index.
    ISBN 13: 978-0-87101-372-9
    ISBN 10: 0-87101-372-X (alk.paper)
    1. United States—social conditions—1980– 2. United States—Race relations. 3. United States—Ethnic relations. 4. Pluralism (Social sciences)—United States. I. Engstrom, David Wells, 1958– II. Piedra, Lissette M. III. NASW Press.

HN59.2.O97 2006
305.800973'09051—dc22   2006019361

DEDICATION

Our Diverse Society

is dedicated to

Pastora San Juan Cafferty.

CONTENTS

FOREWORD

Pastora San Juan Cafferty

Our Diverse Society is the result of a group of scholars coming together to analyze issues raised by the role that race, ethnicity, and class play in American society at the beginning of the 21st century, as well as the questions that these three factors raise about poverty and inequality in an increasingly prosperous but divided country. The book does so in the context of identifying and discussing public policy issues and their implications for social policy and social work practice.

Thirty years ago, a small study group was created at the School of Social Service Administration at the University of Chicago to attempt to come to terms with race and ethnicity as a social phenomenon, and to understand the implication of that phenomenon for the teaching and practice of social work. The papers presented in those meetings were eventually edited into a volume: *The Diverse Society: Implications for Social Policy*, which I edited with Leon Chestang and was published by NASW in 1976. Similarly, chapters edited for this book by David Engstrom and Lissette Piedra were first presented in a symposium, "Race and Ethnicity in American Life: Diversity and Society," held at the School of Social Service Administration at the University of Chicago in the spring of 2005.

Much has changed in the past three decades. Thirty years ago, we were all reading Ellison's *Invisible Man* (1947), discussing Nathan Glazer's and Pat Moynihan's *Beyond the Melting Pot* (1963), and debating the merits of Michael Novak's *Unmeltable Ethnics* (1972). Joseph Fitzgerald, the wonderful Jesuit sociologist who joined our group, was writing about the Puerto Ricans—"the newcomers" who a worried Oscar Handlin believed would never become Americans (1971); never mind that they were, in fact, American citizens. It was a time, following the heady 1960s, a time of celebrating racial pride and ethnic differences. The 1965 amendments to the immigration laws had repudiated racial and ethnic preferences as racist and exclusionary. It was a time in which scholars argued that to be considered American, immigrants need not shed their culture and that cultural pluralism was the complex reality of the immigrant experience. We had not yet learned to fear the racial and ethnic diversity brought about by the new migration that was to ensue.

Today, we are in an era of renewed—and I would say dangerous—nativism in the United States. Scholars as well as politicians voice an apparently widespread fear that "our Anglo-Protestant culture" is threatened. These fears echo the concerns expressed by the Dillingham Commission (1909–1910), a blue-ribbon commission established to recommend immigration reform, that the "new immigrants" (at that time, the Poles and the Italians) could not assimilate into American society and thus would change all we value about the nation forever.[1] Today, of course, it is the assimilated Poles and Italians, along with the rest of us, who worry that the "new immigrants"—the Mexicans, the Iraqis, the Thais, the Sudanese—cannot become American. Editorials in newspapers and the ubiquitous talk-show hosts on 24-hour cable channels voice fears that resonate with many Americans.

The blatant racism of the Dillingham Commission is not acceptable today. However, fear of, distrust of, and antipathy toward those who are "not like us" echo loudly throughout U.S. history. Our present-day fear that newcomers will change American culture and the complexion of American society are remarkably congruent with the perceived threat to the nation expressed by those learned and august individuals who sat on the Dillingham Commission, and of the scholars who documented their prejudices.

The fear of newcomers is, then, a leitmotif in the history of this nation: a nation of immigrants that not only welcomed, but often recruited, immigrants yet always feared the change each successive migration would bring to American society. It seems to me, however, that in the years at the turn of each of the centuries since the British colonies became an American nation, we have experienced pronounced nativism. It may be a coincidence, or it may be that new centuries, which call for national introspection, bring to the surface a national anxiety about who we are as a people. Certainly the events at the beginning of this 21st century have brought about great anxiety.

This fear of newcomers has been shared by such distinguished Americans as Henry Adams and Frederick Jackson Turner. Thomas Jefferson, in his *Notes on the State of Virginia* (1952), worried that immigrants from nations governed by absolute monarchs would "bring with them the principles of government they leave" and "transmit these principles, with their language . . . to their children." As the government then being established by the new nation was unique in the political experience of the day, Jefferson was, in fact, describing all newcomers, although one must conclude that those who spoke English somehow would better understand the democratic principles of the Enlightenment. This fear of those "who came after" by those "who came before" resonates from the earliest days of the settlers. Those who came to establish freedom of religion for themselves seldom wanted to grant it to others. This may be inevitable in a nation of successive waves of newcomers. Those who came established themselves and their society at great cost; they were not about to let those who came after threaten their way of life.

However, they let them come; in fact, they recruited immigrants. Crevecoeur, in his *Letters of an American Farmer* (1997), asked a particularly salient question: "What is an American?" His answer was neither a political document nor a patriotic tract defining an American: It was written to recruit new immigrants from Europe. The new nation needed workers to build roads and dig canals; later to lay railroad tracks, mine coal, smelt iron, and forge steel; and then, much later, to build automobiles and airplanes.

If we were reluctant to admit new immigrants, we nevertheless eventually welcomed them as fellow citizens. The Founding Fathers defined citizenship in the sense of the Enlightenment, in that no one was to be denied—with the shameful exclusions of African slaves (a compromise to appease the South and satisfy the economic needs of the North that would return to haunt the new nation) and American Indians, whose lands were being taken to satisfy the thirst for land of the "settlers" and those who followed. The writings of the Founding Fathers and early naturalization laws made clear that citizenship would be granted to those committed to the political principles in the Declaration of Independence and the Constitution.

In principle, it was clear: Anyone who pledged allegiance to the principles in the Declaration of Independence and the Constitution could become an American. In practice, there were exclusions. Africans and their descendants and American Indians were not given an opportunity to become citizens, nor were women allowed to establish citizenship except through their husbands. Asians were admitted and then they were excluded. Eastern and Southern Europeans came by the millions until they too were deemed "inferior" and a "danger to the republic," and largely excluded based on the quota system recommended by the Dillingham Commission. Those who were admitted and could become citizens without giving up their language and culture nevertheless largely did so: names were changed, accents hidden, and cultural pasts mostly forgotten. It was the price to be paid to be considered an American, to have full participation in this promised land. Today, America is more restrictive in granting citizenship: Literacy is required, as is knowledge of United States history and political institutions for all but the very young and the very old.

At the turn of the 21st century, there are calls for a recommitment to a primarily Christian country as well as to Anglo-Protestant values—a focus on religion that mirrors the religious revivals at the turn of the last century. There are fears that Americans will not continue to speak English and maintain the country's European cultural heritage. Some express a yearning to return to an America with a homogeneous identity, as eulogized in patriotic tracts and the Thomas Nast cartoons of the Gilded Age. The new nativism expresses fear of a loss of English as the American language, of the realities and myths that define American culture, and of society defined by the Christianity brought by early settlers.

Certainly, the common historical past is important in the definition of a nation, as is the mythology that arises when a national identity is formed. Such common bonds forge national pride, important to creating common goals and values in a society where such common values make for a strong political and (one could argue) economic identity. One can argue that English became the language that made it possible for successive generations of immigrants to participate in the national dialogue that has defined and redefined the nation. Although the first Congress debated the wisdom of a "bilingual nation" and of conducting official business in English and French, English became the common language, the lingua franca, of commerce and increasingly of science and politics throughout the world, not because of an ideology but because of economics. Although Benjamin Franklin and, later, William McKinley, fretted that democratic principles were best stated and understood in English, it was economics rather than ideology or politics that made English preeminent. It has been and it continues to be the language of the American nation. Present-day immigrants, by the second generation, are overwhelmingly English-language dominant; many are English-monolingual in a nation where foreign languages are valued only when taught as a second language to native English speakers. Like the other immigrants and settlers who preceded them, today's immigrants lose their languages and their customs in order to become American.

The fact is that this land was never homogeneous and Americans were never all "Anglo-Protestant." When the first census was taken in 1790, those of African descent outnumbered those of British descent. Even in those original 13 states that hugged the eastern seaboard, though the English language was dominant, different cultures were coming together to define the new nation. And while the English, Germans, and Dutch were "settling" the East Coast, the Spanish were settling the South and the West, all territory that was to become the United States.

However, the past 30 years have seen dramatic increases in the heterogeneity that is these United States. This diversity resulted from the 1965 Immigration Act, the effects of which were becoming readily apparent by the 1980 Census. The demographic changes occasioned by the immigration resulting from the 1965 amendments (and subsequent immigration reforms) have been augmented by a global migration, reflecting the will of those living in impoverished and often war-torn nations to go to safer, more developed countries to find work and security for themselves and their families. The 2000 Census showed that the non-Hispanic white population has grown older: Hispanics, African Americans, and Asian and Pacific Islanders make up 40 percent of the 18.6 million children under five years of age in the country. Those children are now in our public schools and are being joined by others whose parents continue to come to what is seen as a land of opportunity.

All these demographic changes are taking place while issues of race and color continue to plague U.S. society. Poverty, overcrowding of schools, the inaccessibility of health care, an ever-growing demand for highly skilled and educated workers; growing religious diversity, and questions of language loyalty must be addressed in the context of an increasingly diverse nation. The historic definition of race as Black or White is challenged not only by a growing multiracial population, but also by those who come from countries where race and class have definitions differing from those that have traditionally ordered U.S. society.

The fact is that America has once again dramatically become a nation of immigrants. One in 10 Americans is an immigrant: one-half of these are Hispanic and one-fourth Asian American. Questions of national allegiance and of inclusion loom large at the beginning of the 21st century. In the 20th century, religious inclusion led to a definition of this country as a "Judeo-Christian" nation, but that inclusion is being tested by the unprecedented growth in those identifying as Buddhist, Muslim, and Hindu.

These changing demographics—the unprecedented diversity of the population—is the leitmotif that runs through any discussion of American society in the 21st century. Those who would create social policies that result in a better society for all must understand and address questions raised by race, ethnicity, and poverty: characteristics that continue to be aligned in any serious discussion of social policy and social work practice.

END NOTE

1. The complete Dillingham Commission reports may be found at http://library.stanford.edu/depts/dlp/ebrary/dillingham/body.shtml

REFERENCES

Cafferty, P. S. J., & Chestang, L. (1976). *The diverse society: Implications for social policy.* Washington, DC: NASW.

Crevecoeur, J. H. St. John de. (1997). *Letters from an American farmer.* New York: Oxford University Press.

Ellison, R. W. (1947). *Invisible man.* New York: Random House.

Glazer, N., & Moynihan, D. P. (1963*). Beyond the melting pot: The Negroes, Puerto Ricans, Jews, Italians, and Irish of New York City.* Cambridge, MA: MIT Press.

Handlin, O. (1971). *The newcomer: Negroes and Puerto Ricans in a changing metropolis.* Cambridge, MA: Harvard University Press.

Jefferson, T. (1952). *Notes on the State of Virginia.* Chapel Hill, NC: University of North Carolina Press. (Original work published 1743–1826)

Novak, M. (1972). *The rise of the unmeltable ethnics.* New Brunswick, NJ: Transaction Press.

PREFACE

David W. Engstrom and Lissette M. Piedra

Global immigration and unprecedented levels of intermarriage between groups are transforming the United States. Historically a multiethnic and multiracial country, the United States is increasingly becoming even more so as a consequence of population shifts set in motion in the 1960s through social movements and landmark legislation, most notably the civil rights movement and the 1965 Immigration Act. In 1976, when Cafferty and Chestang edited *The Diverse Society,* the implications of these powerful demographic changes and their effect on the structure and culture of our society were only beginning to emerge.

Now, 30 years later, the increasing diversity of the United States is readily apparent, although we are still grappling with its meaning and implications. Perhaps the best way to summarize the growing diversity is how we measure race. In 1976, the Census Bureau classified race by three categories: "white," "black," and "other." Three decades later, the Census Bureau has expanded its racial categorizations to include American Indian and Alaska Native, Asian, and Native Hawaiian and other Pacific Islanders; also, for the first time, it allows people to identify themselves as biracial. Further, the Census Bureau added an ethnic identifier, "Hispanic," to measure the demographic consequences of large-scale immigration from Latin America.

Since 1976 approximately 70 million people have been added to the U.S. population. Much of the population increase has resulted from immigration from Asia and Latin America and from the higher fertility rates of immigrant parents. The racial and ethnic diversity that now characterizes the United States is abundantly visible both in the country's large metropolitan areas and in many of its smallest towns. It is literally reshaping our country, and several examples illustrate that fact. In two of the most populous states, California and Texas, the white population is no longer the majority. For the first time since the founding of the United States, the black population no longer constitutes the country's largest minority group, having been overtaken by Hispanics in 2001.

Our Diverse Society builds on the foundation laid by Cafferty, Chestang, and their colleagues. Like *The Diverse Society*, this volume frequently uses historical analysis in an attempt to understand the context of diversity, and it uses an interdisciplinary approach to investigate the complexity of racial and ethnic diversity in the United States. Unlike *The Diverse Society*, which had to argue for the inclusion of ethnicity in the analysis of social problems and policy, this volume takes that point as a given; that debate has been settled. Instead, debate now centers on the implications of diversity, how diversity shapes and is shaped by social institutions, and what role social policy plays in enhancing or restricting diversity.

ABOUT THIS BOOK

This book, a long-overdue follow-up to the original *Diverse Society*, was conceived of as a culmination of scholarly work presented at a symposium, "Race and Ethnicity in American Life: Diversity and Society," held at the School of Social Service Administration at the University of Chicago in April 2005. The symposium was organized to honor the scholarly legacy of Pastora San Juan Cafferty upon her retirement from the University of Chicago, and to offer a fresh look at the implications and effects of racial and ethnic diversity in the United States.

Our Diverse Society is the product of scholars from a range of disciplines and professions, who examine how diversity shapes contemporary U.S. society and how social institutions have responded to the diverse demography that is the United States. Specifically, Our Diverse Society explores how race, ethnicity, and social class interact with social institutions and communities in ways that influence the ability of individuals and families to enjoy basic freedoms: the right to adequate education, health care, social services, employment opportunities, and equal protection and treatment under the law. The nature of these institutional interactions affects people's capacity to harness their sense of agency, pursue their ideals, and constructively participate in society.

Racial and ethnic diversity has always been a source of creativity and strength, but it has also been a catalyst for significant social unrest and conflict. Consequently, it is of utmost importance to understand the role that diversity plays in how social problems are constructed. Understanding diversity as critical in the analysis of social problems promotes effective social action and advocacy. Faulty conceptualization of diversity results in poor public policy and misdirected advocacy efforts. To this end, we have set aside all celebrations of racial and ethnic diversity to focus instead on how diversity is being structured and reflected in communities and institutions. Placing a value on American heterogeneity precludes critical examination of how that heterogeneity is structured, promotes particular agendas, and ultimately obfuscates issues that give rise to social tensions.

Our Diverse Society presents a synthesis of what is known and the implications of that current knowledge. Each chapter provides an analytical treatment of factual information and raises new questions about the creation and implementation of social policy in a diverse society. As important as the facts may be, we believe it is the questions raised by these analyses that are important; the answers will change over time.

Each chapter is strong in narrative. Because this material is intended to be "user-friendly" for public policymakers, social workers, and students, the chapters not only discuss things as they are, but also raise issues for the rest of the 21st century. Whenever possible, the scholar-authors have situated their discussions of current and projected issues in a historical context, as well as in the contemporary social and political context of the United States. Taken together, the chapters in this book lay the foundation for a comprehensive understanding of how ethnic and racial diversity is affected by U.S. social institutions and communities and the transformational influence racial and ethnic groups have on those same institutions and communities.

The book is organized into four parts, the first of which, "America's Changing Landscape," explores demographic change and analyzes how diversity creates tensions and potential conflicts that policy must address. In his provocative introductory essay, "Why Can't They Be More Like Us?," Father Andrew Greeley argues that ethnic diversity is an asset, and reminds us that public demand for quick assimilation falsely assumes that to be an "American" requires a shedding of one's original culture. In short, he declares, people have the right to be different. Theresa Sullivan, a labor-force demographer, discusses how strongly demographic trends affect the demand for social services. Her analysis uses public education and Social Security to explore the issues of intergenerational and interethnic justice. The impact of immigration is explored by David Engstrom, who contends that the outsider status of immigrants is reinforced by exclusionary policy and that such policy is counterproductive to the goal of incorporating newcomers. In "Beyond the Rainbow: Multiraciality in the 21st Century," Gina Miranda Samuels examines the implications of multiracial identity, challenging notions of monoracial loyalties and identity. While recognizing that multiracial and multiethnic populations are not new, Samuels posits that the way some people experience their mixed-race heritage—as a result of identity options made available by contemporary society—is a departure from the racial essentialism, racism, and more recently colorblind individualism that typically have framed contemporary discussions of multiraciality. Samuels argues that this recent development of multiracial identity formation and empowerment challenges social work practice to abandon essentialist and decontextualized frameworks of human development.

The second part of the book, "Conduits of Values and Beliefs," explores how language, religion, and education transmit and transform cultural beliefs. The transmission of values and beliefs through social institutions affects individuals' ability to navigate life in a heterogeneous society. Lissette Piedra notes that the United States has always been a multilingual society; she highlights the fact that the incorporation of non-English-speaking immigrants poses institutional challenges, but argues that these are the realities of a sizeable group making a linguistic transition, rather than a threat to the predominance of English. Religious historian Charles Lippy argues that religious expression in America historically has been pluralistic, not one-dimensional as is often asserted. However, religious pluralism is being expanded further by immigrants, many of whom are non-Christian. These immigrants bring new religious beliefs and traditions, which they are adapting as necessary. Moreover, in the course of transporting religious beliefs, immigrants are also changing older religious traditions.

Perhaps no institution is more important for the transmission of social values than public education. Nora Ishibashi and Noriko Ishibashi Martinez trace how public education has responded to racial and ethnic diversity, often in an exclusionary and oppressive manner. They submit that we are not bound to that history, but can, instead, create public schools that unify differences instead of fostering conflict and separation.

The third part of the book, "Access to Institutions in a Diverse Society," addresses how diversity is structured in American institutions: the workplace, the political system, and the criminal justice system. Institutions directly affect individuals' quality of life by signaling social inclusion or exclusion. The intersection of race, ethnicity, and social class is most disturbing when it results in systematic institutional inequalities. The issue of inequality in the labor market is examined by Anna Haley-Lock and Sarah Bruch, whose approach moves us beyond documenting over- or underrepresentation of certain racial or ethnic groups in specific occupations. Instead, they focus on how workplace benefits such as health insurance and child care shape the lives of workers and, because those benefits are not available to all, result in inequality. Damian Martinez extends the analysis of race, ethnicity, and imprisonment to understand disproportionate incarceration; he argues that socioeconomic inequality is the central problem confronting the criminal justice system. He points out that incarceration most directly affects low-income minority families and communities, often worsening the social ills that are associated with crime in the first place. In "Democracy and Diversity: Expanding Notions of Citizenship," Maria de los Angeles Torres aptly observes that authoritarian societies are associated with monoculture, whereas democratic societies tolerate degrees of cultural differences. Reviewing U.S. political history, she shows that although the universal right to participate politically in government has been the cause of conflict and sometimes violence, the political franchise has been extended. According to de los Angeles Torres, the issues now before us are how to incorporate immigrants into our political community and how to respond politically to the often conflicting interests of racial and ethnic groups.

The final section of *Our Diverse Society* examines the role of health care and social services, two institutions that play a critical role in shaping what people are able to do and able to be. These institutions, perhaps more than any other, address the stark disparities between the wealthy and the poor and struggle to assist those with different cultures and capacities. Edward Lawlor advances a "nondisparities" approach to understanding and addressing health disparities. Although current approaches to health disparities lead to disease-specific and group-specific interventions, Lawlor argues that organizing research, policymaking, and intervention by community, without an initial disease or group focus, could yield more productive approaches to addressing the underlying conditions that give rise to health disparities. Katherine Tyson focuses on the features of practice models that can help social workers enhance their clients' power and dignity, so that the client-worker partnership can be more responsive to an increasingly diverse client population confronted by continuing injustices.

ACKNOWLEDGMENTS

Both the symposium and *Our Diverse Society* were made possible by the strong endorsement and financial commitment of two deans at the School of Social Service Administration (SSA), Edward Lawlor and Jeanne Marsh. We offer them our heartfelt thanks. We wish to thank Loring Jones of San Diego State University; Christopher Larrison of the University of Illinois, Urbana-Champaign; and Rose Perez and Harold Richman of the University of Chicago for their insightful comments on the draft chapters and for serving as moderators of the symposium. In addition, we acknowledge and thank Dolores Norton of the University of Chicago for her steadfast support of our project. The administrators and staff at the SSA played an instrumental role in the early stages of editing the book and in the organization of the symposium. Keith Madderom, Mary Jane Keitel, Tanya Hines, and Betty Bradley deserve special recognition.

A number of friends and colleagues offered support and guidance throughout the process of editing this book. David W. Engstrom thanks Anna Walton, Daniel Finnegan, Amy Okamura, Concepcion Barrio, Alvin O. Korte, and Katie McDonough. Lissette M. Piedra thanks Wynne Korr, Susan Cole, and Sachiko Bamba.

The copyediting skill of Brooke Graves greatly improved *Our Diverse Society* and we are grateful to work with her. We also wish to acknowledge the staff at NASW Press, especially Marcia Roman, Paula Delo, Shandale Kornegay, and Cheryl Y. Bradley, for their efforts that made this book a reality.

Finally, we acknowledge Pastora San Juan Cafferty, whose teaching, scholarship, mentorship, and friendship have greatly influenced our lives. This book is a reflection of what she has taught us: that American diversity is complex and deserves to be studied within its context. We are grateful to be part of such a legacy.

PART 1

AMERICA'S CHANGING

LANDSCAPE

CHAPTER 1

INTRODUCTORY ESSAY: "WHY CAN'T THEY BE MORE LIKE US?"

Andrew M. Greeley

In 2006 one does not have to argue, as one did a quarter-century ago, that ethnicity is an important dimension of American life. However, one still has to argue that ethnic diversity is an asset rather than a liability.

The United States, in an almost absent-minded interlude, decided to let in far more immigrants, both legal and illegal, and became once again a nation of immigrants. Indeed, there are more immigrants now than at the time of the Dillingham Commission and passage of the first restrictive immigration laws (though the immigrants are a smaller proportion of the population). Although there is much unhappiness in the country about the new waves of immigrants, so far no massive demand to introduce more restrictive laws has emerged.

Consider three streets: Atlantic Avenue in Brooklyn (New York), Central Avenue in Los Angeles, and Devon (da-VON in Chicago-speak) in Chicago. More ethnic groups live on these three streets than on almost any street in America in the first decade of the 20th century—representatives, it often seems, of every nation under heaven: Koreans, Filipinos, Chinese, Vietnamese, Cambodians, Thais, Indians, Pakistanis, Bengalis, Lebanese, Palestinians, Israelis (of various religious types), Mexicans, Colombians, Haitians, Dominicans, Syrians, Greeks, Arabs, Sri Lankans, Russians, Georgians, Turks, Nigerians, Ukrainians, Poles, Lithuanians, Brazilians, Assyrians, Cubans, Kurds, Mayan-speaking highlanders from Guatemala, and even a few Irish illegals. Add to the mix Puerto Ricans and various kinds of Native Americans and Appalachians (who are not technically immigrants), and one has a melting pot that could compare favorably with any in the world, at any time.

Moreover, most of these groups resist the existing labels for ethnic groups. The Haitians will insist that they are Catholic and speak French and do not belong in the same group as black Americans. None of the other Spanish-speaking groups is willing to be lumped under the title of "Hispanic" or "Latino" with which the Mexicans and Puerto Ricans are perhaps satisfied. The Dominicans come from Hispaniola, as do the Haitians, but they will insist that they are different peoples. How many Haitian Sammy Sosas are there? The Mayan highlanders in Los Angeles bring in their own priests to say Mass because the local "Hispanic" parish does not seem friendly. The Lebanese are mostly Arabs, but they hardly identify with the Palestinians or the Syrians. Brazilians do not think of themselves as Hispanic (because they speak Portuguese), and Cubans are Cuban (even if they do speak Spanish—or, as they would say, Castilian). Georgians and Ukrainians are not Russian. Kurds are not Turks and not Iraqis either.

Almost all of these groups have their own stores with signs in their native languages (and sometimes, as on Central Avenue, their own street signs); their own restaurants, which serve their own food (much to the delight of connoisseurs of exotic cuisines); their own form of America-speak; their own religious centers (perhaps in storefront churches); their own emergent political groups, seeking their share of the pie (which in traditional American politics means "more"); their own historical and religious animosities; and their own fervent claims to be Americans, albeit with the hyphenated ethnic identity preceding.

Many of these people are illegal immigrants (perhaps all the Guatemalan highlanders in Los Angeles are). Others are in the United States on one sort of visa or other, expired or unexpired. Periodically, Immigration (the Immigration and Customs Enforcement agency, formerly the INS) sweeps the office buildings in downtown Chicago to collect the Polish cleaning women who work long and hard hours keeping the floors as clean as the sidewalks in front of Polish homes. It also collects skilled Irish craftsmen, suspicious-looking folks with dark skin who look like they may deal drugs, and Eastern Europeans who may be attached to their own respective Mafias. Yet ICE has no effective control over illegal immigration, especially when the illegal immigrants can blend into a neighborhood of their own kind where they receive shelter, protection, and jobs. Many Americans know this and suspect that all the members of certain groups might be illegal. In the contemporary United States, no one is hated more than an illegal immigrant. They are breaking the law and they are taking jobs away from Americans—or so most Americans believe (despite all the evidence to the contrary). The new ethnics had to contend with suspicion even before the terrorist attacks on the World Trade Center.

There are 31 million immigrants in the United States, constituting roughly 10 percent of the population (as opposed to 15 percent in the early 20th century). One in nine Americans is an immigrant; half of the immigrants are Hispanic, another quarter Asian American.

Unlike turn-of-the century immigrants, many of these groups are clearly not run-of-the-mill white Anglo-Saxon Americans. Not only are they foreigners, like the Irish and the Italians and the Poles were a century ago, they have dark skins, which makes some Americans suspect that they are terrorists. This is the second important change in the climate for ethnicity in the United States: Men and women with dark skin and "funny" pronunciations are suspected of being terrorists, particularly if the women wear headscarves and the men scowl. After the World Trade Center attacks, immigrants face more bitter and more outraged suspicion than ever. "We should not let those people into our country," many Americans believe. "They are taking away our jobs and they want to take away our freedom. God bless America and send them home where they belong."

Xenophobia has waxed and waned in this country across the decades. Today the combination of the new immigration, distrust of dark-skinned "foreigners" as probably illegal and possibly dangerous, the presumed threat to U.S. jobs, and the threat of terrorism have fanned the flames of nativism. This sentiment is now at an all-time high, at least since the days of the second Ku Klux Klan. U.S. jobs are outsourced overseas. American jobs are being taken over by illegal immigrants. American life and freedom are under attack. Our borders are not safe, our jobs are not safe, our lives are not safe. President Bush's plan for quasi-amnesty for illegal Mexican immigrants, advanced in the winter of 2004, won little support from most Americans and did not stand a chance of getting through Congress.

On the one hand, therefore, there is more ethnic diversity than ever, and on the other hand more suspicion of the strangers among us. Minimally, we demand that they assimilate quickly or go home "where they belong." The diversity they represent is an affront to our American patriotism. The demand for assimilation addressed to every earlier immigrant group is broadcast again across the land, but now it is even more urgent: You must become Americans like the rest of us or we don't want you here. Moreover, you must prove to us right now that you are capable of assimilation.

The demand implicit in "why can't you be like us" is impossible to meet, and would not be desirable even if it could be. The blend in the "stewpot" of Virgilio Elizondo is richer and thicker and tastier than it has ever been before. The official standard for being an American is the same as it always has been: acceptance and support of the Constitution and the Declaration of Independence, with perhaps some ability in English as an additional quasi-requirement. All ethnic groups have the same right to their own language, their own religion, their own family patterns, their own political style, their own cuisine, their own manner of conversation (no one has ever successfully cured Italians of gesturing while they talk), and their own concern for the political situation in their homeland. Acceptance and success as Americans (which is what most members of these newly arrived ethnic groups want) require some level of assimilation, but not total acculturation. However, the new immigrants' path to acceptance in this country may be longer than for other groups because of the handicaps of skin color, religion, and language. The U.S. creed says they should be given a chance, just like everyone else. If they must jump more hurdles to prove that they are American, that is unfair. If they are denied acceptance as Americans, that is intolerable.

Those of us who argued, a couple of decades ago, that diverse ethnic groups are an essential part of the U.S. landscape have been vindicated, perhaps more decisively than we had expected. Those of us who have argued that ethnic diversity is a national asset are, however, under more suspicion than ever. Why can't they be like us?

"Multiculturalism" often means only that one is ready to accept the fact that certain groups have a cultural contribution to make to this country: Native Americans, Samoans, Aleuts, Hispanic Americans, African Americans (as the census question puts it). What can the Dominicans, the Kurds, the Palestinians, the Turks, the Arabs, and the Georgians (for example) have to contribute to American life—any more than the Irish and the Italians and Poles and the French Canadians did a century ago?

Nativism will be with us for a long time to come. Four of five farm workers are immigrants, but immigrants hold one-quarter of the patents. These numbers stir up all the old nativist fears of the foreigners taking over our country. Patronizing "viewers with alarm" wonder whether these new immigrants will be "assimilated," whatever that means (generally, become like us). Patronizing writers like Herbert Gans and Steven Thernstrom dismiss the immigrants from the turn of the 20th century as already like us. The Irish, the Italians, and the Eastern Europeans are already Americans, they tell us, yet anyone who lives in a city like New York or Chicago knows that is not true. Irish, Italians, Poles, Greeks, Albanians, Serbs, Hungarians, Jews all have distinctive family relationships, different political orientations and styles, different expectations of intimate role opposites. Interestingly enough, none of those advocates of the total assimilation of the "Euro-Americans" include Jews in their list of assimilationist success. It is all right, it would seem, for Jews to be different (and I agree completely), but not all right for the Poles or the Italians. It would be wrong to stereotype African Americans or Native Americans on television, but it is perfectly all right to stereotype the Italians (as does the unspeakably vicious television series "The Sopranos").

If the patronizing expectation of the neonativists—that the new immigrants will assimilate like the rest of us have—comes true, then it will be a much less complete assimilation than these folks who see themselves as cultural rulemakers and arbiters would like.

Will all these new immigrants assimilate? The answer, I think, is that it is up to them, not up to the rest of us. They have the right to make their own decisions in these matters, and no one else has the right to stand in judgment over them. They have the right to decide, individually and collectively, what of their heritage they will keep and what they will give up.

My guess is that they will follow the same path as did those of us who came a hundred years ago. They will master English because it is necessary if one is to live and work in our society. Some, however, will maintain their ancestral language within the family. More power to them. They will rapidly catch up to and then surpass native-born Americans in educational attainment, by the second generation; by the third generation, they will be at least as successful as the top tier of Americans, despite their somewhat darker skin color and their funny accents and their strange customs.

As Tamar Jacoby wrote in the best essay in her book, *Reinventing the Melting Pot* (2004):

Today as in the past there are many empirical tests of whether immigrants have become American: how well they speak English, whether they live among their own group or in an integrated community, how much education they have, the kind of occupations they hold, how much they depend on welfare, whether they become citizens, whether they vote, who they marry and so on. By most of these tests, there is no significant evidence that today's immigrants are much different from yesterday's. They still enlist in our armies and fight our wars. They still become American citizens. They still learn English, work and pay taxes." (p. 71)

I would disagree that they have to live in integrated communities or eliminate differences in accents. There is plenty of room in America for different accents.

Ms. Jacoby shrewdly noted that assimilation works:

more easily than in the past . . . . [It] accommodates more than one identity and more than one loyalty. Immigrants continue to identify with the old country, its institutions and its politics. But this is not necessarily cause for regret—for they also forge an identity as Americans. (p. 71)

So, the hyphen is okay now, it would seem.

What about the dark-skinned immigrants, it is asked? The United States has not been able to resolve its racial problem. Can it cope with yet more dark-skinned residents? Will Dominican Americans, Haitian Americans, and some Asian Indian Americans, and Latino Americans (Spanish-speaking) be compressed into an inescapable underclass? For most Latino Americans, the answer is clearly no. For the rest, it depends on educational opportunities, and perhaps on the recognition that the schools do a lousy job with the poor of whatever color and will continue to do so until the country begins to realize how desperately educational competition and freedom of choice are needed for the very poor. Clearly, however, Jamaican Americans, Haitian Americans, and Dominican Americans have no intention of being left behind.

Why is there so much distrust of immigrants, not only among ordinary people, but also among the kind of elites who contributed to Ms. Jacoby's book? Leaving aside for the moment the understandable if unjustified economic fears, why do we dislike the stranger?

The answer is because they are strange, darn it!

I delight in Spanish accents (and in black English and Appalachian English, too, for that matter). But I have a hard time with the sounds of Arabic, which has nothing to do with Islam or terrorists; the breaths sounded sinister long before the World Trade Center disaster. I absolutely deplore the failure of Asian Americans to speak up in class. I once tried to teach a class of 400 students because my very distinguished colleagues had cancelled their classes at the last minute and a priest can't turn down any young person who begs for help (whether sincerely or not). Unfortunately, it seemed to me, two-fifths of my students were Asian Americans, with their pernicious respect for teachers. No way could I persuade them to disagree, argue, or express an opinion. They were good kids and they wrote excellent papers, but they simply would not talk, not even when I called on them.

In my more irenic moments, I understand that Arabs have the right to talk any way they want and that we in the West would barely know of Aristotle or arithmetic without their ancestors. I also understand the right of students of any nationality not to speak up, especially if their cultures teach them to respect teachers. Still, when you're trying to sustain a class without falling back on the cheap academic cop-out of lecturing, their silence is infuriating. Why can't they be like us?

I console myself with the thought that Irish students were silent long ago, at least until they figured out how the game was played. I also console myself with the hope that in a generation or two the Asian Americans will be as gregarious as everyone else, arguably more so.

Yet—and this is the crux of it all—they are entitled to be quiet. They are entitled to stand by their own customs, even if they are somewhat dysfunctional in the context of the educational experience. They don't have to be like us. They are entitled to be "strange."

Just as the rest of us are.

REFERENCE
Jacoby, T. (Ed.). (2004). *Reinventing the melting pot: The new immigrants and what it means to be American.* New York: Basic Books.

CHAPTER 2

DEMOGRAPHY, THE DEMAND FOR SOCIAL SERVICES, AND THE POTENTIAL FOR CIVIC CONFLICT

Teresa A. Sullivan

During the past two-plus decades, the United States has changed fundamentally in ways that are shaped by demographic processes. This chapter offers a systematic view of how demographic trends affect the demand for social services. In particular, the discussion emphasizes how demographic structures bear on some of the pressing social policy issues that face Americans at the beginning of the 21st century.

HOW DEMOGRAPHIC STRUCTURE GENERATES SOCIAL STRUCTURE

As all introductory demography students learn, demography is the study of the size, density, and heterogeneity of human populations, and of the changes that occur in the population through fertility, mortality, and migration (Ross, 1985). These topics and their sequelae are important to all workers in the human services. Indeed, basic demographic facts shape the types of problems that social workers face. To give some simple examples, the size of the population affects the quantity of services required; the density of the population affects the efficiency with which services can be delivered; and the heterogeneity of the population—its variations in age, gender, race and ethnicity, religion, and migrant status—affects the types of services needed.

Social service workers also encounter the effects of the dynamic demographic processes of fertility, mortality, and migration. Births and deaths are significant milestones for each family and are associated with large health expenses; assistance in coping with such issues is an important part of social work practice. Migrant communities historically face issues of societal adjustment and incorporation. Many problems that people encounter in their individual and family circumstances result from intersection with these basic demographic processes. More important, though, these processes writ large have important effects on larger societal groupings.

At a structural level, the demographic processes of fertility, mortality, and migration create large-scale and long-range demographic effects that bear importantly on many social services and many issues of social policy. One of the most important ways in which demography affects social policy is through the age structure.[1] The age structure of a

9

population is shaped by mortality and migration, but it is especially shaped by fertility (Coale, 1987; Ridley, Sheps, Lingner, & Menken, 1967; Ryder, 1990). A very young population needs different types of medical care, education, and income support than a population of elderly people. Migrant flows, which tend to favor young adults, pose additional different issues of housing, employment, and civic integration (Chiswick & Sullivan, 1995).

The sex ratio, which is the typical descriptive measure of sex composition[2], is also affected by fertility, because 105 baby boys are typically born for every 100 baby girls. It is also affected by mortality, because in most societies men have shorter life expectancies than women (Gutentag & Secord, 1983). It is not an accident that the population in most nursing homes is disproportionately female. Short-distance migratory streams tend to be predominantly female, and long-distance migratory streams predominantly male. Classically, immigrant streams were predominantly male, and even today young, single men are overrepresented in many immigrant neighborhoods.

STUDYING RACIAL/ETHNIC GROUPS IN THE POPULATION

In a diverse society such as the United States, there are many reasons for examining diverse groups, both by themselves and in interaction with one another. Each racial or ethnic group may be considered a population by itself and may be analyzed in the same way as the larger national population. That is, one may again turn to size, density, heterogeneity, fertility, mortality, and migration as the linchpins of a structural analysis. In addition, exogamy, or the rate of marital exchange with other groups, also may be an important consideration. The popularity of the "mixed" racial category, introduced by the 2000 Census, shows that, as a practical matter, the children of exogamous unions would like the opportunity to classify themselves and not be forced to choose among their heritages (Prewitt, 2005).

Many political issues, such as elected representation and coalition formation, turn on the relative size and density of racial and ethnic groups (Morrison, 1998). Politicians who are redistricting geographic areas are very aware of these characteristics. Let us say, for the sake of simplicity, that two ethnic groups, which we call A and B, live in the same geographic area.

Group A is characterized by low fertility, low mortality, and low immigration; over time, these characteristics will lead group A to be relatively old. Because older people are more likely to vote, and because group A is more likely to be native-born, the rates of voter registration and participation in group A are potentially high. Group B is characterized by high fertility, moderate mortality, and high levels of immigration. These characteristics will lead group B to have a relatively young native-born segment and an older foreign-born segment. Both groups A and B are entitled to political representation, but Group B is much less likely to contain voters, both because its immigrant population members cannot register and vote unless they become naturalized, and because its youthful native-born generation may be too young to vote and may have fewer role models of civic engagement. Thus, it is very much to group A's advantage to draw districts that incorporate some of the group B members. Because group B will be less likely to vote, in effect every group A vote will gain somewhat greater weight.[3]

As this example implies, racial and ethnic groups with relatively high fertility and with relatively high immigration will, in turn, have distinctive age and sex structures. High fertility contributes to a relatively young population (Coale, 1987). To some extent, early fertility (that is, childbearing at relatively young ages) also rejuvenates a population even if each woman does not bear numerous children. High immigration also contributes to a relatively young population, in part because typical immigrants are themselves young adults and in part because they are of the right age to have children. A group that is growing both through relatively high fertility and high immigration (such as the Mexican American population) will be younger than a population that is growing only through relatively high fertility (such as rural African Americans) or principally through immigration (such as Chinese Americans) (Sullivan, 2000). High fertility and high immigration also both favor somewhat higher sex ratios (Gutentag & Secord, 1983).

These distinctive age structures have ramifications for the types of services that are needed. Education, prenatal care, child care, and vaccination services will be very high priorities for the high-fertility populations and for the geopolitical areas characterized by high fertility. The high-immigration populations or geopolitical areas may have a greater interest in housing and job-location services. The low-fertility and low-immigration populations will tend to be older and have greater interest in medical care, rehabilitation services, adult day care, and social security (Treas & Torrecilha, 1995).

The sheer heterogeneity of ethnic groups is in itself a matter of considerable interest and creates situations of much greater complexity than in the preceding, simple political example of groups A and B. At least since the immigration reforms of 1965 were instituted, U.S. policymakers have been very aware of the rapidly diversifying ethnic character of the United States (Passel & Suro, 2005). Especially in large cities, a wide variety of national-origin, religious, and ethnic groups have changed the political and economic landscapes as they settle in neighborhoods and parishes. This diversification is especially notable in large cities such as New York and Chicago, but it is also readily identifiable in smaller cities.

Signs of racial and ethnic diversity flourish everywhere. Even in medium-sized cities, tourist guides may list ethnic restaurants of 20 varieties. High schools offer bilingual education in dozens of languages. Courts, hospitals, and government service providers are routinely prepared to translate documents and conversations into a variety of languages. Politicians routinely consider the effects of legislation on many different groups.

Projections of population growth in the United States indicate that the racial/ethnic diversity of the population will continue to increase. Hispanics and Asian and Pacific

Islanders—two groups that account for most international migration—will between them add nearly 9 million people to the United States population by 2020. This additional growth will follow closely on two decades of substantial growth. Between 1980 and 2000 the Hispanic population of the United States grew by 20.7 million; by 2020, it is expected to grow by an additional 4.4 million. The Asian and Pacific Islander population grew by 7 million, but is also expected to grow by another 4.4 million. By comparison, no growth is expected among the Native American population, and only small additional growth among the non-Hispanic black population, from an additional 7.5 million to an additional 9.7 million. Perhaps most surprising, the non-Hispanic white population, which grew by 14.3 million during the two decades after 1980, will add 1 million less during the first 20 years of the new century (Pew Research Center, 2005).

In summary, both the absolute numbers of ethnic minority groups, and their relatively higher rates of growth, will continue to transform the United States and its institutions in many ways.

SOCIAL POLICY INTERACTING WITH DEMOGRAPHIC STRUCTURE

The preceding comments shed light on some aspects of U.S. domestic politics. A large number of American social policies tend to be age-graded. The parents of young children have a strong interest in quality public schools and all the policy issues associated with schooling, such as bilingual education, accountability, and access to higher education. In addition, a range of health issues is especially important to this segment of the age structure, such as the Children's Health Insurance Program (CHIP); Women, Infants, and Children (WIC) program; vaccination policies; prenatal care; childhood obesity; sex education; and access to family planning. In addition, adoption policies, the Food Stamp program, and similar matters will be of great interest to children's advocates.

Of the 18.6 million children ages five or younger in the United States in 2000, about 60 percent were non-Hispanic white, 20 percent were Hispanic, and 15 percent were African American. Only about 5 percent were Asian and Pacific Islander or Native American/American Indian or other ethnic minority group (U.S. Census Bureau, 2000). Who, then, will be interested in child welfare issues? To some extent, everyone will be, and there is no denying that many elderly, childless Americans care deeply about what happens to children. Nevertheless, there is a sort of natural constituency for children's issues that is now more than one-third Hispanic and African American, and the population projections suggest that ethnic minority populations will increasingly focus interest on children's issues.

This picture, however, is drawn only at the national level. Put the focus on a local level, and potential conflicts emerge. In some school districts in western Texas, the children in the public schools are overwhelmingly Hispanic, often born in Mexico or the children of Mexican immigrants, and the younger children who have not yet entered school are even more likely to be Hispanic. The older population of these same districts is overwhelmingly native-born and white. The middle-aged population is mixed in ethnicity, but many of the adult children of the elderly white population have moved away to find work. Because Texas relies heavily on property taxes to fund schools and because the probability of owning property increases with age and relative income, the white population disproportionately funds the school systems that the Hispanic children disproportionately populate. In such demographic situations, a taxpayer revolt may have both intergenerational and interethnic roots. The analyst who tries to understand school finance without understanding this underlying demographic dynamic may reach the wrong conclusions.

A similar conflict can arise by a different demographic route. There are other parts of the country, most notably Florida and Arizona, where the native migrant community is disproportionately native-born, white, and relatively affluent. These couples, who have already raised their children, seek a retirement home in a sunnier, warmer clime. They add to the economic base of the communities where they settle, and they are often eager volunteers in local activities, but they may nevertheless balk at school bond elections that seem distant from their current interests. Many analyses of the so-called tax revolt have failed to take such demographic trends into consideration.

Today's prototypical middle-aged taxpayer group, the baby boomers, is worth a bit of separate analysis. The early boomers, born between 1946 and 1955, are approximated by the group ages 45 to 55 in the 2000 Census.[4] In 2000 there were 37.3 million of these early boomers (U.S. Census Bureau, 2000). As children, these boomers experienced extremely crowded public schooling, sometimes attending school in half-day shifts, in part because the country had not built the school infrastructure to accommodate them. The launch of Sputnik in 1957 led to a frenzy of efforts to improve their math and science education and skills, but when they reached college they again found that their great numbers increased the level of competition and limited their access. Similarly, the bulge of new workers led to higher unemployment when the boomers entered the labor market, and to rising real estate prices when they began to bid up the cost of housing. Although not disadvantaged in terms of the general prosperity of postwar America, the early boomers have nonetheless encountered high levels of competition, in part because of their sheer numbers (Jones, 1981).

The early boomers are 76 percent non-Hispanic white, only 8 percent Hispanic, and almost 11 percent African American, with 3.7 percent Asian American (many of them foreign-born) and fewer than 1 percent Native American/American Indian (U.S. Census Bureau, 2000). Notice how much more "white" and how much less Hispanic the early boomers are compared with the youngest children in the current population (described earlier). Three of every four boomers are white, compared with six of every 10 young children. Only 8 percent of the boomers are Hispanic, but one in every five of the youngest children is Hispanic.

What are the concerns of the baby boomers? They are very interested in health issues, because they are beginning to experience the aches and pains of aging, and many of them are unsure about whether they will be able to maintain health insurance until Medicare becomes available. They are worried about their children and often grandchildren, but many of them are also caring for their own elderly parents. Having enough time to care for these dependents, and also enough time to work, is a pressing issue. The boomers are increasingly concerned about their retirement income. Private pensions, their investments and savings (if any), the cost of their children's college educations, and Social Security are very salient issues.

The baby boomers, because of their current life stage, are politically active, and they form the backbone of many civic and volunteer efforts. As the first generation to attend college in relatively large numbers, they are also articulate in expressing their concerns. For the country as a whole, the baby boomers remain the largest single demographic group; consequently, their political concerns carry disproportionate weight with elected officials.

This perspective makes the current controversy concerning Social Security reform more comprehensible (Fry, Kochhar, Passel, & Suro, 2005). Once they retire, the baby boomers will be the largest group of elderly people that the United States has ever had to support. The early boomers will, of course, be those who reach retirement age before their younger siblings who are also boomers. The anxiety about whether Social Security will be available, and in what amounts, is significant among boomers (although, understandably, some denial about aging is still apparent).

If we look at the population who are generally considered the retired (and current recipients of Medicare and Social Security), we find even more pronounced interethnic differences. Of the 34.7 million Americans over the age of 65 in 2004, 82 percent are white, 8 percent are African American, and 6 percent are Hispanic. Perhaps even more striking, about 15 percent of the white population is currently 65 years of age or older, compared with only 5 percent of the Hispanic population (U.S. Census Bureau, 2000). Also politically important and active, the retired population will play an important role in the national debate over changes in Social Security.

Intergenerational Justice and Interethnic Justice
Social Security and public education are paramount vehicles of intergenerational justice, but, as the preceding analysis indicated, such programs will increasingly involve substantial interethnic transfers. Between 2005 and 2050, the U.S. labor force will grow by 39 million, but the Hispanic labor force will grow by 27 million (Fry et al., 2005). Thus, the majority of the new taxpaying workers will be paying into a system that will, for at least a substantial part of the new century, disproportionately benefit a white, elderly population with Social Security and Medicare—but it will also provide public education to a racially and ethnically mixed school-age population.

The programs for the elderly population will be funded federally through payroll taxes and the federal income tax. Workers and employers will be the principal payers. The intergenerational transfers will have significant geographic results, because elderly and youthful people will not be equally distributed across the landscape. Still, although the effects may be experienced locally, the taxing efforts will be national and more or less equivalent in each state and region. Furthermore, although the benefits will be disproportionately enjoyed by white people, this result will usually be regarded as fair because the retirees paid into the system in earlier decades. Thus, there is likely to be a greater perception that Social Security and related programs are fair in the sense that they impose equal burdens and potentially equivalent benefits.

Such is not the case with public funding of schooling. A mixture of federal, state, and local funds currently supports schools. The issue of fairness of educational resources will be much more controversial. Similarly situated taxpayers may not pay the same amount of taxes, even within a single state, and almost surely taxpayers will pay different amounts from state to state. School funding is currently unequal within states (a fact that is being litigated in a number of states), principally because of the differences in local property taxes. These facts, combined with great local differences in the ethnic composition of the children who use the local schools, set the stage for conflict. From the taxpayer perspective, this variance may not be fair. Moreover, the quality of the schooling may vary substantially by geographic area, a fact that may not seem fair to parents. Whether it is fair to have equal access to education, or whether fairness requires access to an equal education, remains to be seen.

The school funding issue probably holds the greatest potential for interethnic political conflict. Ethnic shifts within the school-aged population are larger and more variable among districts than shifts within the Social Security recipient population, and so even the types of political conflicts cannot be predicted. It is, however, predictable that issues that seem superficially to concern federalism, local school control, and taxpayer equity may mask deeper underlying issues of the differing age compositions of ethnic groups.

The Confounding Issue of Wealth
Age structure also strongly affects the distribution of wealth. As a rule, younger families have lower incomes because the breadwinners have less seniority and more mouths to feed. Thus, it is a commonplace observation that there are more children in poverty than elderly people. As workers age, they are more likely to earn higher incomes. Also, as their children reach school age, formerly stay-at-home spouses may devote more hours to the labor force, raising the family income further. Families with middle-aged breadwinners are also likely to have greater savings and may begin to acquire some wealth, such as a home and other durable goods. Advantaged workplace positions continue to benefit the retired after their work lives end, even with public benefits, because the size of the Social Security check is based on the recipient's earnings during his or her work life.

Age structure is obviously not the only factor at work, however. Workers from ethnic minority groups continue to hold lower-paying and less secure jobs (Sullivan, 2003, 2005).[5] These workers are less likely to accumulate wealth during their work lives. In 2001, 74 percent of white families owned a primary residence, and those homes had a median value of $130,000. By contrast, only 47 percent of not white and Hispanic families owned a home, and their homes had a median value of only $92,000 (U.S. Census Bureau, 2004). The contrast is even starker when all assets are considered. The median net worth of white families in 2001 was $120,900, and the median net worth of not white and Hispanic families was $17,100 (U.S. Census Bureau, 2004). For the ethnic minority families, this net worth represented a decline from 1995 ($18,300) and 1998 ($17,900).

As a result of these workplace differences, when ethnic minority workers become eligible for Social Security, they receive smaller checks. In 2003 the average Hispanic retiree received an annual Social Security benefit of $8,497, compared with an average benefit of $10,621 for white recipients and $8,828 for black recipients (Fry et al., 2005). In addition, eligibility itself varies by racial group: 91 percent of white people qualified for Social Security, compared with 85 percent of African Americans and 76 percent of Hispanics. Thus, only three-quarters of Hispanics qualified for Social Security after their work lives.

The benefits of relative economic advantage go well beyond greater Social Security benefits. Public goods, such as Social Security or public schooling, are of much less import when families and individuals can spend personal resources to buy private versions of the same goods. Private schools, private pensions, and private medical care are readily available in the marketplace, but the wealth to spend on these goods is still concentrated disproportionately in the white population. The striking increase in economic inequality during the past 20 years has also tended to benefit the white population rather than ethnic minority groups. Thus, although many elderly people of all races are in at least some economic distress (Draut & McGhee, 2004), there is a substantial group of relatively well-off, politically active older people who are insulated from the pinch of poverty—but for whom tax burdens may well be a salient issue.

Demography and Justice

Demographers would argue that many issues in the United States that are currently framed in terms of intergenerational justice or interracial justice are partly the result of distributional differences in age structure and geography. Because of the U.S. federal system, geography plays a key role in access to some important social services, especially education. Geography is, in turn, strongly related to migration, labor force opportunities, and housing adequacy.

This is not to argue that prejudice and discrimination have disappeared or to minimize the effects of differences in race, ethnicity, language, native origin, or religion.

There is no question that these issues still remain and are key sources of social distress. Nevertheless, an analysis that stops at these characteristics, without looking at the deeper demographic issues, will miss the locus for some important potential solutions. Litigation to equalize school funding and other services within states, changes in tax policy, and changes in federal wage and hour legislation are important potential vehicles for change that might otherwise be overlooked. Other policy issues that are already on the national agenda, such as immigration reform and Social Security reform, would also be illuminated by demographic analysis.

The recent national debate over affirmative action brought a call for "race-neutral" approaches to college admissions. I am not here advocating a race-neutral approach to Social Security, school funding, or other issues. It is true, however, that an emphasis on analytic (and seemingly neutral) factors such as age structure and geographic dispersion tends to be less polarizing. Every individual has an age and a location; the emphasis on age structure and geographic concentration emphasizes the aggregate impact of these characteristics in a way that is less prone to dismissal as mere identity politics.

END NOTES

1. The age structure of the population is often described by a pyramid, a special type of bar chart that shows the proportion of the population at each age. The median age, the dependency ratio, and the proportion of the population above and below certain ages (for example, above age 65 or below age 18) are the typical measures that appear in the literature.

2. The sex ratio is conventionally defined as the number of males per 100 females, often specified for a particular age group. In the young adult years, the sex ratio is typically close to 100 except where there is considerable long-range migration. In the west coast Chinatowns of the late 19th century, sex ratios in excess of 1,000 were reported, principally because the Chinese Exclusion Acts did not permit the immigration of women from Asia.

3. For the same reason, it is to the advantage of voters to have prisons, jails, and military installations nearby, because they increase the population entitled to representation but do not increase the number of voters to the same extent. In effect, a nearby prison gives greater weight to the vote of its neighbors. For an editorial view of this prison effect, see "Phantom Constituents in the Census," 2005).

4. In fact, the baby boom continued, according to some analysts, until 1964, but the peak fertility occurred in 1957–1958. I have chosen the earlier group partly because of its members' characteristics and partly for the ease of taking the data from the 2000 Census. I have calculated the numbers in this section myself, using the 2000 U.S. Census data.

5. The reasons for this disadvantage in the labor market are numerous and beyond the scope of this chapter. There are, however, indications in the literature that some Hispanics, especially Mexican Americans, suffer unique disadvantages (see, for example, Dohan, 2002).

REFERENCES

Chiswick, B. R., & Sullivan, T. A. (1995). The new immigrants. In R. Farley (Ed.), *State of the union: America in the 1990s* (Vol. 2, pp. 211–270). New York: Russell Sage Foundation.

Coale, A. (1987). How a population ages or grows younger. In S. W. Menard & E. W. Moen (Eds.), *Perspectives on population: An introduction to concepts and issues* (pp. 365–371). New York: Oxford University Press.

Dohan, D. (2002). *Making cents in the barrio: The institutional roots of joblessness in Mexican America. Ethnography, 3,* 177–200.

Draut, T., & McGhee, H. C. (2004, February). *Retiring in the red: The growth of debt among older Americans.* Washington, DC: DEMOS Institute.

Fry, R., Kochhar, R., Passel, J., & Suro, R. (2005). *Hispanics and the Social Security debate.* Washington, DC: Pew Hispanic Center.

Gutentag, M., & Secord, P. F. (1983). *Too many women? The sex ratio question.* Beverly Hills, CA: Sage Publications.

Jones, L. (1981). *Great expectations: America and the baby boom generation.* New York: Ballantine.

Morrison, P. A. (1998, June). Demographic influences on Latinos' political empowerment: Comparative local illustrations. *Population Research and Policy Review, 17,* 223–246.

Passel, J. S., & Suro, R. (2005). *Rise, peak and decline: Trends in U.S. immigration 1992–2004.* Washington, DC: Pew Hispanic Center.

Pew Research Center. (2005*). Trends, 2005.* Washington, DC: Pew Research Center.

Phantom constituents in the census. (2005, September 26). *New York Times*, p. A-16. Retrieved February 24, 2006, from http://www.newyorktimes.com

Prewitt, K. (2005, Winter). Racial classification in America. *Daedalus, 134,* 5–17.

Ridley, J., Sheps, M., Lingner, J., & Menken, J. (1967). The effects of changing mortality on natality. *Milbank Memorial Fund Quarterly, 55,* 77–97.

Ross, J. A. (Ed.). (1985). *International encyclopedia of population.* New York: Free Press.

Ryder, N. (1990). What is going to happen to American fertility? *Population and Development Review 16,* 433–454.

Sullivan, T. A. (2000). A demographic portrait. In P. S. J. Cafferty & D. W. Engstrom (Eds.), *Hispanics in the United States: An agenda for the twenty-first century* (pp. 1–29). New Brunswick, NJ: Transaction Books.

Sullivan, T. A. (2003). Work-related social problems. In G. Ritzer (Ed.), *Handbook of social problems* (pp. 193–208). Beverly Hills, CA: Sage Publications.

Sullivan, T. A. (2005). Labor force. In D. L. Poston & M. Micklin (Eds.), *Handbook of population* (pp. 209–225). New York: Springer.

Treas, J., & Torrecilha, R. (1995). The older population. In R. Farley (Ed.), *State of the union: America in the 1990s* (pp. 47–92). New York: Russell Sage Foundation.

U.S. Census Bureau. (2000). *American fact finder.* Retrieved October 15, 2005, from http://factfinder.census.gov

U.S. Census Bureau. (2004). *Statistical abstract of the United States* (124th ed.). Washington, DC: U.S. Government Printing Office.

CHAPTER 3

OUTSIDERS AND EXCLUSION: IMMIGRANTS IN THE UNITED STATES

David W. Engstrom

INTRODUCTION

Throughout the history of the United States, immigration has shaped and transformed the nation, changing its demographic and affecting its political, social, and economic institutions. Despite the significance of immigration in defining American society, the United States, for the most part, lacks a consistent and coherent policy for incorporating immigrants into American society. Indeed, the policy that is in place is entirely inadequate for the 21st century. At a time of globalization and reshaping of boundaries, immigrant policy has grown increasingly exclusionary, resulting in negative consequences for immigrant families, many of which have citizen children.

In the context of this chapter, it is important to understand the demographic changes created by the high level of contemporary immigration to the United States. Today, nearly one in 10 people living in this country is foreign born, and a foreign-born adult heads one in seven U.S. families. Given the presence of so many immigrants, this chapter necessarily explores the distinctions that the United States makes between immigrants and citizens. Recent policy changes have enhanced the value of citizenship, and by doing so have correspondingly weakened the rights of immigrants, resulting in increased exclusion.

This analysis provides a context for understanding the societal institutions with which immigrants interact. The extent and nature of immigrants' interactions with societal institutions shape their incorporation into U.S. society, their well-being, and their quality of life. This is especially true for immigrant families that face the challenges of raising children while beginning life anew. Although all immigrant families experience the stressors of cultural and social adaptation, this chapter pays particular attention to low-wage and low-income immigrant families. These families, with the fewest private and public resources, are affected the most by exclusionary policies. The final section of the chapter reviews the implications of the preceding analysis for social work.

DEMOGRAPHIC CHANGE

The influx of immigrants to the United States in the last four decades is remarkable in its size and diversity. Since passage of the 1965 Immigration Act, which ushered in the new era of immigration, the country has experienced a steady growth in the number of immigrants arriving at its borders. Between 1967—the year the changes took effect—and 2002, the country received more than 24.6 million legal immigrants. Legal immigration averaged 450,000 per year in the 1970s, 734,000 per year in the 1980s, 910,000 per year in the 1990s, and 945,000 per year in the 2000s.[1]

Undocumented immigrants further add to demographic change. Precise estimates of the total number and yearly flow of undocumented immigrants are difficult to derive. Nevertheless, the most current research suggests that the total number of undocumented immigrants in the United States ranges between 7 and 12 million (Passel, 2006; Passel, Capps, & Fix, 2004; BCIS, 2003). The Bureau of Citizenship and Immigration Services (BCIS) estimates that the undocumented immigrant population grew by 3.5 million people during the 1990s, with more arriving at the end of the decade than at the beginning (BCIS, 2003).

Not all immigrants, whether documented or undocumented, stay permanently in the United States. This outmigration alters the demographic effect of immigration. Historically, about one in three immigrants eventually returns home or emigrates to yet another country. Country of origin, reasons for coming to the United States, family ties, and economic success all factor into an individual's decision about whether to stay or leave (Reagan & Olsen, 2000; Woodrow-LaField, 1996). The U.S. Census Bureau estimated that approximately 195,000 foreign-born people per year left the United States during the 1980s (Ahmed & Robinson, 1994). Using different immigrant cohorts, Borjas and Bratsberg calculated that outmigration rates range between 18 percent and 20 percent (1996).

Another way to consider the demographic impact of immigrants is to examine the Census 2000 data on the foreign-born people living in the United States; the decennial census counted 28.4 million foreign-born people in the United States, compared with 19.8 million in 1990 (U.S. Census Bureau, 2001). However, because the U.S. population has constantly increased, a better way to understand the effect of immigration is to look at change in the proportion of the foreign-born population to the total population of the United States—a proportion that has steadily increased over the past three decades. In 1970, the foreign-born constituted 4.7 percent of the population; in 1980, 6.2 percent; in 1990, 7.9 percent; and in 2000, 10.4 percent. Though these numbers are high by contemporary standards, they have not yet approached the historic benchmarks of the late 19th and early 20th centuries, which ranged from 13.3 percent to 14.8 percent (U.S. Census Bureau, 2001).

The racial and ethnic heterogeneity of current immigration is unprecedented. Before 1965, Europe sent the majority of all immigrants to the United States, but that has changed. Presently Latin America (38 percent) and Asia (35 percent) account for nearly 73 percent of all immigrants; Europe is the origin of only 14 percent. Also, though African immigration is still relatively light (approximately 7 percent of all immigrants), it has more than doubled, from 27,086 in 1992 to 66,309 in 2004 (U.S. Department of Homeland Security, 2006). Presently, more Africans are immigrating to the United States on a yearly basis than at any point during the slave trade (Roberts, 2005).

The regional data from around the world is informative, but country-level data yields even more detail on diversity. According to the latest data from the BCIS, in 2003 the United States received legal immigrants from more than 200 countries and territories (U.S. Department of Homeland Security, 2004). Many of these countries and territories send only modest number of immigrants; indeed, 56 of them accounted for 100 people or less. More significantly, immigrants from 20 countries represented approximately 70 percent of all immigrants. As has been true for the past three decades, Mexico has been the single largest sender of immigrants—in 2003, one in six legal immigrants came from there. The four other top sending countries—India, China, the Philippines, and Vietnam—account for an additional 20 percent of all immigrants. That a handful of countries contribute more immigrants than all the rest is not a historical anomaly, but the size of the flow coming from Mexico does represent a break with the past.

Approximately 70 percent of all immigrants live in only a few states: California, Texas, Florida, New York, Illinois, and New Jersey.[2] California alone is home to approximately 30 percent of the nation's foreign-born population; slightly more than one in four Californians is foreign born. This geographic concentration of immigrants in select states (and regions) is also not a new phenomenon. At the turn of the 19th century, states such as New York, Illinois, Michigan, and Pennsylvania received the lion's share of immigrants. Nevertheless, data from the 2000 census indicate that increasing numbers of immigrants are taking up residence in southern states, such as Virginia, North Carolina, Georgia, and Maryland, that previously were not much associated with immigration. Indeed, the great European migrations of the 19th and early 20th centuries for the most part bypassed the South. Unlike the states that have traditionally received immigrants, many of the new immigrant growth states have little experience with incorporating newcomers; in fact, they had a history of excluding those who differ from the majority population.

Immigrants from particular countries tend to settle in specific states and regions. For example, most Dominicans can be found in the New York region, just as most Vietnamese reside in southern California. San Diego has a large concentration of Chaldean Iraqis; Minneapolis has large numbers of Hmong. Networks based on ethnicity, family, and friendship serve to draw immigrants to certain areas (Massey, 1999). Other factors that influence the settlement patterns of immigrants include ethnic networks, businesses and enclaves, religious institutions, and employment opportunities.

One immediate effect of contemporary immigration is that immigrants from Africa, Asia, and those of Indian ancestry from Latin America find themselves settling in a country with a history of difficult racial relations and a definition of race that may be considerably different from that in their country of origin. Racial-group allegiances may not make sense to Asians or black people from more homogeneous societies such as the West Indies or countries in Africa. For groups that can be characterized as Hispanic, the saliency of race as an indicator of social class may seem alien. Thus, this 21st-century immigration is moving American society well beyond the black/white framework that has so long dominated our conceptualization of race in the United States.

SOCIETY

Wherever they settle, immigrants are, to some degree, outsiders. As immigrants, they live under the conditions and terms set by the host country and, because immigrants are not full members of that country, they have fewer rights and privileges than its citizens (Aleinikoff & Klusmeyer, 2002). Another way of framing this issue is to recognize that immigrants encounter some degree of exclusion wherever they live. Exclusion can take the form of prohibiting immigrants from direct participation in political life; granting them less legal protection; or limiting access to important social benefits such as labor markets, education, and health care, to name only a few. All immigrant-receiving countries practice some mixture of de facto and *de jure* exclusion. The question is the degree to which a country's policies and practices promote distinction between citizens and immigrants.

The world's largest receiver of immigrants, the United States, historically has varied in its exclusionary policies and practices. A few examples from our past highlight the ebb and flow of policy regarding exclusion. For instance, throughout much of the 19th century, immigrants could vote in local and state elections,[3] and the federal government actively recruited immigrants to settle U.S. farmland and plow its prairies. However, toward the end of that same century, the United States legally barred Asians from immigrating (Takaki, 1989) and prevented those Asian immigrants already here from naturalizing (Lopez, 1996). The country has had a checkered history on the issue of exclusion.

It should be noted from the outset that the various immigration statuses developed by the United States are themselves highly associated with exclusion. The further one moves from the "gold standard" of immigration status—that is, permanent residency—the more exclusionary the applicable U.S. policies and practices generally become. At the lowest status, undocumented immigrants can expect little from our society, and know that U.S. immigration authorities will remove them if they are caught. For the purpose of the following analysis, this chapter focuses on legal permanent residents, rather than other categories such as temporary (that is, tourists, students, temporary workers) and undocumented immigrants.

Because immigrants do not have the same rights as citizens, they are more vulnerable to government authority and private exploitation. Deportation—or removal, as it is now termed—is one of the best illustrations of the fundamental difference in legal rights afforded to citizens and immigrants. The Supreme Court ruled in 1893 that deportation was not a form of punishment. Because deportation was not deemed a criminal matter, but rather an administrative action, deportation cases did not require a jury trial (or potentially multiple levels of appeals) or the right to an attorney. This decision has long been upheld in spite of the fact that deportation effectively deprives immigrants of their livelihood and right to remain in the country (with their families). Moreover, one agency, Immigration and Customs Enforcement (ICE; formerly the Immigration and Naturalization Service or INS), has almost complete jurisdiction over immigration cases. ICE serves as the judge, jury, and executor of administrative decisions, and its authority extends to detention (jailing) of immigrants during removal proceedings and until they are physically removed from the country. Such a concentration of authority is unheard of in legal proceedings for citizens.

In the 30-year span from the Civil Rights era until the mid-1990s, U.S. policy steadily narrowed the distinction between citizen and legal immigrant. Schuck (1998) referred to this period as one in which citizenship was devalued. While citizens continued to enjoy political rights denied to immigrants (such as voting and jury service), had broader constitutional due process protection, and had better opportunities to sponsor family members to immigrate, legal immigrants nevertheless enjoyed increasing access to public institutions and greater government protection,[4] including more involvement of the federal courts in examining immigration administrative decisions. Several examples illustrate the point. If immigrants worked in low-wage jobs, they could receive Food Stamps. If they became disabled or were too elderly to work, Supplemental Security Income (SSI) provided a modicum of protection against destitution (U.S. Congress, Ways and Means Committee, 2004, j-9). If immigrants who ran afoul of the law served out their sentences, immigration judges were allowed discretion in determining whether deportation served the interests of the community and the nation, rather than having conviction of a crime automatically trigger deportation. Multiple levels of due process protected people seeking asylum, to ensure that the federal government did not mistakenly return them to their home countries to face persecution.

The passage of immigration and welfare reforms, which began in the mid-1990s and continue today, dramatically recast immigrant rights and responsibilities. A partial list of federal legislation and policy initiatives highlights the reduction in social protection and legal rights of immigrants: the Illegal Immigration Reform and Immigrant Responsibility Act of 1996 (IIRIRA), the Antiterrorism and Effective Death Penalty Act of 1996 (AEDPA), the Personal Responsibility and Work Opportunity Act of 1996 (PRWOA), the USA PATRIOT Act (2001, renewed 2006), and Operation Liberty Shield.[5] All these policy changes shape the lives of immigrants, as is discussed later.

These immigration and welfare reforms were spurred by public perceptions that poor and unskilled immigrants were increasingly drawn to the United States to live on welfare; that crime perpetrated by immigrants had reached epidemic levels; that growing numbers of immigrants neither spoke nor made an effort to learn English; and (after

9/11) that terrorist cells comprised of immigrants posed a grave threat to the country. Ongoing concern over illegal immigration also factored into a climate less welcoming to legal immigrants. Some critics of immigration policy likened the policies to a "moral panic" over immigrants and the perceived ruination of American society (Welch, 2002). Ironically, the devaluation of immigrants is occurring even while the vast majority of immigrants comply with societal expectations. An overwhelming majority of immigrants work for a living (U.S. Census Bureau, 2001). Immigrants start businesses that offer employment to the native-born and immigrant alike (Raijman & Tienda, 2003; Light, Bernard, & Kim, 1999; Razin & Light, 1998). Immigrants have strong family values and are more likely to raise their children in married-couple households than are native-born families (U.S. Census Bureau, 2001). Immigrant parents value and support education.[6] Within a generation, the majority of children of immigrants have learned English (Portes & Schauffler, 1996), as have many of their immigrant parents.[7] Immigrants have increased their rates of naturalization over the past 10 years, signifying a symbolic and legal commitment to the United States.[8] Immigrants serve in the U.S. military and have died for their adopted country.[9] Immigrants pay taxes[10] and participate in the civic and religious lives of their communities (Lippy, Chapter 6). These are the very values that have defined U.S. society from its inception: hard work, thrift, respect for the institutions that create community, and the family as the core of community. Both in the reality of public policy and in the mythology of Norman Rockwell paintings, these American values constitute the ideals that define American society, its politics, and its governance. Still, immigrants find that access to the social institutions that shape U.S. society is deliberately made problematic because of policy emphasizing exclusion. How these policy changes affect immigrants is discussed in the following section.

INSTITUTIONS

In a liberal welfare state such as the United States, no institution may be more important to immigrants than the labor market (Esping-Andersen, 1990). Indeed, the authorization of a work permit by the immigration bureaucracy is one of the most important documents an immigrant can possess. American society values work, and major public policies are founded on the assumption that paid work (or ownership of a business) will provide the means to acquire important goods and services such as housing, food, and health insurance. With generally unfettered access to labor markets, legal immigrants participate fully in the U.S. economy, with the same right as citizens to contracts, employment protection,[11] occupational advancement, and contributory social welfare programs such as unemployment insurance and Old-Age, Survivors, and Disability Insurance.

Open access to labor markets was not always the case. Until the Supreme Court ruled the practice unconstitutional in 1971, states could exclude immigrants from certain categories of employment by denying them the necessary licenses to practice trades or professions.[12] For example, in 1943, North Dakota made it illegal for immigrants to hunt and trap,[13] and in 1957 Idaho prohibited immigrants from teaching.[14] Presently, with the exception of positions that require security clearances, legal immigrants freely participate in the same labor markets as do citizens (Aleinikoff & Klusmeyer, 2002).

Only certain categories of immigrants, such as the undocumented and amnesty seekers, are legally excluded from paid work, although clearly, in the case of the former, the prohibition is largely ineffective. The issue for immigrants is not one of being barred from employment; rather, it is of finding work that pays a sufficient wage and grants benefits such as health care, child care, pension, disability insurance, and life insurance (Haley-Lock & Bruch, Chapter 9). Admittedly, this is a struggle for all too many native-born workers, but most immigrant workers are excluded from the public safety net. Moreover, the ability of immigrant (and native-born) workers to earn adequate wages has been reduced by the steady erosion of the buying power of the minimum wage. Having full-time, year-round employment is no longer a guarantee of having income above the poverty line.[15]

Just as access to and participation in labor markets is the defining institution for adult immigrants in the United States, access to public education is the defining institution for immigrant children. Public education is the only true universal benefit in the United States: all children are supposed to be provided it. Through court cases such as *Plyler v. Doe*,[16] public policy has affirmed that public education should be available to all immigrants as well, including those who are undocumented.[17] Public schools socialize immigrant children to American values and provide one of the major means for them to acquire human capital to advance themselves. Indeed, public education is one of the primary reasons why immigrant parents come to the United States in the first place (Farkas, Duffett, & Johnson, 2003). The universality of public education is less the issue for immigrant children than is its quality. Most immigrants live in central cities and attend schools in the poorest urban education districts; thus, the poorer quality of education impedes access to the labor market and assimilation into American society (Fry, 2005; Roderick, 2002).

Although school systems have become more adept at teaching non-English-speaking (or ESL) students, the enrollment numbers and the linguistic diversity represented in that population have steadily increased (Capps, Fix, Murray, Ost, Passel, & Herwantoro, 2005). Instruction of current ESL student populations is a daunting task both for traditional immigrant states, such as California, and for others that are experiencing increasing numbers of immigrant students. Despite changes in state and federal funding that have brought greater resources into low-income, urban school districts, these schools nevertheless have fewer resources with which to educate (Corcoran, Evan, Godwin, Murray, & Schwab, 2004) and are increasingly populated by immigrant students.[18] Many immigrant children (along with other ethnic minorities) are taught by noncredentialed, inexperienced teachers, fear for their safety, have fewer academic and extracurricular programs available, and have classes in decrepit buildings.[19] It is, of course, paradoxical that the very institution the United States relies on to socialize and acculturate immigrant children—an institution that embodies the aspirations of immigrant families for providing their children with the human capital to succeed in their new homeland—is chronically underfunded and poorly staffed. Adding to the pressure on school budgets are underfunded federal mandates, such as those in No Child Left Behind legislation, under which all U.S. schools must operate; these laws further sanction failing schools with the complete loss of federal assistance.

Labor markets and public education are among the few American institutions that, in theory at least, confer the same opportunities and benefits on immigrants as they do on citizens. With most other societal institutions, immigrants face some degree of exclusion and lesser protection. Two examples come readily to mind: welfare and criminal justice/immigration enforcement. Welfare reform, most notably the PRWOA of 1996, has disproportionately placed the responsibility of caring for low-income immigrant families on the states, relatives and friends, community groups, and nonprofit organizations—a return, in many ways, to pre-New Deal welfare practices.[20] Federal public assistance programs, such as Temporary Aid to Needy Families (TANF, formerly AFDC), Food Stamps, Medicaid, and SSI, for which legal immigrants were once largely eligible, are now, for the most part, off-limits. Welfare reform created a bewildering and complex set of eligibility rules based on immigration entry date, immigration status,[21] and work history credit. Moreover, the federal government gave states discretion over using their own resources to allow legal immigrants to participate in joint federal/state programs such as TANF and Medicaid.[22] Even for immigrants who lived in states that permitted enrollment in TANF, participation meant that they ran the risk of having the removal category "likely to become a public charge" levied against them.[23]

In the area of immigration enforcement, a series of immigration reforms, most importantly IIRIRA and the USA PATRIOT Act, have lessened the due process protection granted to immigrants. A telling example of that change has been in the area of mandatory detention and removal of "aggravated alien felons." Under IIRIRA, legal immigrants whose convictions result in sentences of one year or longer (even suspended sentences) are classified as "aggravated felons," and immigration authorities are required to detain them until they can be removed from the United States. Until a Supreme Court opinion brought relief, ICE interpreted the law to apply retroactively, meaning that immigrants who had long since served their time could be detained and removed.[24] IIRIRA allowed little judicial oversight of or intervention in removal proceedings (Fragomen, 1997; Weissbrodt & Danielson, 2005). Designed to hasten the removal of dangerous felons, IIRIRA has resulted in the detention and removal of thousands of immigrants, many of whom have citizen children and citizen spouses, for offenses such as check fraud and minor drug possession (Dow, 2004; Smith, 2005).

Actions taken under the auspices of the War on Terror demonstrated that the federal government could interpret immigration law so that even minor violations could be used to round up and detain immigrants, sometimes indefinitely (Cole, 2003). Basic rights enjoyed by citizens, such as the right to be represented by an attorney and the right to be charged with a crime or released, were denied to immigrants (Cole, 2003). After the September 11th attacks, the Bush Administration required that all adult males originating from countries with alleged ties to terrorism (North Korea was the only non-Muslim country on the list) register with and be interviewed by U.S. security officials. This process resulted in the detention and removal of thousands of immigrants, often on the basis of minor immigration violations (Akram & Karmely, 2005). No known terrorists were apprehended, or successfully prosecuted, as a consequence of registration. Critics of the program noted its resemblance to the World War II-era internment of Japanese Americans, and pointed out that its legacy is primarily fear and resentment (Ahmad, 2002). These legislative and administrative policies demonstrated basic and fundamental distinctions between the constitutional protections afforded to citizens and those given to immigrants.

IMMIGRANT FAMILIES

Our society traditionally values the family, and defines it as the institution most important to preserving American values. The movement of so many millions of immigrants to the United States over the past three decades means that the American family is increasingly made up of immigrants. Depending on when they arrived, these immigrant families have become, are becoming, and will become the new American family. Policies that emphasize exclusion and social institutions that carry out exclusionary practices affect the well-being not only of immigrant families but ultimately of the American family as well.

As stated earlier, slightly more than one in seven families in the United States is headed by a foreign-born adult. Increasing numbers of children have at least one immigrant parent, even though most children in such families are born in the United States. The U.S. Census reported that slightly more than 14 million children (approximately one in five) live in immigrant families; the percentage is even higher (22 percent) for children under the age of six (U.S. Census Bureau, 2001, 2003a). Children of immigrant parents are the fastest growing "segment of the nation's child population" (Capps, Fix, Ost, Reardon-Anderson, & Passel, 2004, p. 1). For children in some racial and ethnic groups, the immigrant family (as opposed to the native-born family) is the norm rather than the exception. Approximately 83 percent of Asian and 58 percent of Hispanic children live in immigrant families, compared with only 6 percent of white and 12 percent of black children (U.S. Census Bureau, 2001, 2003a).[25] On average, immigrant families are larger than the families of the native born and have more children in them—including those of the head of the household and related children such as nieces and nephews. The children of immigrant families are more likely to reside with a married couple than are the children of native-born families (U.S. Census Bureau, 2001).

A distinguishing feature of many immigrant families with children is the fact that these families are composed of members with different immigration statuses (for example, citizen, legal immigrant, undocumented). Fix and Zimmerman (2001) classify these as mixed-status families and estimate that they make up 9 percent of U.S. families. The typical mixed-status family is composed of U.S.-born children with at least one immigrant parent, who may or may not have legal immigration status.[26] These different statuses bring with them varying rights and privileges, among the most important of which are eligibility for government benefits and ability to sponsor family members to immigrate to the United States.

Immigrant families are disproportionately poor compared to the native-born population. Immigrant families have almost twice the poverty rate (15.7 percent) of native families (8.3 percent). Certain characteristics are associated with the variation of poverty among immigrant families. For example, foreign-born children related to a foreign-born head of household have even higher rates of poverty, nearly 30 percent (U.S. Census Bureau, 2001). Twenty-seven percent of children under the age of six living with immigrant parents are in poverty, with an additional 29 percent near the poverty line (Capps et al., 2004).[27] Recently arrived immigrant families have higher poverty rates compared to immigrant families with longer periods of settlement in the United States (Douglas-Hall & Koball, 2004).

Poverty, food insecurity, and hunger go hand-in-hand. Food insecurity means that at least one member of a household went without food sometime during the year because of insufficient resources. Given their high rates of poverty, it is not surprising that immigrant families experienced some of the highest rates of food insecurity in the nation. One study conducted in three high-immigrant states found that 83 percent of immigrant households with children were food insecure, with 45 percent of the families reporting moderate to severe hunger (Physicians for Human Rights, 2000).[28] In sharp contrast, the most recent national food-insecurity prevalence study found that 17.6 percent of all households with all children are food insecure; of those, only 0.7 percent indicated that hunger existed (Nord, Andrews, & Carlson, 2004).

Unlike poor native-born families, many immigrant families, especially recent arrivals, are barred from participating in the Food Stamp program, which is a main source of protection against hunger for poor people in this country.[29] Deprived of any legal claim to government-sponsored food assistance based on citizenship status, ineligible immigrant households are thus denied the opportunity to be free from hunger. Because hunger is associated with a host of other problems, including poor health and poor academic performance by children, this deprivation has long-term and far-reaching consequences.

A very troubling aspect of food insecurity among immigrant families is the prevalence of poverty and hunger despite family members' active participation in the labor force. As noted earlier, the labor force participation rate of immigrants is impressive. Slightly fewer than eight in 10 male immigrants, and 54 percent of female immigrants, work. Work is the norm for immigrants, whether or not they have children. Douglas-Hall and Koball (2004) reported that 62 percent "of children living with low-income, recent immigrants, live with parents who work full-time, year-round" (p. 5). Generally, immigrants are more concentrated in the low-wage, blue-collar sectors of the economy than are native-born workers. For example, 53 percent of female and 45 percent of male foreign-born workers earn 200 percent or less of the minimum wage, compared with 40 percent of female and 26 percent of male native-born workers (Capps, Fix, Passel, Ost, & Perez-Lopez, 2003).

Because immigrant families earn less in the labor market, they have less capacity to purchase necessary goods and services through private exchanges. The lack of purchasing power is not the only disadvantage they encounter. Because employment-based benefits, such as health insurance, child care, and pensions, are associated with better-paying jobs, immigrants in low-wage sectors of the economy do not often benefit from them.[30] Indeed, low-wage immigrant workers are often not covered either by public social welfare programs or by private, employer-based benefits.

The area of health care coverage illustrates the gaps in both private and public availability. In 2003, approximately 35 percent of the foreign-born population had no health insurance, compared with 13 percent of the native population (U.S. Census Bureau, 2003b). As most immigrants live in families, it is not surprising that immigrant families also have high rates of being uninsured for health care (Ku & Matani, 2001). Whereas employers provide health insurance for 54.6 percent of native-born workers, only 44.5 percent of immigrant workers are so covered. The rate of insurance coverage for recently arrived immigrant workers is even lower (36.2 percent) (U.S. Census Bureau, 2001). Capps and colleagues (2003) reported that in 2002, only 22 percent of children with at least one noncitizen parent had private health insurance. Just as with Food Stamps, the public health care safety net crafted to cover low-income families is often inaccessible to immigrant families. The 1996 welfare reforms made many low-income immigrant families ineligible for Medicaid and state child health insurance programs (SCHIPs). The reforms also depressed participation rates for those who remained eligible for the two programs.[31] Between 1995 and 1999, the percentage of immigrant children participating in publicly funded health care programs dropped from 36 percent to 28 percent (Ku & Blaney, 2000).

To deal with the problem of uninsured immigrant children, 23 states have opted to use their own resources to extend Medicaid and SCHIP eligibility to low-income legal immigrant families. Even with improved coverage, though, Fremstad and Cox (2004) reported that 51 percent of noncitizen children had no health care coverage in 2003 (p. 3).

Exclusion has an almost radioactive nature, in that it is difficult to contain and manage. Target efficiencies that restrict public benefits to all but a few select categories of immigrants often result in limiting access by those who do qualify. This dynamic is largely a result of confusion and fear. Regardless, it means that many eligible immigrant families go without health care, remain hungry, and forgo income support because they believe that U.S. policy excludes them.

IMPLICATIONS FOR SOCIAL WORK

Despite the presence of tens of millions of immigrants living in the United States, the country has no comprehensive policy to facilitate their incorporation. Indeed, U.S. policy takes largely a laissez-faire approach to integrating immigrants into our communities and social institutions. Instead, immigrants are brought into the fabric of American life via family, friends, ethnic networks, mutual support associations, religious organizations, immigrant-based social service agencies, and businesses. Immigrant communities have social capital that contributes to the economic and social well-being of their members. Nevertheless, these mechanisms of inclusion are often poorly supported by public policy, a reality all too many social workers know firsthand. Social workers also understand that the lack of policy to foster inclusion is yet another form of exclusion. In reality, the United States maintains an exclusionary climate even for those immigrants it welcomes to start their lives anew. Especially for the families of low-wage immigrant workers, this climate casts a shadow over the well-being of immigrants and constrains their opportunities.

Although it is true that lesser legal protection applies to all immigrants, those with modest means have fewer resources to challenge negative legal actions, such as removal, or to petition for an adjustment in legal status. The same point applies to workplace benefits or educational opportunities: high-wage immigrant workers are more likely to have private benefits, such as health care and health insurance, and to have educational alternatives to public schools for their children. For upper-income immigrants, the tattered and frayed public safety net has little relevance—but it is a crucial element in the lives of low-wage immigrant workers.

This exclusion is not without cost to the larger society. An "us-versus-them" perspective harks back to our darker traditions and, as any student of history knows, the harms such traditions produce are not easily remedied. Poor-quality education, high rates of hunger and poverty, lack of health care, and a climate of fear constitute a poor foundation upon which to build a productive future, but this is exactly what many immigrants face in this country. In the long run, divorcing ourselves from the responsibility to assist immigrants can only mean that an increasingly large segment of our population has less agency and capacity than it might otherwise have had.

The social work profession, by its very nature, must question all exclusionary policy, for at its core social work is about fostering inclusion in both policy and practice.

Beyond resisting and working to repeal policy that reinforces immigrants as outsiders, social workers must articulate a vision of policy that bridges the distance between citizen and immigrant so that the historic tradition of becoming an "American" is facilitated, rather than hindered, by government policy. An inclusionary vision specifies rights and responsibilities and the means to realize them both. An inclusionary vision builds on core American values such as work, family, and community engagement, and creates policy that strengthens those values. An inclusionary vision recognizes that the vast majority of immigrants embrace American values and resists the crafting of policy that treats those who violate those values as if they were the majority.

It is in the fundamental interests of the United States to adopt inclusionary immigration policies. If the United States is to remain globally competitive, it must permit a productive future for immigrants and their children. Investing in immigrants is central for growth of the economy and continuation of the American dream. Providing immigrants an environment in which they can thrive is essential for the economic well-being of the Baby Boomers whose retirement and health care will be increasingly funded by immigrant members of society. Bolstering the agency and capacity of immigrants is crucial for maintaining and enhancing civil society and democratic ideals.

END NOTES

1. Author's calculation of data (based on U.S. Department of Homeland Security, Office of Immigration Statistics, 2006).
2. Data indicates that the residential distribution of legal and undocumented immigrants is equally concentrated in those six states.
3. It was relatively common practice in the 19th century for states to allow immigrants the right to vote if they declared an intention to naturalize. As Ueda noted, "it was not until 1928 that the first national election occurred in which no alien in any state possessed the right to vote" (2001, p. 298).
4. For example, Congress passed a range of laws granting protection to persecuted people such as refugees and asylees in 1980, conferring legal immigration status on undocumented immigrants in 1986, and designating certain vulnerable populations (such as battered immigrant women) as meriting governmental protection.
5. Operation Liberty Shield was an executive policy used by the Bush Administration after September 11, 2001, for mandatory detention of all asylum seekers from countries with alleged ties to terrorism.
6. For example, the author's analysis of data from the National Opinion Research Center's General Social Survey (2006) showed that 63 percent of foreign-born adults opined that the country is spending too little on education (compared with 66 percent of native-born adults); 92 percent of foreign-born adults indicated that government should definitely or probably assist low-income college students (compared with 86 percent of native-born adults).
7. A survey of adult immigrants found that 87 percent of the sample thought immigrants had a responsibility to speak and understand English, and 85 percent of the sample stated that it was hard to get a job or to get ahead without learning English (Farkas, Duffett, & Johnson, 2003, pp. 24, 26). Age of immigration and level of education are associated with adult immigrants' acquisition of English (Fennelly & Palasz, 2003; Stevens, 1999).

8. Naturalization rates are highly variable year by year. Nevertheless, the naturalization rates in the late 1990s, up to 2004, are all higher than the rates for the early 1990s (BCIS, 2004, Table 32).

9. The war in Iraq has highlighted the service of immigrants in the armed forces. A cursory review of newspapers will find frequent mention of immigrants serving, fighting, and dying beside citizen soldiers. Approximately 37,000 immigrants are serving in the military, and 80 of them have died in Iraq ("Foreign-Born GIs," 2005).

10. This is also true of undocumented immigrants. It is estimated that undocumented workers presently contribute approximately $7 billion to the Social Security Trust Fund—money that they will never collect (Porter, 2005).

11. The Immigration Reform and Control Act of 1986 created the Office of Special Counsel for Immigration Related Unfair Employment Practices within the U.S. Department of Justice. Two of the tasks of this office are to educate employers that U.S. law prohibits employment discrimination based on citizenship status or national origins, and to enforce that law.

12. Graham v. Richardson, 403 U.S. 365 (1971).

13. N.D. Rev. Code § 20-0110 (1943).

14. Idaho Code § 33-1303 (Supp. 1957).

15. The last year in which the yearly earnings from a minimum-wage job equaled the poverty line for a family of three was 1968.

16. 457 U.S. 202 (1982).

17. The right to public education is not entirely secure, because it springs from the plenary power of the federal government, meaning only that the federal government has the right to confer or deny benefits based on "alienage." If Congress grants to states the authority to discriminate against immigrants (as it did with welfare reform), universal education that is available to all may well disappear.

18. The U.S. Census Bureau reported that 44 percent of the foreign-born, compared with 27 percent of the native-born, live in a central city of a metropolitan area (U.S. Census Bureau, 2004).

19. Because of data limitations, it is difficult to assess the education of immigrant children nationally. The Urban Institute has used limited English proficiency as a proxy measure for immigrant children. See Capps et al. (2005) on the issue of teacher qualifications. I have taken Phillips' and Chin's analysis of educational disparities based on race/ethnicity and social class and extrapolated their findings on teacher qualification, physical plant, student safety, and academic program to low-income immigrant children (Phillips & Chin, 2004).

20. At the same time, legal immigrants remain eligible for the hallmark programs of the New Deal, Social Security and unemployment insurance, and more recently created tax-based programs such as the earned income tax credit.

21. For example, refugees, asylees (those people granted asylum), and individuals covered by the Violence Against Women Act remain eligible for federal benefits. See the current edition of the Ways and Means Green Books for a description of the eligibility rules for each program.

22. Welfare reformed permitted states the option of allowing immigrants to participate in TANF and Medicaid after a five-year bar. It also allowed states to enroll immigrants in those programs before the five-year waiting period, at their discretion and expense (Zimmermann & Tumlin, 1999).

23. The "likely to become a public charge" provision was created by Congress in 1882, long before the emergence of the modern welfare state.

24. INS v. St. Cyr, 533 U.S. 289 (2001).

25. Author's calculation of U.S. Census Bureau data. Immigrant families are defined as having one or more family members who is foreign born (U.S. Census Bureau, 2003a).

26. Researchers from the Urban Institute estimated that "almost 30 percent of young children of immigrants have an undocumented parent" (Capps, Fix, Ost, Reardon-Anderson, & Passel, 2004, p. 7).

27. Fifty-four percent of young immigrant children live in families with income 200 percent or less of the federal poverty level (Capps et al., 2004).

28. The lead researchers noted, "Hunger was very prevalent among the legal immigrants we surveyed, and the rate of hunger, at 41%[,] was more than double the rate found in the general population of low wage families"(p. 1630; see also Kasper, Gupta, Tran, Cook, & Meyers, 2000).

29. The Food Stamp Restoration Act of 2003 restored eligibility to immigrant children. However, parents who have arrived since 1996 are still prohibited from participating in the program until they have lived in the country for five or more years. The permanency of the restoration remains in question. At the end of 2005, Congress unsuccessfully attempted to bar any immigrants from receiving food stamps.

30. A Kaiser Commission on Medicaid and the Uninsured report noted, "The vast majority of immigrants have a full-time worker in the family, but a disproportionate number of immigrants work in low-wage jobs that are less likely to offer health benefits" (Fremstad & Cox, 2004, p. ii).

31. Fix and Passel found that even in groups that remained eligible for Medicaid, such as refugees, participation rates dropped significantly between 1995 and 1999 (Fix & Passel, 2002). Because most children in immigrant families are born in the United States and therefore are citizens, they remain eligible for Medicaid and SCHIPs. Recent efforts to enroll citizen children of immigrant parents in SCHIPs and Medicaid have made progress in reducing the number of uninsured children in immigrant households (Capps, Fix, Ost, Reardon-Anderson, & Passel, 2004; Capps, Kenney, & Fix, 2003).

REFERENCES

Ahmad, M. (2002, Fall). Homeland insecurities: Racial violence the day after September 11. *Social Text, 20*(3), 101–115.

Ahmed, B., & Robinson, J. G. (1994). *Estimate of emigration of the foreign-born population* (Population Division Working Paper No. 9). Washington, DC: U.S. Census Bureau.

Akram, S. M., & Karmely, M. (2005). Immigration and constitutional consequences of post-9/11 policies involving Arabs and Muslims in the United States: Is alienage a distinction without difference? *U.C. Davis Law Review, 38*, 609–699.

Aleinikoff, T. A., & Klusmeyer, D. (2002). *Citizenship policies for an age of migration*. Washington, DC: Carnegie Endowment for International Peace.

BCIS, U.S. Immigration and Naturalization Service. (2003). *Estimates of the unauthorized immigrant population residing in the United States: 1990 to 2000*. Retrieved January 16, 2005, from http://uscis.gov/graphics/shared/aboutus/statistics/Ill_Report_1211.pdf

BCIS, U.S. Immigration and Naturalization Service. (2004). *Yearbook of immigration statistics*. Washington, DC: U.S. Government Printing Office. Retrieved January 16, 2006, from http://uscis.gov/graphics/shared/statistics/yearbook/Yearbook2004.pdf

Borjas, G. J., & Bratsberg, B. (1996). Who leaves? The outmigration of the foreign-born. *Review of Economics and Statistics, 78*, 165–176.

Capps, R., Fix, M., Murray, J., Ost, J., Passel, J., & Herwantoro, S. (2005). *The new demography of America's schools: Immigration and the No Child Left Behind Act.* Washington, DC: The Urban Institute. Retrieved January 14, 2006, from http://www.urban.org/publications/311230. html

Capps, R., Fix, M., Ost, J., Reardon-Anderson, J., & Passel, J. S. (2004). *The health and well-being of young children of immigrants.* Washington, DC: Urban Institute.

Capps, R., Fix, M., Passel, J. S., Ost, J., & Perez-Lopez, D. (2003). *A profile of the low-wage immigrant workforce.* Washington, DC: Urban Institute.

Capps, R., Kenney, G., & Fix, M. (2003). Health insurance coverage of children in mixed status families. *Snapshots of America's Families, 3*(12), 1–4.

Cole, D. (2003). *Enemy aliens.* New York: New Press.

Corcoran, S., Evan, W. N., Godwin, J., Murray, S. E., & Schwab, R. M. (2004). The changing distribution of education finance, 1972 to 1997. In K. M. Neckerman (Ed.), *Social inequality* (pp. 433–465). New York: Russell Sage Foundation.

Douglas-Hall, A., & Koball, H. (2004). *Children of recent immigrants: National and regional trends.* New York: Columbia University, Mailman School of Public Health.

Dow, M. (2004). *American gulag: Inside U.S. immigration prisons.* Los Angeles: University of California Press.

Esping-Andersen, G. (1990). *The three worlds of welfare capitalism.* Princeton, NJ: Princeton University Press.

Farkas, S., Duffett, A., & Johnson, J. (2003). *Now that I'm here: What America's immigrants have to say about life in the U.S. today.* New York: Public Agenda. Retrieved January 23, 2005 from http://www.publicagenda.org/research/research_reports_details.cfm?list=12

Fennelly, K., & Palasz, N. (2003). English language proficiency of immigrants and refugees in the Twin Cities metropolitan area. *International Migration, 41*(5), 93–125.

Fix, M., & Passel, J. (2002). *The scope and impact of welfare reform's immigrant provisions* (Discussion Papers). Washington, DC: Urban Institute.

Fix, M., & Zimmermann, W. (2001). All under one roof: Mixed-status families in an era of reform. *International Migration Review, 35,* 397–419.

"Foreign-born GIs have special cause." (2005, September 20). Cox News Service. Retrieved January 16, 2006, from Lexis-Nexis database.

Fragomen, A. T. (1997). The Illegal Immigration Reform and Immigrant Responsibility Act of 1996: An overview. *International Migration Review, 31,* 438–460.

Fremstad, S., & Cox, L. (2004). *Covering new Americans: A review of federal and state policies related to immigrants' eligibility and access to publicly funded health insurance.* Washington, DC: Kaiser Commission on Medicaid and the Uninsured.

Fry, R. (2005). *The high schools Hispanics attend: Size and other characteristics.* Washington, DC: Pew Hispanic Center.

Kasper, J., Gupta, S. K., Tran, P., Cook, J. T., & Meyers, A. F. (2000). Hunger in legal immigrants in California, Texas, and Illinois. *American Journal of Public Health, 90,* 1629–1633.

Ku, L., & Blaney, S. (2000). *Health coverage for legal immigrant children: New census data highlight importance of restoring Medicaid and SCHIP coverage.* Washington, DC: Center on Budget Policies and Priorities.

Ku, L., & Matani, S. (2001). Left out: Immigrants' access to health care and insurance. *Health Affairs, 20,* 247–256.

Light, I., Bernard, R., & Kim, R. (1999). Immigrant incorporation in the garment industry of Los Angeles. *International Migration Review, 33,* 5–25.

Lopez, I. F. (1996). *White by law.* New York: New York University Press.

Massey, D. (1999). Why does immigration occur? A theoretical synthesis. In C. Hirshmas, P. Ksinitz, & J. De Wind (Eds.), *The handbook of international migration* (pp. 34–52). New York: Russell Sage Foundation.

National Opinion Research Center. (2006). *General social survey.* Retrieved February 22, 2006 from http://sda.berkeley.edu

Nord, M., Andrews, M., & Carlson, S. (2004). *Household food security in the United States, 2004* (Economic Research Report No. ERR11). Washington, DC: U.S. Department of Agriculture. Retrieved January 10, 2006, from http://www.vidyya.com/18pdfs/erril.pdf

Passel, J. S. (2006). Size and characteristics of the unauthorized migrant population in the U.S. Washington, DC: Pew Hispanic Center. Retrieved September 16, 2006, from http://pewhispanic.org/reports/report.php?ReportID=61

Passel, J. S., Capps, R., & Fix, M. (2004). *Undocumented immigrants: Facts and figures.* Washington, DC: Urban Institute. Retrieved January 15, 2005, from http://www.urban.org/UploadedPDF/1000587_undoc_immigrants_facts.pdf

Phillips, M., & Chin, T. (2004). School inequality: What do we know? In K. M. Neckerman (Ed.), *Social inequality* (pp. 467–519). New York: Russell Sage Foundation.

Physicians for Human Rights. (2000). *Hungry at home: A study of food insecurity and hunger among legal immigrants in the United States.* Boston: Author.

Porter, E. (2005, April 5). Illegal immigrants are bolstering Social Security with billions. *New York Times*, p. A1.

Portes, A., & Schauffler, R. (1996). Language and the second generation: Bilingualism yesterday and today. In Portes (Ed.), *The second generation* (pp. 8–29). New York: Russell Sage Foundation.

Raijman, R., & Tienda, M. (2003). Ethnic foundations of economic transactions: Mexican and Korean immigrant entrepreneurship in Chicago. *Ethnic and Racial Studies, 26,* 783–801.

Razin, E., & Light, I. (1998). Ethnic entrepreneurs in America's largest metropolitan areas. *Urban Affairs Review, 33,* 332–360.

Reagan, P. B., & Olsen, R. J. (2000). You can go home again: Evidence from longitudinal data. *Demography, 37,* 339–350.

Roberts, S. (2005, February 21). More Africans enter U.S. than in days of slavery. New York Times, p. 1, §A, col. 3.

Roderick, M. (2002). Hispanics and education. In P. S. J. Cafferty & D. W. Engstrom (Eds.), *Hispanics in the United States* (pp. 123–174). New Brunswick, NJ: Transaction Books.

Schuck, P. H. (1998). *Citizens, strangers, and in-betweens: Essays on immigration and citizenship.* Boulder, CO: Westview Press.

Smith, J. F. (2005). United States immigration law as we know it: El clandestine, the American gulag, rounding up the usual suspects. *U.C. Davis Law Review, 38,* 747–814.

Stevens, G. (1999). Age at immigration and second language proficiency among foreign-born adults. *Language in Society, 28,* 555–578.

Takaki, R. (1989). *Strangers from a different shore: A history of Asian Americans.* Boston: Back Bay Books.

Ueda, R. (2001). Historical patterns of immigrant status and incorporation. In G. Gerstle & J. Mollenkopf (Eds.), *E pluribus unum?* (pp. 292–327). New York: Russell Sage Foundation.

U.S. Census Bureau. (2001). *Profile of the foreign-born population in the United States: 2000* (Current Population Reports P23-206). Retrieved January 20, 2005, from http://www.census.gov/prod/2002pubs/p23-206.pdf

U.S. Census Bureau. (2003a*). America's families and living arrangements* (Detailed Tables, Table C5). Retrieved March 15, 2005, from http://www.census.gov/population/www/socdemo/hh-fam/cps2003.html

U.S. Census Bureau. (2003b). *Income, poverty and health insurance coverage in the United States: 2003.* Washington, DC: Author.

U.S. Census Bureau. (2004). *The foreign-born population in the United States: 2003* (Current Population Reports P20-551). Washington, DC: Author. Retrieved January 23, 2006, from http://www. census.gov/prod/2004pubs/p20-551.pdf

U.S. Congress, Ways and Means Committee. (2004). *Green Book: Appendix J—Welfare Benefits for Noncitizens.* Washington, DC: Author.

U.S. Department of Homeland Security, Office of Immigration Statistics. (2004). 2003 *Yearbook of immigration statistics.* Washington, DC: Author. Retrieved January 25, 2005, from http://uscis. gov/graphics/shared/statistics/yearbook/2003/2003Yearbook.pdf

U.S. Department of Homeland Security, Office of Immigration Statistics. (2006). 2004 *Yearbook of immigration statistics.* Washington, DC: Author. Retrieved February 21, 2006, from http://uscis. gov/graphics/shared/statistics/yearbook/Yearbook2004.pdf

Weissbrodt, D., & Danielson, L. (2005). *Immigration law and procedure.* St. Paul, MN: West Publishing.

Welch, M. (2002). *Detained: Immigration laws and the expanding INS jail complex.* Philadelphia: Temple University Press.

Woodrow-LaField, K. A. (1996). Emigration from the USA: Multiplicity survey evidence. *Population Research and Policy Review, 15,* 171–199.

Zimmermann, W., & Tumlin, K. (1999). *Patchwork policies: State assistance for immigrants under welfare reform.* Washington, DC: Urban Institute. Retrieved February 2, 2005, from http:// www.urban.org/publications/309007.html

CHAPTER 4

BEYOND THE RAINBOW: MULTIRACIALITY IN THE 21ST CENTURY

Gina Miranda Samuels

I am new. History made me. . . .
I was born at the crossroads
and I am whole.
—*Aurora Levins Morales (1990)*

INTRODUCTION

The inclusion of this chapter within a text that explores race and ethnicity in the United States is in part a testament to changes in both the concept of race and increased identity options officially available through Census 2000. Nevertheless, some suggest that Census 2000's "check all that apply" approach is at best a shift that still mirrors our racialized history and reifies existing norms and obsessions with race (Graves, 2004). Others argue that allowing U.S. citizens to select multiple categories on the census form threatens programs, legislated during the civil rights movement, that depend on national demographic statistics to justify their ongoing existence (Spencer, 1997, 1999). Added suspicion is levied at multiracials who claim their white racial heritage through the use of various labels other than socially sanctioned single-race identifications. Publicly choosing multirace labels (for example, biracial) is interpreted as an attempt to escape more stigmatized categories and move toward an in-between group with assumed socioeconomic privileges. Examples that validate this concern exist not only in the United States (both past and present), but also in South Africa's "colored" population and among the prados in Brazil (Daniel, 2003). These varied responses to multiraciality have profound implications for multiracial people and also for the communities and individuals who claim single-race identification.

This chapter advances three points of discussion. First, it proposes that multiracial and multiethnic populations are not new. What may be new is the way in which some people experience their mixed-race heritage and what identity options are made available to them, either informally or officially, in contemporary society. How existing institutions and structures legitimate, sanction, or constrain these identities (for example, racial classification systems) is an important dimension of this discussion. Secondly, this chapter uses the example of black–white multiracials to illustrate how the contemporary debates surrounding multiraciality are generally framed by a history of racial essentialism, racism, and (more recently) colorblind individualism.[1] Black–white mixed-race people have always attracted disproportionate attention, fascination, and concern from media, social science, law, and the general public. It is here that a rich discussion of the myths and realities of multiraciality can be gleaned. The effects these constructions have on today's public perceptions of all multiracials, and the ability of multiracial individuals and communities to be self-determining beyond a black–white paradigm, are examined. Finally, this chapter explores contemporary constructions of multiraciality. This discussion includes a challenge to social work practice to abandon essentialist and decontextualized frameworks of human development. To that end, this chapter is a call to move beyond outdated notions of racial/ethnic identity formation and "cultural competence" that conflate race, class, culture, and ethnicity and imply that these social identities are biologically fixed and inherited master statuses.

In this chapter, race is understood as a social construct, but one that continues to operate in the United States as real and primarily biological. Although race is largely deemed a fiction among social scientists, the general public overwhelmingly endorses a folk biology that legitimates race as a meaningful human distinction in social life and central in developing a personal/group identity, particularly for people of color (Daniel, 2002; Graves, 2004; Kennedy, 2004). Essentialist phraseology such as, "It's in my blood," and even titles of movies (for example, "White Men Can't Jump") are cultural markers of our continued commitment to notions of inherence and race: implying causal relationships between race and our abilities, talents, limitations, and traits.[2] However, racial labels also signify distinct sociopolitical histories (for example, histories of immigration and migration, social injustices, slavery) around which individuals and families have coalesced, through group solidarity, and crafted affirming cultural identities and ethnic group loyalties. Indeed, many of us embrace such identities; they can be sources of healing and great pride, and offer a sense of belonging and community grounded in that shared history. They are also group identities around which communities have gathered to advocate for civil rights and social change efforts.

As a recognition of the power of these group identifications in the United States, racialized and ethnic labels will sometimes be used as proper nouns when discussing these populations as socially constructed groups (for example, blacks, whites). Multiracial and mixed-race are used interchangeably as panracial labels, and refer to people with more than one racial or ethnic heritage. The term "racialized" denotes the social and legal process by which populations and people become racial beings, as well as the reification of that meaning system within a racialized community. To that end, the term "racialized identity" is used in place of "racial identity" to remind us that race is not a natural biological fact; rather, it is something we ascribe to a body based on phenotype. Ethnicity is understood to include a racialized identity, but extends beyond this to one's self-identified history of immigration or migration, region, and values that are integrated into one's daily practices and awareness through one's family and community (Root & Kelley, 2003). "Cultural identity" is used to signify a broader identity, and includes class, gender, and ethnicity. Cultural identity is learned, and evolves intergenerationally through family and community memberships and experiences. It is not assumed that these experiences and identifications necessarily match one's biological heritage or racialized phenotypes (Root & Kelley, 2003). Likewise, people who use multiracial labels or identities may not actually have biological parents who claim different racial categories, or may have parents who each represent or claim some "pure" racial heritage.

It is important to note here that substantial debate continues about the use of racialized labels as reifying racism and racial essentialism. Myriad labels are used by multiracial populations to name themselves and their experiences as unique and tied to a specific set of racial or ethnic heritages and histories.[3] This chapter will not enter into that debate, though the merits and hazards of reclaiming and inventing racialized labels to assert a group identity are explored in the final section. This chapter ultimately argues that an individual's choice of racial label is not a proxy for his or her cultural experiences or background. It is also important to note that people who are multiracial are not automatically multicultural; not all multiracial people have had access to their cultures of origin as children or even as adults (Miranda, 2003a). These issues are relevant to the discussion of identity development and to an understanding of how essentialist notions of authenticity and race shape identity work. References will be made to contemporary multiracial research and literature that offers insight into how identity politics and constructions of race come to bear upon one's identity across the life course.

THE HISTORY OF MIXED-RACE AMERICA

The experience of multiracial America has undergone radical transformations (Daniel, 2002; Root & Kelley, 2003; Talty, 2003; Williamson, 1980; Winters & DeBose, 2003). Some of these transformations have been invisible to social science or have been ignored; others have received overwhelming attention (Baird-Olson, 2003; Morning, 2003). To understand contemporary debates tied to racial identity and multiraciality, one must first begin by looking back in history. Although today, people of black heritage are least likely to officially claim other racialized heritages (according to the U.S. Census 2000), most arguments against multiple racial recording and multiraciality seem to disregard this reality. It is argued here that this has everything to do with the ways in which racial constructions were formed during the inception of what we now call the United States of America, particularly in the context of U.S. slavery and colonialism. This history of mixed race is overviewed here to precede a later demonstration of the ways in which the unique histories of ethnic populations in the United States matter, as individuals from these communities express multiple ethnic identities in the 21st century.

The history of black–white multiracial people United States is one of the most poignant examples to use in exploring the social, scientific, and political establishment of a binary racial classification system rooted in the philosophies of colonialism in the United States (Davis, 1991; Foeman & Nance, 1999; Korgen, 1998; Lopez, 1996; Williamson, 1980). The creation of an institutionalized caste structure tied to the assumed "natural" and mutually exclusive categories of racial group membership, and the implication this has for asserting multiracial identities today and into the future, is central to this discussion. To that end, three primary dimensions within U.S. history are examined, as they illustrate the treatment of black-white multiracial heritage (hereafter referred to as biracial) and either validate or deny individual and group identities. They are the legal regulation of racial inheritance (biracial identity in the context of hypo-descent laws); the development of blood theories and the "muleology" of mixed race; and the shifting of racial identity during the Harlem Renaissance (internalizing the one-drop rule).

Constructing Race through Law

The contemporary understanding of race stems from the historical merging of class, geographic, ethnic, political, and biological constructs both real and imagined (Anzaldua, 1987; Awkward, 1995; Davis, 1991; Gabard & Cooper, 1998; Ignatiev & Garvey, 1996; Williamson, 1980). The following discussion explores the evolution of race as a binary system, the contributions of law in supporting a racialized power structure, and the function of legislative regulation of family systems to ensure that the racial-group membership of multiracial people remained within the established racial hierarchy. Readers are reminded that the regionally diverse treatment of mixed-race status not only represents the variance in contemporary understandings of racialized identities, but also reflects the North American struggle to maintain the power structure that racial designations represent and ultimately reinforce (Zack, 1993).

The first liaisons between people of African and European descent predated slavery and produced America's first biracial children within a structure initially more classist than racist: indentured servitude (Davis, 1991; Williamson, 1980). Indentured Europeans and African slaves were originally viewed as members of the same social caste, that is, servant. Within this system of servitude, it is speculated that the first biracial Americans were born and occupied a free but "lower class" status (Davis, 1991; Korgen, 1998; Williamson, 1980). This is not to suggest, however, that black-white coupling was ignored or even somewhat tolerated by colonists (Davis, 1991; Williamson, 1980). There are numerous accounts of public whippings of white people and black people whose sexual relationships were understood within colonial Christianity as a "dishonor of God," and by the 1700s as bestiality (Davis, 1991; Williamson, 1980).

As the slave economy took hold and indentured servitude dwindled, colonists struggled to legislatively protect their vested interests in maintaining power and a socially privileged position (Williamson, 1980; Zack, 1993). Although African enslavement had already received moral and legal support among colonists (Williamson, 1980), they were challenged by the existence of biracial children and the thought of enslaving whiteness (Zack, 1993). It was during this time that some of the first language regarding the social status of so-called mulattoes appears in the law.[4] Although most were considered socially inferior to whites (Davis, 1991; Williamson, 1980), this was not the legal status of many mulatto children in the upper South (Russell, Wilson, & Hall, 1992). Consequently, Virginia initiated the break from traditional English law that granted children the class status of their fathers, and legislated social status, and ultimately racial identity, as maternally inherited (Williamson, 1980).

Particularly troubling, therefore, were the biracial offspring of white women. Virginia's previous legislation appears an irrelevant precedent for determining the status of these children, most of whom were legally free (Williamson, 1980). By the late 17th century, Virginia's courts had declared white mothers of mulatto children subject to a five-year sentence of indentured servitude, and their children to slavery until the age of 31 (Davis, 1991; Russell, Wilson, & Hall, 1992). Consequently, the freedom of mulattoes with white mothers was revoked so as to match their already informally established subordinate social positions as black/slave. These laws, however, still proved insufficient in deterring miscegenation, and the mulatto population continued to grow.

Eventually, many states in the upper South and in the North adopted a "one-drop rule" for determining blackness (Williamson, 1980). Designating blackness by hypo-descent, or, in other words, "one drop of black blood," made no distinction between someone of "pure" African heritage and those whose appearance and racial ancestry were more white than black. The literature in this field notes that these laws were even stricter than those used by the Third Reich in identifying Jews (Zack, 1993). Arguably, the one-drop rule was in part a pragmatic consequence of the "whitening" of slavery: the mulatto population in the upper South had increased by 66.9 percent between 1850 and 1860, as compared to the black population's increase of 19.8 percent (Zack, 1993). The one-drop rule protected the slave economy from losing its natural resources through the obvious continuation of miscegenation (Williamson, 1980). Subsequently, as whiteness was being constructed as racially pure, blackness was becoming racially mixed. Not surprisingly, current estimates suggest that anywhere from 75 to 90 percent of today's "black" population has some white heritage (Davis, 1991; Winters & DeBose, 2003).

Beyond its economically pragmatic function, the law of hypo-descent made clear statements about the U.S. theory of race. First, this rule defined race as a white and not-white dichotomy, and sanctioned the legal system as a mechanism for regulating an individual's racial-group membership by quantums of "blood." Moreover, in establishing what blackness could include, it reserved whiteness as its ontological opposite. In other words, just as one could not be both free and slave, a person could not be both black and white.

Second, this law ascribed biological and social potency to blackness in its capacity to trump the inheritability of whiteness and its ascribed social privileges for descendents

41

of racially mixed white heritage.[5] In a context of slavery that already regarded whiteness as inherently superior, this construction protected the concept of purity as being solely attached to whiteness. This notion of race purity was reinforced by definitions of the word pure in various dictionaries that used phrases such as "not mixed or adulterated with any other substance . . . of unmixed origin or descent . . . Innocent or morally good" (Pearsall, 2002) and "not mixed . . . free of dirt, defilement, pollution . . . complete . . . having no faults; perfect, chaste, virgin, of unmixed blood or ancestry . . ." (Pickett, 2004). These modern definitions of "pure" mirror colonial constructions of whiteness as a social privilege tied to racial (and moral) purity and ultimately, biological superiority (Anzaldua, 1987; Lopez, 1996; Williamson, 1980). Thus, once an individual crosses the race line in creating a family, all of that person's descendents have impure blood, and therefore can no longer be white—by definition. It seems reasonable to suggest that the legislation surrounding the status of mulatto children as black and thus second-class in states in the upper South was enacted largely to protect the future of whiteness as one of social power and privilege reserved only for those biological descendents of genetically pure white family systems (Zack, 1993). Because the presence of children with black heritage would challenge the whiteness of future family members, the laws relegated mulattoes to the social and racial position of blackness.

New Orleans and Free Mulatto Elites

Despite these laws in the upper South, not all mulattoes in the United States were automatically subjected to the one-drop rule. In some areas of the lower South, free mulatto descendants of wealthy plantation owners were themselves members of prosperous, developed, elite societies, and occasionally were slave owners (Davis, 1991; Williamson, 1980). Although the majority of all mulattoes in the Deep South were slaves, approximately 75 percent of the relatively small free black population in those states comprised free mulattoes and their descendants (Zack, 1993). The stricter laws of miscegenation and hypo-descent eventually made their way to these areas, but South Carolina's courts in particular refused to automatically apply the one-drop rule to all mulattoes (Williamson, 1980). In one case, a judge verified a mulatto's whiteness by acceptance by whites as an insider and his or her reputation as such in the white community (Davis, 1991; Korgen, 1998). Clearly, South Carolina did reflect early American constructions of whiteness as both a privileged social and racial status. However, that state did not automatically join the rest of the country in its definition of blackness under the laws of hypo-descent; instead, it created a middle caste occupied by free mulatto elites, also referred to as Blue Vein Societies (Davis, 1991; Williamson, 1980).

This again makes the case that where one experiences his or her multiraciality matters, especially with regard to the range of viable identity options (and attached privileges) available under law and social sanction. It also begins to illustrate how the identities of mixed-race populations became tied to their value and function in protecting the social privileges of whiteness.

The legal sanction of this three-tiered racial structure had practical functions. The lower South had a long history of slavery, and a significantly larger slave population than the upper South. Many white people viewed the existence of an established, but small, free mulatto population as a protective barrier to prevent slave uprisings (Williamson, 1980). Initially, mulattoes were prevented from marrying either blacks or whites, to ensure the survival of this "buffer" class (Davis, 1991). Over time, the careful orchestration of family lineage among free mulatto elites, both voluntary and imposed, resulted in the formation of entire mulatto communities, which enjoyed a position higher than that of blacks, but not equal to that of white people (Russell, Wilson, & Hall, 1992; Williamson, 1980). Free mulattoes established elite societies for which membership relied upon extremely light skin tone, as evidence of one's white heritage. Here the formation of distinct mulatto identities was tied to French Catholic cultural influences, particularly in New Orleans and Charleston (Russell, Wilson, & Hall, 1992; Zack, 1993). Subsequently, a free mulatto identity and social status were secured through increasing one's white heritage, or at the very least preventing additional black heritage. Within this treatment of race, it is not surprising that labels were used to mathematically establish racial pedigree in fractions of blackness (for example, quadroon, octoroon, etc.). Given the looser enforcement of antimiscegenation laws between white and mulatto elites, arranged unions to protect the three-tiered system did not always remain within the small circle of free mulatto families (Davis, 1991; Russell, Wilson, & Hall, 1992; Williamson, 1980).

Perhaps the most distinct and gendered treatment of mulatto heritage resulting from mulattoes' established racial position as "other" were the quadroon balls, attended exclusively by white men and extremely fair-skinned mulatto women. These institutionalized and widely popular social events ultimately provided, through formal contracts, mulatto concubines to wealthy southern white men. In exchange, the women and the children these unions produced were financially provided for through the duration of the relationship. An added benefit was the mulatto family's continued membership among the free mulatto elite, and the children's genetically strengthened chances to "pass" into whiteness (Davis, 1991; Williamson, 1980; Zack, 1993). Although many of these relationships ended when the men entered "respectable" marriages with white women, some relationships continued informally despite the marital status of the men involved (Williamson, 1980). The exotified beauty and sexual/social desirability ascribed to these mulatto women is a dimension of mixed race that continues today, particularly for multiracial women (Funderburg, 1994; Gordon, 1995; hooks, 1992, 1989; Jones, 1994; Luke, 1994; Root, 1992, 1996; Streeter, 2003, 1996).

One interpretation of this response to the one-drop rule is as a resistance against the structures imposed upon mulattoes in other regions as black/second class, and a carving-out of racial identities as neither black nor white. Likewise, in using their class privileges to arrange marriages within the mulatto elite and formally institutionalize intimate relationships between mulatto women and wealthy white men, they challenged the construction of mulatto identity within a context of antimiscegenation laws that rendered the mulatto's existence synonymous with illegitimacy and lower-class status. Subsequently, the lighter skin and European features of the mulattoes in the lower South became associated with higher economic class and socially distinguished family heritage.

Another interpretation, one that became more widespread after emancipation, was that of internalized oppression, and free mulatto adaptation to and acceptance of a classist, racist, and colorist system that acted to further oppress those with darker complexions. The fictitious credo of the mulatto elite often known as the Blue Vein Society, discussed in Wallace Thurman's *The Blacker the Berry* (1970), is an excellent example of this:

> Whiter and whiter, every generation. The nearer white you are the more white people will respect you. Therefore all light Negroes marry light Negroes. Continue to do so generation after generation and eventually white people will accept this racially bastard aristocracy, thus enabling those Negroes who really matter to escape the social and economic inferiority of the American Negro. (p. 37)

These interpretations of mulatto adaptation to a racist social structure, through the formation of separate societies and, ultimately, their ability to defy the construction of blackness by entering whiteness through "passing," became increasingly upsetting to both white and black America, particularly after emancipation. What was clear, however, was that in North America mulattoes could either be black or "other." If they attempted to be white, it was only because their skin color allowed them to "pass" as interlopers into that privileged world.

Emancipation: Replacing Slavery with Jim Crow

As slavery ended, laws of segregation were quickly erected to uphold the institutional-ized structures that maintained social and political distance between blacks and whites. Eventually, white support for the three-tiered racial organization of the lower South buckled under the growing endorsement of the one-drop rule (Williamson, 1980). In balancing the power structure on a binary racial system of hypo-descent, the racial designations of "black" and "white" held increased significance for establishing social status outside of the slave system. Subsequently, the previous dichotomy of slave/free and all of its symbols became fully collapsed into the dichotomy of black/white (Davis, 1991; Williamson, 1980; Zack, 1993).

Still, some newly freed mulattoes joined preexisting communities of free slaves who had intermarried with white people and Native Americans, forming what today is referred to as "triracial isolates"; many of these individuals denied their black heritage and lived isolated from both whites and blacks (Williamson, 1980; Zack, 1993). Research conducted by E. Franklin Frazier in the 1930s portrayed these small communities of mixed-race people, including the well-known "Moors of Delaware" and the "Jackson White," as having rich histories and distinct racial identities. This is reflected in one descendant's description of the attitudes toward established triracials, the white community, and newly freed slaves:

> The tribe is all mixed up now more than they used to be. During the old times we had a separate feeling. We did not belong to the Negro or the white people. That's what started them to marrying first cousins. I guess you know how people just freed feel toward people of this settlement who had been free all the time. We was what was considered the "Old Free Issue" . . . . They did not like us and we did not like them. They felt that they could not accept their inferiority. (Zack, 1993, p. 9)

In fact, the 1950 Census had specific instructions to record these populations by their family names, which were synonymous with their racially mixed lineage: the Moors, the Tunicas, the Croatans, and so on (Morning, 2003). Arguably, many mulattoes from the lower South expressed an "other" identity and also sought to maintain this status after emancipation. Without the distinction of freedom, many of the mulatto elite clung to the advantages of light skin tone, resisting the one-drop rule by reinforcing their mixed-race identities within exclusive and colorist social clubs and institutions. These organizations' members were required to pass "brown paper bag" and "comb" tests to prove that their genetic heritage was enough removed from blackness that a comb could glide easily through the hair, or that the skin was lighter than a paper bag or allowed the veins underneath the skin to show (Korgen, 1998; Williamson, 1980). These institutions, which included preparatory schools, colleges, churches, fraternities and sororities, and professional clubs (many of which are still in existence today), no longer have official skin-tone requirements (Russell, Wilson, & Hall, 1992; Williamson, 1980). However, many are suspected of continuing to hold skin-tone preferences that privilege European features, thereby informally perpetuating their more blatantly colorist and classist beginnings (Davis, 1991; Russell, Wilson, & Hall, 1992; Williamson, 1980).

Not all mulatto elites chose to participate in upholding a distinct mulatto identity. Some, whose skin color and physical appearance permitted, completely broke ties with their black ancestry and entered white society through a process referred to as "passing" (Korgen, 1998; Williamson, 1980; Zack, 1993). Although passing occurred before this time, many white people became obsessed with the possibility of "invisible blackness" in the years following emancipation (Williamson, 1980; Zack, 1993). The secretive nature of passing fueled a fear among many white people of having a child with a person who was "really" black but had defied the one-drop rule and was passing—blackness and black blood camouflaged beneath white skin. Consequently, the mulatto elite became the target of these hostilities, as their family systems were known suspects—a result of more than two centuries of miscegenation and careful construction of family lineage. The fear of having a child with black blood was not, however, limited to the realities of hypo-descent laws or the existence of social racism.

Contributing to these fears was the steadily growing body of scientific racism (Korgen, 1998). Although the initial quest was to prove the moral, genetic, and intellectual inferiority of African/black people, it now explicated the dangers of miscegenation and the plight of people with "mixed blood" (Williamson, 1980; Zack, 1993). Therefore, not only were white southerners concerned with maintaining their white identities that were tied to a sociopolitical power structure, but they also sought to avoid the literal destruction of this assumed pure race through the mixing of blood.

Blood Theories and the "Muleology" of Mixed Race
Much of the American understanding and pathologizing of mixed race and racial-group membership is rooted in the epistemological traditions of essentialism (Davis, 1991; Favor, 1999; Ferber, 1997; Frankenberg, 1995; Gabard & Cooper, 1998; Pope-Davis & Liu, 1998; Stubblefield, 1995; Williamson, 1980; Zack, 1993). We must briefly explore the premises on which this philosophy is founded if we are to fully grasp the contemporary implications it holds for racial identity theories, and the inimical environment it has created for the expression of individual racial and cultural identities—particularly for multiracial populations.

From the 1860s to the mid-1900s, the scientific community contributed its share in support of the essentialist American folk theory of race as a natural human designation representing both seen and unseen human qualities (Allport, 1954; Appiah, 1990; Hirschfeld, 1995; Williamson, 1980; Zack, 1993). Important is the fact that many of the early theories regarding mixed-race psychology and biology were fundamentally tied to the influential writings of Charles Darwin, whose full book title reveals the position of this theory regarding the possibilities of natural group superiority among animals and humans: *The Origin of Species by Natural Selection: The Preservation of Favored Races in the Struggle for Life* (1859). Darwin's theory directly and indirectly validated white domination as the result of a natural selection process that had produced a superior race—a race whose survival was put at risk by the existence of racial hybrids and breeding with other "not-white" races (Ferber, 1997; Williamson, 1980; Zack, 1993). Although strict social Darwinism did not receive extended endorsement, vestiges of its logic remain in the underlying explanations of mixed-race identity as a threat to whiteness as pure, and in the theoretical pathologizing of multiracial people that continues into the 21st century (Daniel, 2002; Kennedy, 2004; Root & Kelley, 2003; Talty, 2003). The only comfort offered to antimiscegenists was the reassurance that eventually the descendants of mixed-race unions, being naturally inferior, would become infertile and die out (Williamson, 1980). Consider the following statements from Dr. W. A. Dixon (1883), whose documented medical observations of mulattoes in Ohio yielded the following conclusions:

> Those of the first cross were robust; those of the second were paler more ash like in complexion, of slender form, plainly bearing many of the characteristics of . . . inevitable tendencies to special diseases. The third union resulted in less fertility and greater predisposition to disease. The fourth union, still less fertile than the others, brings forth a progeny largely suffering from cutaneous affections, ophthalmia, rickets, dropsy of the head, white swelling of the knee joints, morbus coxrius, diseased glands, [and] suppurating sores until the whole generation is quite extinct. (Zack, 1993, p. 123)

This lengthy illustration is captured succinctly within the very word "mulatto," which originally meant young mule, a mule being a sterile mixed breed (Williamson, 1980). What Williamson (1980) refers to as the "muleology" of mixed racial heritage fits well within the language already established in naming this group. In addition to the biological frailty of mulattoes, scientists advanced "blood theories" explaining the mysterious transmission of a racialized inheritance and attached personal traits through one's blood (Allport, 1954; Hirschfeld, 1995; Williamson, 1980).

The earlier notions of black blood potency that led to the one-drop rule became solidified in the American folk biology of race during the late 1800s (Zack, 1993). Slavery had already been justified by paleontologists' earlier classification of black people, as well as Native Americans, as inherently subhuman, amoral, and animalistic (Baird-Olson, 2003; Korgen, 1998). However, without the institution of slavery, the additional scientific "proof" offered by these theories relegated the identities of all black descendents to an inferior essence intergenerationally transmitted through the blood (Hirschfeld, 1995; Williamson, 1980; Zack, 1993). Consequently, whiteness, as a racially pure essence, was assumed to be everything positively opposite to blackness (Williamson, 1980). Therefore, even if one's black heritage was not visibly apparent, one could not avoid embodying the invisible essence of black blood, within which lurked all of the subordinate, amoral personality traits of blackness (Ferber, 1997; Williamson, 1980; Zack, 1993). To further support the pathology of mixed race, some neurologists theorized differences in electronic currents that allegedly ran through the bodies of white people in an opposite direction than in black people. In people of mixed race, these currents supposedly became crossed, resulting in severe psychopathologies (Zack, 1993). Considering this collection of scientific racism, it becomes clear how the tragic mulatto could emerge as the poster-child image of multiraciality: ascribing the racialized essence of psychological frailty and biological inferiority caused by one's "racial impurity."

It is also important to note that this essentialist and racist construction of race and mixed race was experienced among other racialized populations, as their communities of origin held them to essentialist notions of identity and group allegiance. Here is a quote, from 1927, from a mixed-race Native American named Mourning Dove Cognea The Half Breed:

> Yes, we are between two fires, the Red and the White. Our Caucasian brothers criticize us as a shiftless class, while the Indians disown us as abandoning our own race. We are maligned and traduced as no one but we of the "despised breeds" can know. (Baird-Olson, 2003, p. 212)

Another piece of evidence that extends the muleology of mixed race beyond blackness was noted by Spickard (1989) in a white minister's public comment on a mixed-race Asian-white couple living near his home:

> Near my home is an eighty-acre tract . . . . On that tract lives a Japanese. With that Japanese lives a white woman. In that woman's arms is a baby. What is that baby? It isn't white. It isn't Japanese. It is a germ of the mightiest problem that ever faced this state; a problem that will make the black problem in the South look white. (p. 25)

Although biologists and anthropologists increasingly recognized the scientific fallacy in blood theories of racial inheritance, an essentialist folk theory of race continues to shape many Americans' conceptions of mixed-race identity, particularly in supporting the one-drop rule. Research conducted in 1995 by anthropologist Lawrence Hirschfeld found that among black and white children and college students in his sample, disproportionate numbers endorsed the one-drop rule of inheritance in predicting both the racial appearances and identities of biracial children. Likewise, in research and literature on culture and race, it is still common to see the terms "blood" or "mixed blood" (Ferber, 1997; Zack, 1993). Arguably, essentialist understandings of racial-group membership and personal identity have survived despite advances in science that challenge these explanations of human racial inheritance.[6]

Considering this scientific and social war levied against mulattoes in the late 1800s, and their loss of a unique identity based on their status as "free," it is not surprising that many joined the newly freed black community in reconstructing a postcolonial blackness outside of slavery. This period of history produced rich literature, music, and art, and established the beginnings of a unified black American identity that internalized the one-drop rule and self-regulated racial-group memberships, and subsequently racial identities.

MULTIRACIAL IDENTITY THEORIES FROM 1900 TO 1950

As noted earlier, studies conducted before the 1920s on mixed race employed the etic perspective, and were propelled more by racist assumptions than rigorous scientific inquiry or empirically informed theories (Korgen, 1998; Williamson, 1980; Zack, 1993). It is not surprising, therefore, that the first theories of "racial identity" appearing during the 1920s sought to explain the phenomenon that later in the Harlem Renaissance was described by DuBois as a "double consciousness," but in 1928 by theorist Park as a "marginal man" (see Park 1928, 1931). Park's theory targeting all "non-white people" was eventually extended specifically to "racial hybrids," as he described a human life in the margins of blackness and whiteness (Park, 1928, 1931). It is interesting to note, however, this was not initially viewed as pathological and was in fact theorized to produce exceptional intelligence and resiliency. Park cited the life success of W.E.B. DuBois as evidence of the mental agility produced by such psychologically challenging life conditions (Park, 1931).

The notion of the marginal man, however, was later adopted by Everett Stonequist (1937), who constructed a stage process of identity development resembling the more pathological understandings of mixed race of the time. The literary works of both black and white authors complemented these theoretical descriptions. Through viewing the tragic mulatto, the exotic quadroon, and those who "passed," Americans watched mulattoes resolve their inevitable "identity crises" as predicted by Stonequist (1937). Lacking any empirical scientific evidence, the art and aesthetics of the Harlem Renaissance era are the only supports for the validity of this theory. Arguably, this conceptualization of mixed-race consciousness is carried on in the subtle and overt pathologizing of biracial identity within more contemporary racial identity theories that emerged in the years following the Harlem Renaissance (Daniel, 1996; Ferber, 1997; Herring, 1995; Hirschfeld, 1995; Renn, 2004; Root, 1992, 1996).

The Harlem Renaissance: Blackness as a Cultural Identity

The leaders of the Harlem Renaissance were disproportionately members of the lower South's mulatto elite (Korgen, 1998; Sollors, 1997; Williamson, 1980; Zack, 1993). With them they brought their generations of higher education and familiarity with white elite customs and culture (Korgen, 1998). During this time, their role in the black community shifted, and they began to move into positions of leadership within the black community. As Williamson noted, "They changed the mission of the mulatto elite from one of carrying white culture to the Negro mass to one of picking up the black culture within the Negro world and marrying it smoothly to the white culture they knew so well" (1980, pp. 151–152). However, the historical politics between light- and dark-skinned Americans of black descent remained. Likewise, the enduring stereotypes about skin tone and ascribed temperaments were embedded in the art and literary expressions of the Harlem Renaissance (Favor, 1999; Sollors, 1997; Zack, 1993).

Images of the tragic mulatto, the culturally displaced, and the survivalist strength of those with darker skin all had their places within the literary discourse of this era, and are perhaps the most tangible pieces of evidence to use in tracing the beginnings of a unified black identity rooted in laws of hypo-descent, colorism, and quests for political power through racial solidarity.

During the Harlem Renaissance, accepting the one-drop rule became a sociopolitical defiance of blackness as inferior, particularly for those with extremely light skin who could easily "pass" but chose to devote their energies to the "up lift" of the race (Favor, 1999; Sollors, 1997). It is telling, however, that the phrase "up lift" was the one chosen to describe a movement led by the mulatto elite, whose traditions of colorism and classism were now repositioned to benefit a group they had previously scorned and abandoned. Arguably, the suspicions of those who questioned the loyalties of the mulatto elite were not automatically assuaged through their public assertion of a common identity.

This era also began to articulate clear dimensions of what is often referenced as a "positive" or "healthy" black identity, the core essence of which was theoretically independent from, or despite, a racially mixed blackness (Korgen, 1998). Under the umbrella of hypo-descent, the mulatto elite led the creation of a single racialized identity tied not to a pride of racial purity, but to an evolving sense of cultural purity. During the Harlem Renaissance, blackness, or "authentic blackness," became a cultural construct that honored a historically devalued racialized experience. This reinforced the racial dichotomy of black/white through the acceptance of the one-drop rule (Favor, 1999; Williamson, 1980). In other words, what was being challenged was the definition of blackness as inferior, not the construction of black and white as discrete and dichotomous categories. Consequently, people with various degrees of black heritage found their places in this new blackness—some more easily than others.

"Being Black": The Performative Nature of Race and Identity

> Being black is not a color—it's an experience.
> —*Kathy Russell* (Russell, Wilson, & Hall, 1992, p. 62)

In his book, *Authentic Blackness* (1999), Favor presented an unparalleled exploration of the folk understanding of blackness as expressed within the literary works produced during the Harlem Renaissance. Most compelling is his analysis of race as performative, particularly in establishing the identities of black–white Americans, many of whose sociopolitical and ultimately racial loyalties were increasingly held suspect. It was during that time that racial constructions were both challenged and reified through the establishment of the concept of racial authenticity and its demonstration through dress, politics, and behaviors recognized to be fundamentally reflective of the new black cultural consciousness (Favor, 1999). Consequently, inherited blackness was not enough for real racial-group membership, and the writings of many black–white multiracial authors during this era discussed the phenomenon of "performing oneself into a racial community" or relocating to the south to "find" one's heritage (Favor, 1999; Sollors, 1997). Establishing pan-ethnic definitions of a "core" black identity, under the auspices of racial solidarity and empowerment, articulated blackness as a cultural and political state of mind upon which the survival of this new identity, in defiance of whiteness, depended. This positioned many multiracials on the borders of blackness. Light skin represented the historical and current class privileges of the mulatto elite; this history was proof of their predisposition to abandon blackness to protect their own identities (and social status) as not black. The mulatto elite, however, was also viewed as a political asset for leadership and negotiations within white society—a fact that secured some value for their membership and role within the Black Renaissance (Williamson, 1980).

Interpersonally, though, light skin remained a liability and a reason for mistrust when individual racial, and consequently political, loyalties were being determined. A distinct mulatto identity was becoming a conceptual and theoretical threat to the new black identity, and compromised political power to fight racism and discrimination as a unified black community (Favor, 1999; Root, 1992, 1996; Russell, Wilson, & Hall, 1992). It is not surprising, therefore, that the contemporary multiracial empowerment movement is opposed by many civil rights leaders and pan-ethnic organizations largely on the basis of its potentially negative implications in loss of political power for their communities, specifically in protecting civil rights laws and federally funded programs (Leary, 1997; Reed, 1998). These identity politics are not unique to the black community. The National Organization of La Raza and Pan-Indian advocacy groups are also noted in the literature as expressing their opposition to, and the negative consequences of Census 2000 for their communities (Morning, 2003). Not surprising, the legacy of "passing" fuels additional concerns about multiple-race recording as statistical "passing": allowing multiracials to escape the continued social stigma attached to their nonwhite communities of origin (Leary, 1997). It is important to note that these arguments ignore the existence of people who claim multiracial identities and labels (for example, "LatiNegra") that do not include white (Comas-Dìaz, 1996).

This historical movement is also significant because it suggests that although a system for racial designation had been located externally through legislation, "blackness" (cultural blackness) was regulated and negotiated within the black community (Russell, Wilson, & Hall, 1992; Zack, 1993; Williamson, 1980). Although these constructions were not left unchallenged (Hurston, 1937; Johnson, 1912; Larsen, 1986; Toomer, 1923), a distinct mixed-race consciousness was becoming antithetical to the so-called authentic black experience in the United States (Favor, 1999; Williamson, 1980). It is not surprising that by the 1920s the elite mulatto identity became absorbed into an elite black identity (Favor, 1999). It should not be surprising, therefore, to find that that same year marked the last U.S. Census recording of mulattoes as an official racial category (Sollors, 1997; Williamson, 1980; Zack, 1993). The one-drop rule had become firmly established as both a racial and a cultural identity in North America, and arguably a mixed-race consciousness independent from the black community became conceptually and legally meaningless (Williamson, 1980; Zack, 1993).

The Harlem Renaissance began to fade by the mid-1930s with the onset of the Great Depression, but the identities formed during that period were a budding public statement that blacks in the United States were a culturally defined and politically unified community. Group consciousness, firmly rooted in the history of slavery and the political efforts to "up lift" and transform "the race," eventually spread to industrial urban cities in the north and west. Although colorism festered in the black community, a series of political movements drew attention elsewhere—to the broader issues of white racism and segregation. The civil rights movement of the 1960s, advocating integration, along with others calling for black nationalism, and Africentrism that extended American blackness to its African origins, continued the move toward defining authentic blackness as a cultural and racialized identity. Nonetheless, this identity was always fundamentally tied to whiteness as its ontological opposite (Omi & Winant, 1994; Williamson, 1980). Other communities of color joined these pan-ethnic models for coalition, and disenfranchised communities coalesced around their common experiences with social injustice and racism against the white communities and colonialist traditions that continued to threaten their survival both as groups and as individuals (Baird-Olson, 2003).

IDENTITY THEORIES

The 1960s and 1970s introduced a wave of monocentric identity development theories and models that specifically sought the emic perspective, and drew upon the philosophies of black empowerment and resiliency (Chestang, 1972; Cross, 1971, 1991; Helms, 1990; Kahn & Denman, 1997). Literature focusing on "black psychology" challenged notions of blackness as marginal (Jones, 1980), and called for a black American identity as opposed to the "Negro identity" then seen negatively as assimilationist and caused by internalized racism and oppression (Cross, 1971). It should also not be surprising; therefore, that very little attention, if any, was given to the identity development of multiracial people. Conceptually, a biracial identity would have been considered an unhealthy, nonblack (or even white) identity.

The omission of the biracial experience from dominant identity theories, which persisted into the 1980s, resulted in the development of Poston's Biracial Identity Model (1990). Although clearly not a theory per se of biracial identity development, this model was firmly rooted in the theoretical assumptions guiding these earlier monocentric stage theories of identity. It did, however, introduce the concept of a healthy biracial identity, one through which people claim both of their heritages (Herring, 1995; Kahn & Denman, 1997). Existing multiracial research generally considers this and other stage/phase models of identity limited in their understanding of the complexities of racialized identity work; the notion of a single "healthy" identity outcome is now generally rejected (Bolatagici, 2004; Miranda, 2003a, 2003b; Renn, 2004; Rockquemore & Brunsma, 2002; Root, 1998; Tashiro, 2002).

The remainder of this chapter continues this exploration of identity, and extends it to more contemporary issues of multiraciality beyond (but rooted within) the black–white paradigm.

MULTIRACIAL IDENTITY IN THE 21ST CENTURY AND BEYOND

> Who are you, what are you, where are you from, no, where are you really from, where are your parents from, are your grandparents Americans? Are you from here, what's your background, what's your nationality, where do you live? Are you black, are you white, do you speak Spanish? Are you really white, are you really black? Are you Puerto Rican, are you half and half, are you biracial, multiracial, interracial, transracial, racially unknown, race neutral, colorless, colorblind, down with the rat race or the human race? What are you? Where are you coming from? Who are your people? (Jones, 1994, pp. 53–54)

What is now referred to as the "biracial baby boom of 1990" represented 50,000 biracial babies born in that year alone (Root, 1996). The U.S. Census Bureau reported that the number of black–white biracial births had increased by 500 percent from 1960 to 1990, compared to a 27 percent growth in births of black babies (Root, 1996). One of every 40 U.S. citizens officially claimed mixed-race heritage on Census 2000, and some predict that one in five people will claim more than one race on the 2050 census (Lee & Bean, 2004). Phrases such as "the new face of America," "rainbow children/families," and ideals of colorblindness all mark this era. In fact, some have referred to the years from the late 1990s into the new millennium as the "post-race era" (Cowels, 2003). But do changes in the U.S. census of 2000 and the multiracial movement indicate real shifts in American constructions of race? Does this generation of multiracial people in the 21st century represent a "new face" of the United States, with new identities that transcend our history of mixed race and folk theories?

To begin to answer this question, consider 2004. The state of Illinois has a biracial candidate for senator, a man whose father is from Africa and whose mother is white. His name is Barack Obama. He is referred to in the press as "handsome" and "intelligent." He is a graduate of an Ivy League college with a carefully groomed, established career. In a magazine insert of the *Chicago Tribune,* dated October 24, 2004, there is an article titled, "The Skin Game: Do White Voters Like Barack Obama Because 'He's Not Really Black'?" Included in this article is a picture of his face: half in brown, half in white, with color by numbers written inside the white segments. When asked how

53

he identifies (arguably a question of interest to all readers), Mr. Obama asserts a racial identification as black and multiple cultural homes. He notes in this article that racial politics exist and are summoned up when people learn of his mixed-race background: "When people who don't know me well, black or white, discover my background . . . I see the split-second adjustments they have to make, the searching of my eyes for some telltale sign. They no longer know who I am."[7] A white woman who is interviewed as a supporter of Obama's candidacy confirms the title of this article when she states, "I guess . . . I don't think of him as black."

These interpersonal experiences to which Obama refers—the racialized perceptions of others, the fragmented portrayal of a racialized face, and the confusion occasioned by racial ambiguity—are markers of multiraciality that are explored within a growing body of literature and research (Funderburg, 1998; Kich, 1992; O'Hearn, 1998; Renn, 2004; Rockquemore & Brunsma, 2002; Root, 1992, 1996; Root & Kelley, 2003; Twine, 1996; Zack, 1993). This new body of literature, predominantly authored by people who are themselves multiracial, informs the final section of this chapter. It proposes that vestiges of the old are found in the contemporary experiences reported by multiracial people. It ultimately constitutes a challenge to the field of social work, in working with multiracial people and family systems, to move beyond notions of cultural competency toward increased sophistication in understanding race and power dynamics across and within racialized groups.

WHAT SOCIAL WORK CAN LEARN FROM MULTIRACIAL RESEARCH

The multiracial movement and the biracial baby boom gave birth to an abundance of literature and research exploring multiracial identity. One should also note the growing number of multiracial adults who pursued careers in social science and literature in order to challenge the theories and research methods that pathologized and marginalized their experiences (Anzaldua, 1987; Comas-Dìaz, 1996; Daniel, 2003; Funderburg, 1994, Gaskins, 1999; Miranda, 2003a; Nakashima, 1996; O'Hearn, 1998; Rockquemore & Brunsma, 2002; Root, 1992, 1996, 1998; Thornton, 1996; Twine, 1996, 1999; Zack, 1993). Perhaps the most cited work on multiracial identity is found in the two volumes edited by Maria P. P. Root, who is multiracial. Although some have critiqued this body of literature and science for its small-sample-size studies, taken together it stands as a compelling illustration of the inadequacies inherent in traditional identity theories and research methods for exploring the identities of multiracial people. In particular, the second volume, published in 1996, begins to move beyond the micro-level of identity development to actually critique constructions of race and mixed race in a multisystemic and sociohistorical context. Beginning in the mid-1990s and continuing into the 21st century, literature has begun to explore how multiracial people negotiate the additional structural challenges of ambiguous racial appearance, multiple cultural heritages, and quests to legitimize their racialized and cultural identities in various contexts (Renn, 2004; Rockquemore & Brunsma, 2002). This work largely advances ecological frameworks for exploring identity development as fluid, contextually tied, and multidimensional (see, for example, Root, 1998). This discussion introduces some of these findings because of their relevance to social work practice.

Traditionally, multicultural social work education is designed to cover the primary four socially/legally constructed pan-ethnic/racial groupings in the United States (that is, black/African American, Latino, Native American, and Asian). This essentially excludes mixed-race populations (Fellin, 2000; Fong & Spickard, 1995). The field of social work in general has yet to make a connection with this new body of literature in challenging traditional understandings of identity and the transmission of culture as fixed, unidirectional, and biologically inherited (Miranda, 2003b). Though there are myriad areas for discussion, those highlighted here are of particular interest because of their potential effect on the field of social work practice.

Identity in Its Developmental Context

Although antimiscegenation laws were repealed by 1967, and the census now allows multiple racial reporting, interracial families are still not widely accepted in many parts of the United States (Davis, 1991; Oriti, Bibb, & Mahboubi, 1996; Root, 1992, 1996, 1998). In fact, it is not surprising that in southern states, where more rigid racial borders continue to be maintained despite extensive histories of multiraciality (Davis, 1991; Favor, 1999), people were least likely to claim biracial heritage. For example, in a report of the Census 2000 data, Myers and Hacegaba (2001) noted that in Mississippi, 99.1 percent of white people and 99.2 percent of black people claimed monoracial heritage. Even in Louisiana, a state with historical significance for black–white racially mixed people, fewer than 2 percent of the state reported mixed racial heritage (Kelley, Howe, Kawabori, & Meriwether, 2001). The literature also notes the importance of regional and sociohistorical context in constraining or promoting specific identity responses of U.S. citizens (Bolatagici, 2004; Root & Kelley, 2003; Tashiro, 2002).

Moreover, many studies now regard the developmental demands of adulthood as occasioning contextual shifts that require young adults to learn or relearn, with additional complexity, the meaning of their multiracial heritage (Funderburg, 1994; O'Hearn, 1998; Renn, 2004; Rockquemore & Brunsma, 2002; Root, 1998; Senna, 1998). This process frequently includes adding to their repertoires variations on the theme of responding to the hallmark questions of mixed racial status: "What are you?" and "Where are you from?" (Gaskins, 1999; O'Hearn, 1998). Well into adulthood, multiracial people report experiencing external pressures to mold themselves into others' racial and cultural expectations (Daniel, 2002; Root, 1998). This has challenged traditional assumptions about identity development, which regarded it as confined to adolescence. Most research on multiraciality supports a life-course perspective: namely, that adulthood brings ongoing opportunities to shift and reconstruct one's racialized self as one's environment and social networks expand (Miranda, 2003b; Rockquemore & Brunsma, 2002).

Physical Appearance in Context

Understanding of the multiracial experience must acknowledge the limitless diversity in racial appearance within this population. Given the salience of racialized phenotypes and their everyday use to categorize human beings (for example, with the eyeball test), it is crucial for social workers to recognize the significance of racial appearance and the range of phenomenological experiences individuals report based on their physical characteristics. The inclusion of skin tone as a factor in identity development within previous research also suggests that external appearance draws racialized responses, specifically from parents in their preferences and racial socialization strategies, and from peers in relating to the multiracial person as a racial insider or outsider (Folaron & Hess, 1993; McRoy & Grape, 1999 ; Miranda, 2003a, 2003b; Patton, 2000; Vivero & Jenkins, 1999). The identity politics attached to each racialized population, includ- ing preferences and assumptions for the identities claimed by multiracials, shape the experiences of identity work and gaining insider status to each cultural community (Vivero & Jenkins, 1999). Though multiracial people share a common experience in having to navigate these politics, the identity choices they make and the identity work they undergo to sustain and establish these identities may vary greatly (Root, 1998, Winters & DeBose, 2003). As one male biracial adoptee reported:

> Growing up in my town, I was considered to be black. Yet in metropolitan areas . . . I'm viewed as biracial or even white. In Texas, people sometimes think I'm Latino. When I go to New Orleans, I fit in with the general skin tone there. As far as being "ancestryless," that strikes some truth for me. (Simon & Roorda, 2000, p. 238)

How mixed-race people experience their various communities of origin is facilitated by how their phenotypes are interpreted as insider or something "else" by people in these communities (Awkward, 1995; Berry, 2000; Bolatagici, 2004; O'Hearn, 1998; Rockquemore & Brunsma, 2002). A Korean-White biracial woman said:

> My Korean friends said I looked really white. They joked about my . . . hair . . . and eyes. Most Koreans assume I'm white so they don't ask me, "What are you?" I used to think Caucasians thought I was one of them too, but now I'm not sure. Sometimes Spanish (Latino) people start speaking to me in Spanish . . . so I guess they think I'm Spanish. . . . .I'm questioning my race . . . . I feel like I'm going to have to choose one over the other, but no matter which one I choose I'll never fit in because while people will accept me . . .they'll think I'm of a different race. (Williams, 1996, p. 201)

It is important for social workers to remember that although an individual may have a personal identity, the viability of this identity in public, and the person's ability to access a cultural community as an insider, makes that individual's phenotype either an inhibiter or a promoter of this process. This is not to say that phenotypes cause identity outcomes. In a color-conscious world, however, they do contribute to how an individual's racialized status is assessed. This fact is also a reminder that historical movements to patrol cultural membership and authenticity (Dalmage, 2000) are not unique to the black community; they exist in all racialized communities. For example, the Japanese American sports leagues had blood-quantum requirements, and recent literature describes the historical and contemporary discrimination faced by multiracial Asians, particularly those born during the Korean and Vietnamese wars (Espiritu, 2001). Therefore, social workers must develop sophisticated understanding of the ethnic-specific rules that inform how an individual's identity becomes enculturated, tested, or rejected within a particular ethnic community.

The Family System

Finally, it is important to recognize the degree to which being multiracial, and existing in a multiracial family, is a political existence. In the context of one's intimate family space, a family system may feel buffered against the realities of racism. Out in the world, those realities become visible. In fact, some multiracial adults have noted that their white parents were a liability to their acceptance in communities of color. Consider the following from an Asian–white multiracial adult: "White people always saw me as white . . . . Asians told me how I wasn't Asian . . . . I asked my mom one day to leave my dad home so I wouldn't be seen as too white" (Williams, 1996, p. 202). Reports of similar experiences among multiracials suggest that the idea of "choosing" one's identity is not solely a matter of individual, independent decision making; rather, it is a process shared with others who also claim that identification (Funderburg, 1994; Rockquemore & Brunsma, 2002).

A commonly noted experience is the degree to which multiracial families receive inquisitive stares and polite interrogations when out in public, requiring family members to establish their relationships to each other. Not surprisingly, therefore, a common question among parents of multiracial children is often, "Where should we live?" Most multiracial children have parents who do not share their multiracial experience. Therefore, a place where they can connect with other children and families who are multiracial can be a supportive environment. Research continues to suggest generally that a racially mixed community and school setting, where multiracial children can have access both to their parents' communities of origin and to other multiracial children of similar backgrounds, can be helpful (Johnson, 1992; O'Hearn, 1998; Oriti, Bibb, & Mahboubi, 1996; Root & Kelley, 2003). However, where a child lives and the communities she or he is exposed to (or not exposed to) does not cause a child's racialized identity. Nor does simply being around other multiracial children prevent a child from feeling "different" or from having to navigate the micro-aggressions of racial litmus tests. Still, in choosing their residence location, parents are drawing the boundaries of their child's socialization experiences. Gaining access to racial socialization experiences outside of the home can facilitate a child's development of the coping skills necessary to navigate racial litmus tests, racism, and colorism as they manifest within different ethnic and cultural contexts.

SUMMARY AND CONCLUSION

History bears out the realities of mixed-race America and its multiple associations, including those to cultural whiteness or to "otherness." The mixed messages (or missing messages) about multiracial America beyond black–white have not only pathologized this population, but also suggest that without a unified and tangible cultural context outside of the one-drop rule, a person can have no distinct, viable racialized identity (Daniel, 2002; Root, 1998). The experiences of mixed-race people have included learning to negotiate constructions of biological racial-group membership, folk theories of racialized identity, and micro-aggressions via racial litmus tests from those in their communities of origin whose identities are firmly established in this dichotomous racial paradigm (Renn, 2004; Russell, Wilson, & Hall, 1992). There is surely evidence here to support the adage, "The more things change, the more they stay the same." Despite the changes in the U.S. Census 2000, skin tone and perceived race continue to matter in daily life. We have learned from integration and desegregation efforts that proximity alone does not erase barriers. Similarly, we should not think that the existence of multiracial family systems will eliminate racism. As research suggests, people who form interracial partnerships, their children, and the society in which they live can still be racist and colorist.

It is argued here that we should move beyond ideals of colorblindness; beyond the rainbow imagery imposed upon multiraciality as the great hope, the magic cure. This will allow a critical discussion of the ways in which our society is and is not shifting in response to the perceived changes in the U.S. population.

Some new dimensions of this familiar race paradigm can already be discerned from existing literature and research. There are interracial families that are formed by love—and via adoption or by birth, their children are raised in that context. There are multiracial children who are accepted by both their white families and their families of color—this reduces the social need to "pass" as exclusively white. There are multiracial and multiethnic families whose heritage does not include white. To be sure, love is not enough to raise multiracial or multiethnic children in any of these contexts. Nevertheless, the growing presence and visibility of multiracial people and family systems may, at the very least, continue to challenge the pathologies historically attached to multiraciality.

It has also been argued here that social work practice (and research) has a long way to go in understanding the many ways in which race, ethnicity, and culture both constrain and promote well-being in a color-conscious society. Our profession is challenged to develop more racially sophisticated frameworks, to facilitate working relationships with families and individuals whose cultural realities and racialized locations are currently outside the purview of our practice wisdom. This alone is a barrier to our profession's ability to join with these families and identify culturally relevant paths for enhancing and stabilizing their well-being.

As for multiracial people themselves, a generation of mixed-race adults is now framing the discussion for the future. Just as with other racialized groups, they are seeking acknowledgment and the power of choice to name themselves. Not all wish to be named by all of their heritages. Not all claim their heritages all the time, in all contexts, or by using the same labels. Bills of rights authored by researchers who themselves are multiracial insist that this group must be afforded the right to be self-determining (Root, 2003). Like other groups, they do not speak with one voice; there is no one single opinion or authentic multiracial experience. Perhaps multiracial individuals are marked by, and unified through, this diversity and complexity—a truth that in its uniqueness makes it no better nor worse than that of their ancestors and communities of origin.

END NOTES

1. The term "colorblind individualism," coined by Ruth Howe (1995, 1997) in her discussions of transracial adoption, promotes the view that race should not matter in the selection of adoptive parents for children of color who are available for adoption. Its use is extended here to represent a similar philosophy of race within multiracial discourse, particularly among white parents of multiracials, that promotes colorblindness as ideal. It also supports the ability of multiracial children to freely choose their racial identity as individuals, rather than as members of a group determined by their racialized phenotypes and assumed biology.

2. This is further reinforced by social and medical sciences that continue to use race as a causative or main-effect variable in explaining different outcomes in certain communities. In these studies, race is tied to the epidemiology of poverty, crime, education, violence, and so on (Helms, Jernigan, & Mascher, 2005; Kaplan & Bennett, 2003; LaVeist, 2000).

3. For example, the Hawaiian term hapa is often used by U.S. Asian Pacific Islanders of mixed heritage. Interestingly, Amerasian has become a multinational identification grounded in the history of U.S. military men (typically white) who fathered children with women in the Asian countries where they were stationed. Japanese mixed-race children in Japan are noted in the literature as coining the term "doubles" as a alternate view—suggesting that they are both Japanese and another "race" and not halves of a whole. For a more in-depth discussion of the politics associated with these terms, and the histories of multiracial Asians in the United States and in Hawaii, see Edles, (2004) and Tashiro (2002).

4. The term "mulatto" is used here and elsewhere in its historical context. It will later be critiqued as an outdated and racially offensive label. It is important, however, to acknowledge that this term is still used—including by people who are themselves black–white multiracial.

5. This notion of racial purity also extends to mixed-race Native Americans, whose racialized blood quantums were recorded as early as 1870 as "half-breeds." This strategy of categorizing

racial-group membership has continued today, and is accepted by many First Nations communities as the method of establishing rights of tribal membership through one's "blood" line (Baird-Olson, 2003).

6. In addition, some multiracial literature has voiced concern about the use of blood quantums for establishing group membership, as is the case with Native Americans. For a more in-depth discussion of the use of blood quantums in this population, see Baird-Olson (2003).

7. Another example of this experience followed this candidate's speech at the Democratic National Convention, when he was later interviewed by NBC's well-known anchor Tom Brokaw. The first question Mr. Brokaw chose to ask was if there was one race Mr. Obama felt more at home in—to which Mr. Obama replied: "All of them."

REFERENCES

Allport, G. (1954). *The nature of prejudice*. Cambridge, MA: Addison-Wesley.

Anzaldua, G. (1987). *Borderlands, la frontera—The new mestiza*. San Francisco: Aunt Lute Books.

Appiah, K. (1990). Race. In F. Lentricchia & T. McLaughlin (Eds.), *Critical terms for literary study* (pp. 274–287). Chicago: University of Chicago Press.

Awkward, M. (1995). *Negotiating difference, race, gender, and politics of positionality*. Chicago: University of Chicago Press.

Baird-Olson, K. (2003). Colonization, cultural imperialism, and the social construction of American Indian mixed-blood identity. In L. I. Winters & H. L. DeBose (Eds.), *New faces in a changing America: Multiracial identity in the 21st* century (pp. 194–221). Thousand Oaks, CA: Sage Publications.

Berry, C. (2000, February 7). It's time we rejected the racial litmus test. *Newsweek, 135*(6), 13.

Bolatagici, R. (2004). Claiming the (n)either/(n)or of "third space": (Re)presenting hybrid identity and the embodiment of mixed race. *Journal of Intercultural Studies, 25*(1), 75–85.

Chestang, L. W. (1972, November). Character development in a hostile environment. *Occasional Papers, 3*, 1–12.

Comas-Dìaz, L. (1996). LatiNegra: Mental health issues of African Latinas. In M. P. P. Root (Ed.), *The multiracial experience: Racial borders as the new frontier* (pp. 167–190). Thousand Oaks, CA: Sage Publications.

Cross, W. E. (1971). The Negro to black conversion experience: Towards a psychology of black liberation. *Black World, 20*(9), 13–27.

Cross, W. E. (1991). *Shades of black: Diversity in African-American identity*. Philadelphia: Temple University Press.

Dalmage, H. (2000). *Tripping on the color line: Black–white multiracial families in a racially divided world*. New Brunswick, NJ: Rutgers University Press.

Daniel, R. G. (1996). Black and white identity in the new millennium: Unsevering the ties that bind. In M. P. P. Root (Ed.), *The multiracial experience: Racial borders as the new frontier* (pp. 121–139). Thousand Oaks, CA: Sage Publications.

Daniel, R. G. (2002). *More than black? Multiracial identity and the new racial order*. Philadelphia: Temple University Press.

Daniel, R. G. (2003). Multiracial identity in global perspective: The United States, Brazil, and South Africa. In L. I. Winters & H. L. DeBose (Eds.), *New faces in a changing America: Multiracial identity in the 21st century* (pp. 247–286). Thousand Oaks, CA: Sage Publications.

Darwin, C. (1859). The origin of species by natural selection: The preservation of favored races in the struggle for life. In G. Suriano (Ed.), *The origin of species* (1998). Santa Cruz, CA: University of California Press.

Davis, F. J. (1991). *Who is black?* University Park: Pennsylvania State University Press.

Edles, L. D. (2004). Rethinking "race," "ethnicity," and "culture": Is Hawai'i the "model minority" state? *Ethnic and Racial Studies, 27*(1), 37–68.

Espiritu, Y. L. (2001). Possibilities of a multiracial Asian America. In T. Williams-Leon & C. L. Nakashima (Eds.), *The sum of our parts* (pp. 25–33). Philadelphia: Temple University Press.

Favor, J. M. (1999). *Authentic blackness.* Durham, NC: Duke University Press.

Fellin, P. (2000, Spring/Summer). Revisiting multiculturalism in social work. *Journal of Social Work Education, 36,* 261–279.

Ferber, A. L. (1997, June). Of mongrels and Jews: The deconstruction of racialized identities in white supremacist discourse. *Social Identities, 3,* 193–208.

Foeman, A. K., & Nance, T. (1999, March). From miscegenation to multiculturalism. *Journal of Black Studies, 29,* 540–557.

Folaron, G., & Hess, P. M. (1993). Placement consideration for children of mixed African American and Caucasian parentage. *Child Welfare, 72,* 113–125.

Fong, R., & Spickard, P. (1995). A multiracial reality: Issues for social work. *Social Work, 40,* 725–729.

Frankenberg, R. (1995). Whiteness as an "unmarked" cultural category. In K. Rosenblum & T. Travis (Eds.), *The meaning of difference* (pp. 92-98). New York: McGraw-Hill.

Funderburg, L. (1994). Black, white, other. New York: William Morrow.

Funderburg, L. (1998). Crossing the demographic divide: The otherness of multiracial identity. *American Demographics, 20*(10), 24–25.

Gabard, D. L., & Cooper, T. L. (1998, September). Race. *Administration & Society, 30,* 339–356.

Gaskins, P. F. (1999). *What are you? Voices of mixed-race young people.* New York: Henry Holt.

Gordon, L. R. (1995, August). Critical "mixed race." *Social Identities, 1,* 381–394.

Graves, J. L., Jr. (2004). *The race myth: Why we pretend race exists in America.* New York: Penguin Books.

Helms, J. E. (Ed.). (1990). *Black and white identity: Theory, research, and practice.* Westport, CT: Greenwood.

Helms, J. E., Jernigan, M., & Mascher, J. (2005). The meaning of race in psychology and how to change it: A methodological perspective. *American Psychologist, 60,* 27–36.

Herring, R. D. (1995). Developing biracial ethnic identity: A review of the increasing dilemma. *Journal of Multicultural Counseling & Development, 23*(1), 29–40.

Hirschfeld, L. A. (1995). The inheritability of identity: Children's understanding of the cultural biology of race. *Child Development, 66,* 1418–1437.

hooks, b. (1989). *Talking back: Thinking feminist, thinking black.* Boston: South End Press.

hooks, b. (1992). *Black looks: Race and representation.* Boston: South End Press.

Howe, R. A. W. (1997). Transracial adoption (TRA): Old prejudices and discrimination float under a new halo. *Boston University Public Interest Law Journal, 6,* 409–472.

Howe, R. A. W. (1995). Redefining the transracial adoption controversy. *Duke Journal of Gender Law & Policy, 2,* 131–164.

Hurston, Z. N. (1937). *Their eyes were watching God.* New York: Harper & Row.

Ignatiev, N., & Garvey, J. (Eds.). (1996). *Race traitor.* New York: Routledge.

Johnson, D. J. (1992). Developmental pathways: Toward an ecological theoretical formulation of race identity in black–white biracial children. In M. P. P. Root. (Ed.), *Racially mixed people in America* (pp. 37–49). Newbury Park, CA: Sage Publications.

Johnson, J. W. (1912). *Autobiography of an ex-colored man.* Boston: Sherman, French.

Jones, L. (1994). *Bulletproof diva: Tales of race, sex, and hair.* New York: Doubleday.

Jones, R. (1980). *Black psychology.* New York: Harper & Row.

Kahn, J., & Denman, J. (1997). An examination of social science literature pertaining to multiracial identity: A historical perspective. *Journal of Multicultural Social Work, 6*(1/2), 117–139.

Kaplan, J. B., & Bennett, T. (2003). Use of race and ethnicity in biomedical publication. *JAMA, 289,* 2709–2716.

Kelley, M., Howe, C., Kawabori, K., & Meriwether, N. (2001). *Snapshot of Census 2000.* Seattle, WA: MAVIN Foundation.

Kennedy, R. (2004). *Interracial intimacies: Sex, marriage, identity, and adoption.* New York: Vintage Press.

Kich, G. K. (1992). The developmental process of asserting a biracial, bicultural identity. In M. P. P. Root (Ed.), *Racially mixed people in America* (pp. 304–320). Newbury Park, CA: Sage Publications.

Korgen, K. O. (1998). *From black to biracial: Transforming identity among Americans.* Westport, CT: Praeger.

Larsen, N. (1986). Passing. In D. E. McDowell (Ed.), *American women writers series* (pp. 143–242). New Brunswick, NJ: Rutgers University Press.

LaVeist, T. A. (2000). On the study of race, racism, and health: A shift from description to explanation. *International Journal of Health Services, 30,* 217–219.

Leary, R. (1997, May 27). "Multiracial" census listing opposed: Groups fear dilution of civil rights laws. *Philadelphia Tribune, 113*(42), 1-A.

Lee, J., & Bean, F. D. (2004). America's changing color lines: Immigration, race/ethnicity, and multiracial identification. *Annual Review of Sociology, 30,* 221–242.

Lopez, I. F. H. (1996). *White by law: The legal construction of race.* New York: New York University Press.

Luke, C. (1994). White women in interracial families: Reflections on hybridization, feminine identities, and racialized othering. *Feminist Issues, 14*(2), 49–72.

McRoy, R., & Grape, H. (1999). Skin color in transracial and inracial adoptive placement: Implications for special needs adoptions. *Child Welfare, 78,* 673–689.

Miranda, G. E. (2003a). Domestic transracial adoption and multiraciality. In M. P. P. Root & M. Kelley (Eds.), *Multiracial child resource book* (pp. 108–115). Seattle, WA: MAVIN Foundation.

Miranda, G. E. (2003b, Spring/Summer). Reading between the lines: Black-white heritage and transracial adoption. *African American Research Perspectives, 10,* 174–187.

Morales, A. L. (1990). *Getting home alive.* Milford, CT: Firebrand Books.

Morning, A. (2003). New faces, old faces: Counting the multiracial population past and present. In L. I. Winters & H. L. DeBose (Eds.), *New faces in a changing America: Multiracial identity in the 21st Century* (pp. 21–38). Thousand Oaks, CA: Sage Publications.

Myers, D., & Hacegaba, N. (2001). *Multiracial patterns in the United States by state* (Public Research Report, Race Contours 2000, No. 2001-02). Retrieved August 10, 2005, from http://www.usc.edu/sppd/census2000

Nakashima, C. L. (1996). Voices from the movement: Approaches to multiraciality. In M. P. P. Root (Ed.), *The multiracial experience: Racial borders as the new frontier* (pp. 79–100). Thousand Oaks, CA: Sage Publications.

O'Hearn, C. C. (Ed.). (1998). *Half + half: Writers on growing up biracial and bicultural.* New York: Pantheon Books.

Omi, M., & Winant, H. (1994). *Racial formation in the United Sates: From the 1960's to the 1990's.* New York: Routledge.

Oriti, B., Bibb, A., & Mahboubi, J. (1996). Family-centered practice with racially/ethnically mixed families. *Families in Society, 77,* 573–582.

Park, R. (1928). Human migration and the marginal man. *American Journal of Sociology, 33,* 881–893.

Park, R. (1931). The mentality of racial hybrids. *American Journal of Sociology, 36,* 534–551.

Patton, S. (2000). *Birthmarks.* New York: New York University Press.

Pearsall, J. (Ed.). (2002). *Concise Oxford English dictionary.* New York: Oxford University Press.

Pickett, J. P. (Ed.). (2004). *The American heritage dictionary.* New York: Bantam Dell.

Pope-Davis, D. B., & Liu, W. M. (1998, June). The social construction of race: Implications for counseling psychology. *Counseling Psychology Quarterly, 11*(2), 151–160.

Poston, W. S. C. (1990). The biracial identity development model. *Journal of Counseling & Development, 69,* 152–155.

Reed, I. (1998, December 31). Some questions and answers on biraciality. *Black Renaissance/Renaissance Noire, 2*(1), 74.

Renn, K. A. (2004). *Mixed race students in college: The ecology of race, identity and community on campus.* Albany: State University of New York Press.

Rockquemore, K. A., & Brunsma, D. L. (2002). *Beyond black: Biracial identity in America.* Thousand Oaks, CA: Sage Publications.

Root, M. P. P. (Ed.). (1992). *Racially mixed people in America.* Newbury Park, CA: Sage Publications.

Root, M. P. P. (1996). *The multiracial experience: Racial borders as the new frontier.* Thousand Oaks, CA: Sage Publications.

Root, M. P. P. (1998). Experiences and processes affecting racial identity development: Preliminary results from the biracial sibling project. *Cultural Diversity and Mental Health, 4,* 237–247.

Root, M. P. P. (2003). Bill of rights for racially mixed people. In M. P. P. Root & M. Kelley (Eds.), *Multiracial child resource book: Living complex identities* (pp. 32–33). Seattle: MAVIN Foundation.

Root, M. P. P., & Kelley, M. (Eds.). (2003). *Multiracial child resource book: Living complex identities.* Seattle: MAVIN Foundation.

Russell, K., Wilson, M., & Hall, R. (1992). *The color complex: The politics of skin color among African Americans.* New York: Harcourt Brace Jovanovich.

Senna, D. (1998). The mulatto millennium. In C. C. O'Hearn (Ed.), *Half + half: Writers on growing up biracial and bicultural.* New York: Pantheon Books.

Simon, R., & Roorda, R. (2000). *In their own voices.* New York: Columbia University Press.

Sollors, M. (1997). *Neither black nor white yet both: Thematic explorations of interracial literature.* New York: Oxford University Press.

Spencer, R. (1997). *The new colored people: The mixed-race movement in America.* New York: New York University Press.

Spencer, R. (1999). *Spurious issues: Race and multiracial identity politics in the United States.* Boulder, CO: Westview Press.

Spickard, P. R..(1989, Spring). In justice compounded: Amerasians and non-Japanese in America's concentration camps. *Journal of American Ethnic History, 5,* 5-22.

Stonequist, E. V. (1937). *The marginal man: A study in personality and culture conflict.* New York: Russell & Russell.

Streeter, C. A. (1996). Ambiguous bodies: Locating black/white women in cultural representations. In M. P. P. Root (Ed.), *The multiracial experience: Racial borders as the new frontier* (pp. 305–323). Thousand Oaks, CA: Sage Publications.

Streeter, C. A. (2003). The hazards of visibility: "Biracial" women, media images, and narratives of identity. In L. I. Winters & H. L. DeBose (Eds.), *New faces in a changing America: Multiracial identity in the 21st century* (pp. 194–221). Thousand Oaks, CA: Sage Publications.

Stubblefield, A. (1995, Fall). Racial identity and non-essentialism about race. *Social Theory & Practice, 21,* 341–368.

Talty, S. (2003). *Mulatto America at the crossroads of black and white culture: A social history.* New York: HarperCollins.

Tashiro, C. J. (2002, December). Considering the significance of ancestry through the prism of mixed-race identity. *Advances in Nursing Science, 25*(2), 1–21.

Terry, D. (2004, October 24). The skin game: Do white voters like Barack Obama because "He's not really black"? *Chicago Tribune Magazine,* pp. 15–23.

Thornton, M. (1996). Hidden agendas, identity theories, and multiracial people. In M. P. P. Root (Ed.), *The multiracial experience: Racial borders as the new frontier* (pp. 101–120). Thousand Oaks, CA: Sage Publicatiosn.

Thurman, W. (1970). *The blacker the berry.* New York: Macmillan.

Toomer, J. (1923). *Cane.* New York: Liveright Press.

Twine, F. W. (1996). Brown-skinned white girls: Class, culture and the construction of white identity in suburban communities. *Gender, Place & Culture: A Journal of Feminist Geography, 3,* 205–224.

Twine, F. W. (1999). Bearing blackness in Britain: The meaning of racial difference for white birth mothers of African-descent children. *Social Identities, 5,* 185–211.

Vivero, V. N., & Jenkins, S. R. (1999). Existential hazards of the multicultural individual: Defining and understanding "cultural homelessness." *Cultural Diversity and Ethnic Minority Psychology, 5,* 6–26.

Williams, T. K. (1996). Race as process: Reassessing the "What are you?" encounters of biracial individuals. In M. P. P. Root (Ed.), *The multiracial experience: Racial borders as the new frontier* (pp. 191–210). Thousand Oaks, CA: Sage Publications.

Williamson, J. (1980). *New people: Miscegenation and mulattoes in the United States.* Baton Rouge, LA: Louisiana State University Press.

Winters, L. I, & DeBose, H. L. (Eds.). (2003). *New faces in a changing America: Multiracial identity in the 21st century.* Thousand Oaks, CA: Sage Publications.

Zack, N. (1993). *Race and mixed race.* Philadelphia: Temple University Press.

PART II

CONDUITS OF VALUES
AND BELIEFS

———— ⁓ ————

CHAPTER 5

REVISITING THE LANGUAGE QUESTION

Lissette M. Piedra

INTRODUCTION

I teach a graduate-level class on Hispanics and social policy. One day, as we discussed language and culture, a bright student raised her hand and plaintively asked, "Why don't families just teach their language at home?" In response, an entire row of Hispanic students' hands shot up. It was a moment any teacher would have relished, but on that particular morning I was simply curious: the question had struck a nerve.

Language is paradoxical, and its implications for creation of social policy in a diverse society are complex. The physiological and cognitive ability to use a system of shared symbolic communication enables those who share a language to understand each other and participate in the creation of shared meanings, communities, and culture. As a mode of communication, language both has a unifying function within families and communities (Delgado-Gaitan & Trueba, 1991) and is a source of conflict (Rodriguez, 1982). These paradoxes are readily confirmed by my Latino and Latina students who once "knew Spanish." They describe private family decisions made long ago: choice of schooling, tolerance of spoken English at home with peers and siblings, influence of media, and, in many cases, simply not knowing the importance of language retention and accessing resources outside of the home. They also describe personal outcomes: family estrangement, anger, limited reading and writing ability, and the inability to verbally engage even when spoken Spanish is understood.

Language makes intergenerational learning and transmission of culture possible (Suleiman, 2003), and the acquisition of language always occurs through a shared body of cultural meanings. At its core, language is relational. As such, it has the potential to be both inclusive and exclusive, cohesive and divisive. Language operates in a way similar to phenotypical differences, as a tangible cultural marker that signals group membership (Jupp, Roberts, & Cook-Gumperz, 1982). Those who fail to speak the same language or do not speak it well are clearly outsiders. Even an accent serves to connote regional and class differences.

Although language creates social bonds, it also accentuates group differences, fueling social tensions in a diverse society (Cafferty, 2001; Cafferty & Engstrom, 2001; Jupp,

Roberts, & Cook-Gumperz, 1982). For students of social policy and social work, understanding the role that language plays in institutional access and in social mobility is critical to analyzing and crafting policies that address the needs of a linguistically diverse society such as the United States.

This chapter examines the significance of language diversity in this country and the tensions that are created when non-English-speakers are incorporated. Although fears of linguistic and cultural diversity have been classified as xenophobic and even racist, such classifications do little to assuage the legitimate concerns of those who are threatened by a multilingual America. Although every society undergoes some measure of cultural transformation as one generation gives way to another, rapid cultural transformation occurs when sizeable new groups enter a society within a short time span. The unprecedented level of immigration from non-European countries is rapidly transforming the social and political landscape of the United States. Next to phenotype, the most visible marker of otherness is language.

In many respects, fears of cultural change are well founded. The most recent Current Population Survey shows that 28 million Americans are foreign-born and that more than 44 million Americans speak a language other than English (Youdelman & Perkins, 2002). The United States hosts speakers of more than 300 different languages, and as immigrants disperse to nontraditional settings in suburban and rural areas, language issues also disperse and become more complex. Indeed, though the incorporation of a new population will always bring about increased opportunities for contact and conflict with the existing majority group (Blau, 1977), cultural change will be the inevitable result. At the heart of this cultural transformation will be issues of language: not so much concerning the erosion of English, as some would contend, but regarding how institutions will manage issues of language diversity and language access. The question of the hour is not whether linguistic minorities can learn English and integrate into the American scheme; this is not a particularly perplexing question for a country with a long record of incorporating non-English-speaking immigrants. Rather, what is needed is a serious inquiry into how existing public polices and social institutions can shape the cultural transformation that is already underway. At the heart of such an inquiry is the issue of language.

In sharp contrast to the premise of the U.S. "English-only" movement, the central question about language concerns governmental and civic responsibility for meeting the needs of linguistic minorities who are in a transitional phase between acquiring English and being fluent in it. This question assumes that institutions and public policy do have a role in addressing the needs of linguistic minorities. However, to investigate the role of policy and institutions, and to understand the tensions over language in contemporary U.S. society, it is necessary to understand the political history of language in this country, consider the values and social meanings associated with language, and assess the ability of current policies and institutions to serve the needs of individuals and of society. This latter assessment is based on Amartya Sen's "capabilities approach" to social justice (Sen, 1995).

A capabilities approach to meeting social needs highlights the ways in which society sets expectations but fails to provide pathways for people to meet those expectations. This approach also lays the conceptual groundwork for determining how institutions—as well as the professionals who staff them—can meet the needs of linguistic minorities. Addressing the language diversity in this country is an acute problem for social work and social workers, because we are so connected to the communities and services that interact with individuals who have limited English proficiency (LEP). Schools of social work (and other professional academic units) could play a transformational role in the lives of people who struggle with English by creating a cadre of bilingual workers and other language resources. Through interinstitutional cooperation and intrainstitutional resource coordination, social work education could be augmented to address the complex service needs of the LEP population, and serve as an example of ways in which academic institutions can address complex social needs.

LANGUAGE AND SOCIETY: THE FORMATION OF NATIONAL IDENTITY

In the emotionally charged debate over immigration reform, the issue of language invariably emerges. Any discussion of possible citizenship for the 12 million undocumented immigrants currently residing in the United States is punctuated with an expectation of English-language acquisition. The assumption that all immigrants will acquire English, as a sign of truly belonging, is a deeply American notion that coexists with the reality that the United States is and has always been a multilingual society. To name a few, we have had hundreds of Native American languages and dialects, German, French, Italian, Chinese, Polish, Spanish, and Creole—a language distinct to the United States. The 2000 Census grouped reported languages into 380 categories of single languages or language families. Although it has no official national language, the United States operates as a monolingual, English-language-dominant nation in the practice of its daily affairs, despite an everpresent multilingual constituency.

The political history of language reveals values that shape notions of social inclusion. Social attitudes toward language diversity range from periodic ambivalence to high social tension; patriotic loyalties are inevitably (if often mistakenly) tied to linguistic affiliation. Since the early colonial period, the degree of language tolerance has varied considerably (Schmid, 2001; Sollors, 1998), usually along political and economic lines (Crawford, 1996).

The association of patriotic loyalties with language, and with the use of language as a way to preserve a cultural identity, is endemic to every society. The formation of the nation-states and the colonization of the New World were part of a historical process, spanning more than five centuries, of ethnic groups organizing around language consciousness, loyalty, and maintenance. Often, the same word that names the language is used to connote culture: Spanish, French, English. In the contemporary United States, it is not unusual to bemoan the fact that someone speaks "Mexican" or to demand that immigrants speak "American." Given the intimate association between language and culture, language becomes a powerful proxy for culture (Cafferty & Engstrom, 2001) and for other conditions that challenge power relations in dominant groups (Schmid, 2001).

Before the 19th century, language diversity at first got an ambivalent reception, but later was tolerated as a means of garnering political support for the fledgling nation. Nevertheless, in a country that lacked a common history, culture, or customs, it was felt that a common language would serve as a common bond. Although never articulated in either the Articles of Confederation or the Constitution, it was assumed that English would be the common vernacular (Schmid, 2001).

The case of German is a useful example of U.S. ambivalence toward linguistic diversity, and how political forces pushed that ambivalence to outright intolerance. Germans remain the largest ancestry group in the United States, and are regarded as a model immigrant group that is highly assimilated. This was not always so. Benjamin Franklin worried about whether German settlers could be incorporated into the new country, because they retained their native language. Through the 19th century into the early 20th century, the Unites States showed a fairly high capacity to tolerate linguistic diversity, demonstrated through publicly funded German-language schools in states with high concentrations of German-origin individuals. However, once the German language and culture were associated with a threat to national security during World War I, public financial and cultural support evaporated. Supporting the retention of German language became highly unpopular, just as support for anything German signified compromised loyalties during a time when Americans were laying down their lives to fight German aggression.

Another example of cultural preoccupation with patriotic loyalties, in the face of national threat, is the detention of Japanese Americans during World War II. Although their incarceration was fueled by racism, language played a role in both instigating and justifying it. Because so few Americans understood the Japanese language, it was easy to view the use of it by Japanese Americans as subversive. More recently, the use of Arabic after 9/11 has been viewed in the same light. Clearly, cultural and linguistic associations with national loyalties become more closely drawn during periods of national threat (Sollors, 1998).

We define "Americanness" (inclusion) as Anglophone (Franklin, 1989; Gordon, 1998). Part of the symbolic/cultural reality that the United States is an English-speaking nation stems from the American myth that as immigrants assimilate into their new home, they relinquish their cultural ties and loyalties in favor of American identity and democratic ideals. This American mythology, as embodied in Israel Zangwill's melting-pot imagery (Zangwill, 1910), has created an ideal model of assimilation and acculturation that considers the relinquishment of native language and acquisition of English an important milestone in the process of becoming American (Cafferty & Rivera-Martínez, 1981). Although sociological research has long shown that the process of becoming American is complex (Cafferty and Rivera-Martínez, 1981), and that immigrants tend to keep their ethnic identity long into the third and fourth generations, myths die hard; the expectation is that immigrants will learn English and assimilate into American culture as soon as possible. This expectation was reflected most recently in President Bush's March 2006 address on immigration reform. Articulating the importance of reforming immigration as consonant with a lawful society, President Bush went on to state that, "We must also ensure that immigrants assimilate into our society and learn our customs and values—including the English language" (Bush, 2006). This assumption both underlies and fuels the considerable social tensions that are produced within a perceived monolingual society when growing portions of the population use other languages.

We are very concerned about those in our society who are unable or unwilling to learn the English language; in fact, we accept cultural diversity much more readily than we accept linguistic diversity. Legislation that emerged as a result of the civil rights movement prohibits discrimination against individuals on the basis of race, ethnicity, or nationality. However, discrimination on the basis of language remains unprotected unless there is a close association with nationality (Schmid, 2001). Implicitly, the United States has taken the stance that we should have only one national language, and that people who do not conform to that unspoken norm are not fully American. Historic tensions over bilingualism in Canada become examples for those who fear that bilingualism will result from public policy and public resources "catering to" the demands of an ethnic minority group that wishes to maintain its minority culture.

LANGUAGE, DEFENSIVE NATIONALISM, AND THE ENGLISH-ONLY MENTALITY

Some say that the English-only movement represents a new type of nativism in a post-civil rights world, in which cultural disparagements are socially frowned upon but linguistic intolerance still maintains some currency in public policy discourse (Sanchéz, 1999). Others argue that the presence of language diversity and the corresponding ethnic identities in the United States represent an erosion of American life and the values that shape our democracy (Huntington, 2004). Such concerns are founded on the belief that the essence of what it means to be an American is compromised by the incorporation of those who speak another language and hold strong ethnic identifications. Although ethnic identification can persist beyond the third generation, sociologists have shown that native-language retention among the foreign-born diminishes in the second generation and is all but gone by the third (Portes, 2002, 1996; Portes & Rumbaut, 2001a, 2001b; Portes & Schauffler, 1996). There is also evidence that transition to monolingual English is occurring much more frequently and faster in recent immigrant waves as compared to previous waves (Portes & Rumbaut, 2001b)—a fact that prompted one scholar to remark that never in the history of the world has a language needed so little protection (Schmid, 2001). Even so, any discussion of language policy to address the current linguistic diversity in the United States requires an understanding of the motivating forces behind the English-only movement and its effects on legislation for linguistic minorities. Central to this discussion is an exploration of the legitimacy of the official-English claims and the attitudes this movement reflects.

The organized "U.S. English" movement emerged in the early 1980s, as an effort to protect and reify English as the common and official language for and of the nation. The platform of this movement is predicated on the idea that without a common language, U.S. democratic ideals and its national unity and identity are threatened. Although proponents are careful to point out that they do not oppose individual bilingualism, they maintain that institutional bilingualism is anathema to a coherent national identity. U.S. English has galvanized a flurry of legislative activities, much of which is symbolic in nature, to name English as the official state language. As of 2006, the U.S. English, Inc., Web site reported that 27 states have passed legislation making English their official language. In addition, the Web site boasts that the organization has assisted Alaska, Georgia, Iowa, Missouri, Utah, Virginia, and Wyoming to enact some form of official English legislation (U.S. English, Inc., 2005). Momentous as this may at first seem, it is interesting that most states that have enacted such legislation have relatively small linguistic minority populations. In a Census 2000 brief (Shin, 2003), the states most recently mentioned by U.S. English, Inc., have the following percentages of the population that speak English "less than well": Alaska, 5.3 percent; Georgia, 4.9 percent; Iowa, 2.5 percent; Missouri, 2 percent; Utah, 5.2 percent; Virginia, 5.3 percent; and Wyoming, 1.9 percent.

Fueling the official-English legislation efforts are the surprisingly prevalent notion that immigrants are unwilling to learn English and a growing resistance to immigration, not unlike the anti-immigrant sentiment that arose during the immigration waves of the early 20th century. Rapid language and population changes coinciding with uncertain times create fertile ground for a defensive national identity and ethnic intolerance. In the midst of unprecedented immigration, the aftermath of World War I, and industrialization, Theodore Roosevelt succinctly articulated the nation's defensiveness in the face of massive social upheavals in a 1919 letter to the president of the American Defense Society: "We have room for but one language declaration and that is the English language, for we intend to see that the crucible turns our people out as Americans, of American nationality, not as dwellers in a polyglot boarding house" (Roosevelt, 1919/1989).

As history would show, Roosevelt's fears proved unfounded. The United States has a history of being able to incorporate non-English-speaking immigrants while operating as a monolingual society in the presence of a multilingual populace. What is in actual jeopardy is the retention of native languages (Portes, 2002). Portes cited results from the Children of Immigrants Longitudinal Study (CILS), which collected data from 5,200 students of 77 different nationalities. This study showed that if fluency is defined as the ability to read, write, and speak well, no second-generation group was fluent in its mother tongue by the time its members reached the age of 17 (Portes, 2002). The absorptive capacity of the American culture and the lack of broad social frameworks that facilitate language retention contribute to the second generation's rapid transition to monolingual English (Portes & Rumbaut, 2001b).

Despite mounting evidence of the cognitive and self-esteem benefits to children of non-English-speaking families (Portes, 2002; Portes & Rumbaut, 2001a), the United States is a virtual graveyard of native languages. Portes and Rumbaut (2001a) pointed out that linguists have shown that bilingual people have greater cognitive flexibility (Leopold, 1970) and the capacity to "look through language to its intended meaning" (Cummings, 1978). Consistent with these linguists' findings, the CILS study showed a positive association between bilingualism and academic performance. Moreover, the study showed that children who were fluent bilinguals in the early high school years had significantly higher educational aspirations and self-esteem three years later (Portes, 2002). This finding underscores the importance of parental involvement, but also links that relationship with language. Bilingualism among the second generation facilitates parental involvement through communication and fosters greater self-understanding by maintenance of ties to one's cultural roots (Portes & Rumbaut, 2001b).

The maintenance of non-English languages would, however, require institutional support, especially through educational institutions, and this is unlikely except where parents opt to provide private bilingual education for their children. In the face of anti-immigrant sentiment and the perceived threat of national disunity, support for the maintenance of native languages is hard to muster. Indeed, it has been noted that the real issue is less about protecting national interests than it is about protecting the status quo and erecting barriers to social inclusion for those perceived as "other." As Crawford (1996) stated:

> What seems to gall English-only advocates is not the translation of street signs or tax forms or children's lessons, but what these accommodations symbolize: a public recognition that limited-English speakers are part of the community and therefore entitled to services from government, even if that may entail "special" programs and expenditures . . . . [I]t legitimizes diversity, notwithstanding the challenges involved. It implies certain rights that were not previously acknowledged. (p. 31)

Acceptance of language diversity creates pathways to greater social inclusion. Every action that promotes institutional access to needed services transmits a message of inclusion. Ironically, this fact is not lost on the private sector. Companies that have been linguistically and culturally sensitive in marketing have found such efforts profitable

(Cafferty, 2001). The economic lessons from business aside, in our consumer society, the availability of hallmark "American" products and services, such as cell phones, computers, and Internet service, has a facilitative effect on assimilation of linguistic minorities. The real lesson is paradoxical: attention to cultural and linguistic diversity enhances social inclusion and promotes "American" behaviors. As Crawford (1996) pointed out:

> Thus in a small way, when government offers bilingual assistance, it elevates the status of language minorities. It suggests that immigrants and Native peoples need not abandon their heritage to be considered American—or at least to be given access to democratic institutions. In short, it alters structures of power, class, and ethnicity. The demand for language restrictions, by contrast, is a demand to reinforce the existing social order. (p. 31)

English is not in peril, but the dominant cultural norms that English speaking represents may be (Huntington, 2004). The real threat is the cultural manifestations that language diversity reflects (Cornelius, 2002). In a context in which salsa outsells ketchup and "José" outranks "Michael" as the most popular boy's name (Huntington, 2004), the telltale signs of cultural transformation are evident. Even so, demands for language restrictions that reinforce a particular social order must ultimately fail; they cannot stem that transformation. The primary problem is that the social and cultural norms protected by language restrictions are both incompatible with and incongruous in this country's current demographic reality. Such restrictions fan the flames of social conflict by exploiting the fears (founded or otherwise) that often arise in uncertain times. However, the most devastating effects of these restrictions and the attitudes underlying them are felt by those who are excluded from needed services. The most certain way to ensure that an individual will not succeed is to deny that person the very thing most critical for success: access to institutions.

THE CAPABILITIES APPROACH

The "capabilities approach" developed by Nobel laureate Amartya Sen advances an ideal of social justice that judges individual advantage in terms of the individual's capabilities or the degree of freedom she or he has to lead a valued life (Sen, 1995, 1999). With this concept, Sen departed from the utilitarian paradigm of preference and functioning that sets a premium on satisfaction and well-being. Such a utilitarian focus obfuscates the context factors that people have become accustomed to, including poverty and mistreatment. The capabilities approach focuses instead on what people are actually able to do and be, and thus is particularly relevant for study of linguistic minorities, because language barriers affect people's ability to function in society.

To a great extent, language determines whether one can participate in the labor market, take part in civil life, receive educational services or services enhancing access to education, seek and obtain health services, and be protected from crime. The emphasis in an analysis using a capabilities approach is on the processes that lead to exclusion or unfreedoms (Sen, 2003). When society fails to address the needs of linguistic minorities, the resulting social exclusion includes institutional barriers that impede access to important services such as health care and education. These institutional barriers represent a type of unfreedom that keeps linguistic minorities from creating the most optimal life possible, specifically because access to services essential to well-being is made difficult or impossible by linguistic inaccessibility. In a free and democratic society that strives to enhance the capacities of its citizens, social policy would be directed toward reducing or removing access barriers based on language, while at the same time providing the resources for immigrants and other LEP people to acquire English skills.

Martha Nussbaum (2003) built on Sen's arguments by advancing a humanizing conception of social justice that includes the human life span. She conceptualized human life as necessarily including periods of extreme dependency, such as infancy, chronic disability, and old age—a viewpoint that has particular applicability to language minorities (Nussbaum, 2003). The life cycle of a new immigrant also includes periods of heightened vulnerability and need, especially in the beginning when the immigrant is adapting to a new country. Enhancing new immigrants' capacity to adapt to this country does not coddle or encourage dependency. Rather, a political agenda that includes addressing the need of linguistic minorities potentially benefits the larger society by reducing the problems that arise from mistake, frustration, or lack of knowledge and resources. Policies based on such an agenda could help LEP minorities become more productive, thereby increasing their value to the larger society. Most immediately, addressing the needs of LEP adults would improve the quality of care their children receive; many of these children are American citizens upon whom our future depends.

The perception of a human being as both capable and needy is an important starting point in theorizing about people with limited English proficiency. How are we to understand the cyclical nature of dependency and independence? Nussbaum wrote that we need

> a political conception of the person that . . . sees the person from the start as both capable and needy—"in need of a rich plurality of life-activities," to use Marx's phrase, whose availability will be the measure of well-being. Such a conception of the person, which builds growth and decline into the trajectory of human life, will put us on the road to thinking well about what society should design. (Nussbaum, 2003, p. 54)

Acquiring a new language is an ongoing process for adults and a briefer one for children. The slower progress for adults is caused in part by the fact that adults have already cognitively incorporated language and its cultural meanings into their thinking.

Learning a new language forces a cognitive readjustment. However, this is only part of the story. For economic reasons, many LEP adults take jobs in which there is little need for language skills (Capps, Fix, Passel, Ost, & Perez-Lopez, 2003). Though there might be economic gains, such jobs provide little opportunity for LEP adults to learn English. At best, LEP adults might be able to access formal instruction in English as a second language (ESL classes).

LINGUISTIC MINORITIES

Linguistic diversity in the United States has always been a reality. However, the urgency of addressing the needs of a linguistically plural society is driven by the numbers. At the time of the 1970 Census, 19 million U.S. inhabitants (11 percent) spoke a language other than English. In 2000, the Census Bureau estimated that 47 million people—nearly a fifth of the population of the United States—speak a language other than English; this is due primarily to increased immigration to this country. After English and Spanish, Chinese was the language most commonly spoken at home (2 million), followed by French (1.6 million), and German (1.4 million). After Spanish, Asian and Pacific Islander are the fastest-growing linguistic groups. For example, in the past decade, the number of Vietnamese speakers doubled to just over 1 million.

The sizeable numbers of multilinguals in the United States are not distributed equally; non-English-speakers are heavily concentrated in certain cities and states. The West had by far the greatest numbers of non-English-speakers. In seven states, more than a quarter of the population speaks a language other than English: California (39 percent), New Mexico (37 percent), Texas (31 percent), New York (28 percent), Hawaii (27 percent), Arizona (26 percent), and New Jersey (26 percent).

Most people who speak another language also speak English very well. More than half of those who were counted as speaking a language other than English reported that they spoke English "very well." When combined with those who reported that they speak only English, the overwhelming majority of the U.S. population (92 percent) has no problem communicating in English.

This figure is in sharp contrast to those who live in "linguistically isolated" households (the Census term for households in which no one aged 14 years or over speaks only English or speaks English at least "very well"). The Census Bureau tabulates every person in such a household as linguistically isolated, and the 2000 Census identified 4.4 million linguistically isolated households comprising 11.9 million people. These numbers have grown significantly since 1990 (2.9 million households with 7.7 million people).

Non-English-speakers are heavily concentrated in seven states: California (12.4 million), Texas (6 million), New York (5 million), Florida (3.5 million), Illinois (2.2 million), Arizona (1.2 million), and Massachusetts (1.1 million). These seven states grapple with increasingly difficult policy issues because the sizable presence of non-English-speakers necessitates the development and implementation of linguistically sensitive services. However, the challenge of providing such services is most acute in states with the greatest concentration of people who speak English "less than well": Florida, Texas, and California. These states have large concentrations of people who struggle with English and are linguistically isolated. Linguistic isolation is a particularly serious obstacle for local governments and institutions because informal means of translation—family, friends, and neighbors—are virtually nonexistent.

SOCIAL COSTS FOR LINGUISTIC MINORITIES

In today's complex society, access to institutions and services shapes the quality of one's life and one's experience of membership in the United States. Since the beginning of the industrial era and the development of urban centers, human beings have increasingly relied on institutions for service delivery. The highly specialized institutions and complex service delivery systems that now characterize our technologically advanced society create especially challenging problems of access for vulnerable citizens, including those who are linguistically isolated. In this era more than in any other, institutional access and linkage are vital for citizens to achieve any measure of quality in their lives; many of our needs must be met by a host of often unrelated and certainly noncoordinated institutions. For vulnerable populations such as LEP and linguistically isolated people, access to institutions that provide critical medical, psychosocial, financial, and housing services is frequently made difficult or impossible by language barriers.

The greatest social cost for LEP individuals comes in the economic arena. A study by the Urban Institute found that limited English skills are closely associated with low-wage work (Capps et al., 2003). The vast majority of all LEP workers were foreign-born (84 percent), and nearly two-thirds (62 percent) of low-wage immigrant workers are LEP (Capps et al., 2003).

English proficiency opens the door to greater earning potential. One study found that understanding spoken English is paramount for labor-market success; other skills, such as reading, writing, and speaking ability, were not significant after considering language comprehension (Carnevale, Fry, & Lowell, 2001). Another study (Cornelius, Valdez, & Tsuda, 2003) found that in San Diego, foreign workers who understood and spoke English earned 76 percent more than those who understood and spoke English poorly or not at all. Age and education did not improve wages significantly; neither did sex, membership in an ethnic group, or the use of social networks to obtain jobs. With the exception of employment experience, which tends to increase wages by 13 percent for each year with the same employer, language was pinpointed as the most valuable human capital a foreign worker can possess.

The same study surveyed employers, and found that while 12 percent considered education, language, and work experiences important characteristics in immigrant workers, 50 percent cited "work ethic" as important. However, Cornelius, Valdez, and

Tsuda (2003) argued that employers so often conflate "work ethic" with other human-capital factors that the term has lost its distinct meaning. In their study, 58 percent of the employers claimed that English is necessary for the jobs they offer. Given the varied skill levels of jobs available for immigrants, many employers use English as a proxy for potential skill in higher paying jobs.[1] In this way, English-language proficiency translates into higher wages.

LEARNING ENGLISH

In a society where income determines quality of housing, neighborhood, and educational and health care resources, learning English takes on a whole new meaning—and a decided urgency. The importance of learning English is not lost on immigrants: Many share the view that English acquisition is important to their quality of life and also believe that it is their responsibility to acquire these language skills. One way to look at this is to examine public opinion. Despite the existence of numerous surveys of the American public's attitudes toward immigrants, few surveys explore what immigrants think of the United States. In perhaps the most methodologically sophisticated survey of immigrant opinion, Farkas and colleagues found that nearly 9 in 10 (87 percent) of adult immigrants said it is extremely important for immigrants to speak and understand English (Farkas, Duffett, & Johnson, 2003). Sixty-five percent of immigrants reported feeling that the United States should expect all immigrants who do not speak English to learn it. These sentiments are tied to perceived employment opportunities for English-speakers: 85 percent of immigrants who mentioned difficulty with English or knew only enough to get by reported that it was hard to get a job or do well without learning English.

Economic gains aside, speaking English well has other social benefits that affect quality of life. The same study found that 77 percent of respondents strongly agreed that "immigrants who speak good English have a much easier time in the U.S." In daily living, heavily accented English is often taken as an indicator of low literacy, educational level, or cognitive ability. Such a mark of perceived inferiority makes LEP people targets for social mistreatment and exclusion. Immigrants' belief in the importance of learning English complements their beliefs as to how their children should be educated. The majority of immigrant parents felt that public school should teach English to immigrant children (Farkas, Duffett, & Johnson, 2003).

This attitude toward the importance of English-language acquisition is reflected in the large waiting lists for ESL classes. A 2004 study by the Arizona Department of Education found 5,009 adults on a waiting list to get into English classes (Gonzalez, 2005), and revealed that an additional 5,686 had been turned away. In Boston, 3,500 immigrants were reported to be on waiting lists for low-cost or free ESL classes (Rhor, 2004). These figures are consistent with information compiled by the Center for Adult English Language Acquisition (CAELA), showing that both volunteer programs and those operated by school districts and community colleges report long waiting lists for

ESL classes (National Center for ESL Literacy Education, 1995). Most notable are the statewide waiting lists that reach into the thousands, such as Colorado (2,000 to 3,000), Illinois (1,846), and Massachusetts (15,000). Even local areas can have alarmingly high numbers, such as the 4,000-person waiting list in San Jose, California. Wait times can be as long as six months to a year or more.

THE LANGUAGE ISSUE IN EDUCATION

Whenever people from minority cultures interact with a majority institution, the transaction represents an opportunity both for further participation in the larger society and for increased tension and alienation. Tensions over capabilities are best understood by examining how important social institutions deal with individuals who do not speak English, or do not speak it well.

Ensuring that American children have equal educational opportunity was the guiding principle of Brown v. Board of Education.[2] Since the 1960s, the Spanish-speaking community has focused much of its civil rights efforts on equal access to education. Schools play a critical role in structuring diversity in our society. Because they are the primary pathways by which children will come to participate as adults in American life, the ways in which schools negotiate racial, ethnic, and class differences among teachers, staff, parents, and children have lasting effects on children's participation in society as adults. According to Louise Lamphere (1992), institutions such as schools serve to channel political and economic resources, in addition to mediating interactions between people. It is through schools that most children are formally exposed to people who differ from them socially, economically, racially, and ethnically. As a result, school personnel effectively facilitate or impede diversity by the way they shape, structure, and constrain interactions among teachers, students, and parents (Goode, Scheider, & Blanc, 1992; Lamphere, 1992).

Portes and Rumbaut (2001a) and Delgado-Gaitan and Trueba (1991) made it clear that schools play a critical role in language acquisition and cultural assimilation by non-English-speaking children. However, schools often fail to recognize the ability of non-English-speaking children to successfully learn a new language and culture. Portes (2002; Portes & Rumbaut, 2001b) provided convincing evidence that most children learn English fairly quickly and that English-language acquisition coincides with native language diffusion. The CILS study found that by age 18, second-generation bilingualism is an exception. By the end of a three-year period, less than one-third of the sample (28.5 percent) could communicate easily in both English and a foreign language; even among Hispanic children, who were the most likely to be bilingual, 65 percent had lost Spanish-language fluency (Portes, 2002).

The real issue, Portes (2002) contended, is not the ability to learn English, which is usually rapidly acquired, but rather the retention of the native language (and the associated ties to a cultural heritage). Portes advanced the argument that language retention is much easier than language acquisition, and that the language rapidly being lost by the second generation is a cultural resource that schools can help preserve (Portes, 2002).

Scholars also point out that it is not uncommon for educators to assume that children's low achievement is a function of insufficient knowledge of the English language or the communication etiquette expected in school (Delgado-Gaitan & Trueba, 1991). However, an argument can be made that although learning a new language is a cultural variation, it is not necessarily a cause for distress in children. A conflict does ensue when children are taught in English in such a way that their native language and culture are invalidated (Delgado-Gaitan & Trueba, 1991). An often-cited example is Rodriguez's autobiographical account of how the well-intentioned nuns at his school encouraged his parents to speak English to him. Rodriguez recounted how the achievement of English fluency, in the end, was accompanied by an agonizing betrayal of and marginalization from his family:

> For my part, I felt that I had somehow committed a sin of betrayal by learning English. But betrayal against whom? Not against visitors to the house exactly. No, I felt that I had betrayed my immediate family. I knew that my parents had encouraged me to learn English. I knew that I had turned to English with angry reluctance. But once I spoke English with ease, . . . I felt I had shattered the intimate bonds that had once held the family close. This was the original sin against my family told whenever anyone addressed me in Spanish and I responded, confounded. (Rodriguez, 1982, p. 30)

Many children, whether English-speaking or not, whether native-born or foreign-born, have difficulty starting school for the first time. For children of linguistic minorities, though, starting school means not only learning and adjusting to the rigors and routine of an environment vastly different from home, but also adapting to an environment comprised of people from different socioeconomic classes, ethnicities, and languages (Zentella, 2002). One could argue that academic difficulties arise not so much from the need to acquire a new language as from the need to learn and assimilate into a culture radically different from the home culture—a culture that invalidates the legitimacy of the family culture. Although English is necessary to children's success and meaningful participation in the classroom, Delgado-Gaitan and Trueba (1991) argued that the language must be taught appropriately, in the context of real experience with English-speakers, and that acquisition of English does not necessarily preclude use of the native language.

Intentionally or otherwise, schools tend to impede diversity and undermine the importance of native language and culture (critical to maintaining and enhancing familial relationships) by privileging the acquisition of English. English is learned at a personal cost. Practicing English in the context of the family with LEP parents is not the same as having meaningful contact and intimacy with those parents. To a child, the most important function of a family is to provide the physical and emotional resources that support daily living. These emotional supports are needed in whatever language is readily available to the family. Schools would be more facilitative if they fostered increased interaction with peers, rather than encouraging the family to relate in a language that is unfamiliar and uncomfortable. The children of LEP adults need less assistance with the mechanical process of English acquisition and more warmth and support from parents and teachers if they are to make a successful transition from being only a member of a family to also being a member of a school community. All children face this transition, but children coming from linguistically and culturally different households must make additional and larger adjustments. Meaningful partnerships between parents and educators, that honor what each cultural context can contribute to educational development of the child, will validate the perception that educational institutions are a natural extension of community participation, not a choice between two radically different cultural worlds.

THE LANGUAGE ISSUE IN HEALTH CARE

Language has come to the forefront as a critical issue in quality of and access to health care. Language barriers can lead to delays in or denial of services, or result in more costly or invasive treatment. Language difficulties can cause mistakes in prescribing and using medication, and often hinder patient compliance with medical instructions. A report by the Kaiser Commission on Medicaid and the Uninsured assessed how poverty, high levels of uninsurance, and language and cultural factors influenced health care for immigrants in four major cities (Los Angeles, New York City, Miami, and Houston). The commission found that, aside from financial factors, language access—in the form of bilingual providers and staff, translated materials, and interpreter services—was the most important factor in determining immigrants' access to health care. In every city, despite health care providers' efforts to provide language capacity (in compliance with Title VI of the Civil Rights Act of 1964), language difficulties posed a serious barrier to getting medical care and to receiving quality medical care (Ku & Freilich, 2001).

Title VI of the Civil Rights Act of 1964, and President Clinton's later Executive Order 13166 (August 2000), require federal agencies to develop and implement guidance to ensure institutional access for individuals with limited English proficiency, to the extent that doing so does not unduly burden or change the fundamental nature of the department or program (Youdelman & Perkins, 2002). However, the Kaiser Commission found that even for Spanish-speaking LEP patients, who tended to have greater access to bilingual health providers and interpreter services; many could not communicate with their health care providers. Often the large numbers of Spanish-speaking patients needing interpretation or translation services overwhelmed existing resources. Problems with interpreters and translation services were even more pronounced among immigrants who spoke less common languages, such as Vietnamese, Khmer, and Creole. These problems are further compounded by the fact that many patients are poorly educated or even illiterate in their own languages, thus making translated materials useless.

Another troubling feature of treating LEP clients is that needed services may be refused because of a lack of understanding. Language barriers may compound cultural misunderstandings about medication regimes and treatment adherence, leading to tragic results (Fadiman, 1997). Language barriers are a contributing factor in health care disparities among racial and ethic minorities and in the lack of health insurance among immigrants and refugees. Consider, for example, that the Hmong language has no word for cancer, or even for the concept of the disease (Morse, 2003). An inexperienced translator tried to explain radiation treatment to a Hmong patient by describing the treatment process as, "We're going to put a fire in you." Naturally, the patient refused the treatment.

The problems posed by the presence of a significant number of LEP patients are exacerbated by the shortage of bilingual workers, inadequately trained interpreters, and limited opportunities for native bilinguals to develop their language abilities. Consider the example of a nurse aide used as an interpreter for a Navajo woman who was about to receive a course of antibodies (Isaac, 2001). The doctor needed to know if the patient was allergic to the medication. The nurse aide interpreted this inquiry as, "Does the white man's medicine make you vomit?" The doctor, who understood some Navajo, corrected the interpreter, stating that he needed to know about allergies—to which the interpreter responded that she didn't know what "allergy" meant and that he should do the translation himself. This exchange illustrates the frustration of bilingual staffers caused when the differing levels of linguistic proficiency among bilinguals are not taken into account, and when it is assumed that people who have developed conversational proficiency in one language can easily transfer professional skills and knowledge obtained in English to their work with clients who speak that other language. The common practice of using inadequately trained interpreters is problematic at best, and contributes to compromised service for LEP patients and high levels of stress and frustration for bilingual workers (Engstrom & Won Min, 2003).

THE ROLE OF SOCIAL WORK EDUCATION IN ADDRESSING LINGUISTIC DIVERSITY

In all the human services, there is a need for bilingual workers, and there are few service providers who do not bemoan the lack of bilingual workers. Yet, very few institutions of higher education make concerted efforts to develop a bilingual workforce to address the growing need. In *The Politics of Language*, Carol Schmid (2001) wrote that "the growth of limited English-speaking populations (LEPs) has created adjustment problems across the region and anti-immigrant sentiment." (p. 4). Linguistic minorities in the United States live in a technologically advanced society that requires sophisticated language skills; the lack of those skills, combined with the dearth of interpreters, creates a dangerous situation for families with LEP members. Given the importance of language in access to services, it is incumbent on academic institutions, especially in the states with the largest LEP populations, to develop a linguistically competent workforce through educational supports that facilitate language skills and help establish the knowledge needed to work with interpreters of multiple linguistic backgrounds. At the very least, cultural competence includes a sensitivity to linguistic diversity and an understanding of the ways in which language barriers can affect the consumption of services. This mirrors a biopsychosocial approach to social service, ruling out health-related causes of psychiatric symptoms. What is needed, especially in states with high concentrations of limited English proficient people, is to prevent language incomprehension from contributing to perceived symptomology, becoming a reason for refusal of treatment, or causing poor treatment adherence. Language skill is not required for this, just a secondary review process that asks two crucial questions: Is this a language issue? How can we be sure?

Educational institutions such as schools of social work can directly influence the way American society responds to the needs of LEP people by raising consciousness of the linguistic needs of clients. One need not be bilingual to figure out that one's client is not being understood, or that service may be lacking because of language and/or comprehension barriers. The profession can develop a future generation of social workers who are both sensitive to the issues faced by non-English-speakers and equipped with the linguistic skills to mitigate the stresses associated with language acquisition and cultural assimilation.

Although it is unrealistic to suggest that schools of social work can address the totality of the linguistic diversity in our country, we cannot ignore the sizeable group of Spanish-speakers here. Currently, very few schools of social work provide ways for interested students to develop as bilingual social workers. Better training for bilinguals should also include training monolingual social workers to work with interpreters (Engstrom & Won Min, 2003; Tribe, 1999). Schools of social work could collaborate with Spanish and Hispanic Studies departments to provide interested students with real, ongoing opportunities to enhance their linguistic skills while working toward master's or doctoral degrees. This type of interuniversity partnership is not new: many joint programs have been offered through law schools, business schools, and divinity schools. What is different is that this particular joint effort would be organized as a collaboration that would play a facilitative role in the development of social workers with the skills and linguistic functionality to work with the ever-growing Hispanic population. (Note that for LEP Hispanics, cultural competence necessarily entails a level of linguistic competence.)

In this post-civil rights era, many major universities have created courses intended to help students understand the sociological and social policy issues that affect Hispanics. What is needed is coordinated effort that combines this rich body of coursework with opportunities to develop the language skills to adequately serve the Spanish-speaking population. In social work, especially in large urban settings, we are fortunate to have the field placement site as a critical educational component. Field placements with LEP clients can also serve as language laboratories wherein students are exposed to the informal and clinical aspects and uses of language. In certain universities, service agencies with large numbers of Spanish-speaking clients are being used to augment curricula for students majoring in Spanish. For heritage speakers who were raised with conversational language at home, but have had little opportunity to improve proficiency in their home language, an institutional endorsement of bilingualism is a valuable asset, to be drawn upon, fostered, and invested in.

CONCLUSION

The issues of language and language diversity are here to stay. Historically, the United States has presented itself as a monolingual society, and there is little evidence to suggest that English will be replaced by or will share its dominance with any other language. The central problem remains the incorporation of linguistic minorities and the cultural transformations that their absorption will have on the larger society. Although the United States has a long record of successful incorporation of linguistically different groups, it has no coherent strategy for addressing the transitional period of language acquisition. Institutions play a vital role in providing linguistically sensitive service and promoting social inclusion. At the forefront, social work education, along with other social and health professions, can assist U.S. society and its institutions through training students to address language diversity in this country.

END NOTES

1. One poignant example of language trumping education is found in Luis Rodriguez's memoir, *Always Running: La Vida Loca* (1994). In this memoir, Rodriguez described how his father, who in Mexico had been the principal of a school, could not find work in the United States commensurate with his level of education. The best he could do was work as a lab assistant.
2. Brown v. Board of Education, 349 U.S. 294 (1954).

REFERENCES

Blau, P. M. (1977). Size and number. In P. M. Blau (Ed.), *Inequality and heterogeneity: A primitive theory of social structure* (pp. 19–44). New York: Free Press.

Bush, G. W. (2006). Transcript of radio address. Retrieved March 31, 2006, from http://www. whitehouse.gov/news/releases/2006/03/20060325.html

Cafferty, P. S. J. (2001). The language question. In P. S. J. Cafferty & D. W. Engstrom (Eds.), *Hispanics in the United States: An agenda for the twenty-first century* (pp. 69–95). New Brunswick, NJ: Transaction Publishers.

Cafferty, P. S. J., & Engstrom, D. W. (Eds.). (2001). *Hispanics in the United States: An agenda for the twenty-first century.* New Brunswick, NJ: Transaction Publishers.

Cafferty, P. S. J., & Rivera-Martínez, C. (1981). *The politics of language: The dilemma of bilingual education for Puerto Ricans.* Boulder, CO: Westview Press.

Capps, R., Fix, M., Passel, J. S., Ost, J., & Perez-Lopez, D. (2003). *A profile of the low-wage immigrant workforce.* Retrieved April 4, 2006, from http://www.urban.org/url.cfm?id=310880

Carnevale, A. P., Fry, R. A., & Lowell, B. L. (2001). Understanding, speaking, reading, writing, and earnings in the immigrant labor market. *American Economic Review, 91,* 159–163.

Cornelius, W. A. (2002). Ambivalent reception: Mass public responses to the "new" Latino immigration to the United States. In M. M. Suarez-Orozco & M. M. Paez (Eds.), *Latinos: Remaking America.* Berkeley: University of California Press.

Cornelius, W. A., Valdez, Z., & Tsuda, T. (2003, January–June). Human capital versus social capital: A comparative analysis of immigrant wages and labor market incorporation in Japan and the United States. *Migraciones Internacionales, 2*(1), 5–35.

Crawford, C. A. (1996). *Anatomy of the English only movement: Social and ideological sources of language restrictionism in the United States.* Paper presented at the Conference on Language Legislation and Linguistic Rights, University of Illinois at Urbana-Champaign.

Cummings, J. (1978). Metalinguistic development of children in bilingual education programs. In M. Paradis (Ed.), *The fourth LACUS forum: 1977* (pp. 199–217). Columbia, SC: Hornbeam Press.

Delgado-Gaitan, C., & Trueba, H. (1991). The role of culture in learning. In C. Delgado-Gaitan & H. Trueba (Eds.), *Crossing cultural borders: Education for immigrant families in America* (pp. 17–38). Bristol, PA: Falmer Press.

Engstrom, D. W., & Won Min, J. (2003). Perspectives of bilingual social workers: "You just have to do a lot more for them." *Journal of Ethnic & Cultural Diversity in Social Work, 13,* 59–82.

Fadiman, A. (1997). *The spirit catches you and you fall down: A Hmong child, her American doctors, and the collision of two cultures.* New York: Farrar, Straus & Giroux.

Farkas, S., Duffett, A., & Johnson, J. (2003). "Now that I'm here: What America's immigrants have to say about life in the U.S. today." Retrieved April 4, 2006, from http://www.publicagenda.org/research/research_reports_details.cfm?list=12

Franklin, J. H. (1989). Ethnicity in American life: The historical perspective. In J. H. Franklin (Ed.), *Race and history: Selected essays 1938–1988* (pp. 321–331). Baton Rouge: Louisiana State University Press.

Gonzalez, D. (2005, July 26). Immigrants jam English classes. *Arizona Republic.* Retrieved April 4, 2006, from http://www.azcentral.com/arizonarepublic/news/articles/0726english.html

Goode, J. G., Scheider, J. A., & Blanc, S. (1992). Transcending boundaries and closing ranks: How schools shape interrelations. In L. Lamphere (Ed.), *Structuring diversity: Ethnographic perspectives on the new immigration* (pp. 173–213). Chicago: University of Chicago Press.

Gordon, M. M. (1998). Assimilation in America: Theory and reality. In J. Adalberto Aguirre & D. V. Baker (Eds.), *Sources: Notable selections in race and ethnicity* (pp. 105–116). Guilford, CT: Dushkin/McGraw-Hill.

Huntington, S. P. (2004, March-April). The Hispanic challenge. *Foreign Policy, 114,* 30–45.

Isaac, K. M. (2001). What about linguistic diversity? *Communication Disorders Quarterly, 22,* 110–113.

Jupp, T. C., Roberts, C., & Cook-Gumperz, J. (1982). Language and disadvantage: The hidden process. In J. J. Gumperz (Ed.), *Language and social identity* (pp. 232–256). New York: Cambridge University Press.

Ku, L., & Freilich, A. (2001). *Caring for immigrants: Health care safety nets in Los Angeles, New York, Miami, and Houston.* Washington, DC: The Henry J. Kaiser Family Foundation.

Lamphere, L. (Ed.). (1992). *Structuring diversity: Ethnographic perspectives on the new immigration.* Chicago: University of Chicago Press.

Leopold, W. F. (1970). *Speech development of a bilingual child: A linguist's record.* New York: AMS Press.

Morse, A. (2003). *Language access: Helping non-English speakers navigate health and human services.* Washington, DC: National Conference of State Legislatures, Children's Policy Initiative.

National Center for ESL Literacy Education. (1995). *The waiting game.* Retrieved April 4, 2006, from http://www.cal.org/caela/esl_resources/waiting.html

Nussbaum, M. C. (2003). Capabilities as fundamental entitlements: Sen and social justice. *Feminist Economics, 9*(2–3), 33–59.

Portes, A. (Ed.). (1996). *The new second generation.* New York: Russell Sage Foundation.

Portes, A. (2002). English-only triumphs, but the costs are high. *Contexts, 1*(1), 10–15.

Portes, A., & Rumbaut, R. G. (Eds.). (2001a). *Legacies: The story of the immigrant second generation.* Berkeley: University of California Press.

Portes, A., & Rumbaut, R. G. (2001b). Lost in translation: Language and the new second generation. In A. Portes & R. G. Rumbaut (Eds.), *Legacies: The story of the immigrant second generation* (pp. 113–146). Berkeley: University of California Press.

Portes, A., & Schauffler, R. (1996). Language and the second generation: Bilingualism yesterday and today. In A. Portes (Ed.), *The new second generation* (pp. 8–29). New York: Russell Sage Foundation.

Rhor, M. (2004, September 19). On a waiting list for the American dream. *Boston Globe.* Retrieved April 4, 2006, from http://www.boston.com/news/education/continuing/articles/2004/09/19/on_a_waiting_list_for_the_american_dream/

Rodriguez, L. (1994). *Always running: La vida loca.* New York: Touchstone.

Rodriguez, R. (1982). *Hunger of memory: The education of Richard Rodriguez.* New York: Bantam Books.

Roosevelt, T. (1989). Letter to the President of the American Defense Society, January 3, 1919. In A. B. Hart & H. R. Ferleger (Eds.*), Roosevelt, Theodore, 1858-1919: Theodore Roosevelt Cyclopedia* (Rev. 2nd ed., p. 243). Westport, CT: Meckler. (Original letter dated 1919)

Sanchéz, G. J. (1999). Face the nation: Race, immigration, and the rise of nativism in late-twentieth-century America. In C. Hirschman, P. Kasinitz, & J. DeWind (Eds.), *Handbook of international migration: The American experience* (pp. 371–392). New York: Russell Sage Foundation.

Schmid, C. L. (2001). *The politics of language: Conflict, identity, and cultural pluralism in comparative perspective.* New York: Oxford University Press.

Sen, A. (1995). *Inequality reexamined.* Cambridge, MA: Harvard University Press.

Sen, A. (1999). *Development as freedom.* New York: Anchor Books.

Sen, A. (2003). Foreword. In P. Farmer (Ed.), *Pathologies of power: Health, human rights, and the new war on the poor.* Berkeley: University of California Press.

Shin, H. B. (2003). *Language use and the English-speaking ability: 2000.* Retrieved April 5, 2006, from http://www.census.gov/prod/2003pubs/c2kbr-29.pdf

Sollors, W. (Ed.). (1998). *Multilingual America: Transnationalism, ethnicity, and the languages of American literature.* New York: New York University Press.

Suleiman, L. P. (2003). Beyond cultural competence: Language access and Latino civil rights. *Child Welfare League of America, 82,* 185–200.

Tribe, R. (1999). Bridging the gap or damming the flow? Some observations on using interpreters/bicultural workers when working with refugee clients, many of whom have been tortured. *British Journal of Medical Psychology, 72,* 567–576.

U.S. English, Inc. (2005). *About U.S. English.* Retrieved April 4, 2006, from http://www.us-english.org/inc/about/

Youdelman, M., & Perkins, J. (2002). *Providing language interpretation services in health care settings: Examples from the field.* Washington, DC: The Commonwealth Fund (www.cmwf.org).

Zangwill, I. (1910). *The melting-pot: Drama in four acts.* New York: Macmillan.

Zentella, A. C. (2002). Latina languages and identities. In M. M. Suarez-Orozco & M. Paez (Eds.), *Latinos: Remaking America* (pp. 321–338). Berkeley: David Rockefeller Center for Latin American Studies, Harvard University Press and the University of California Press.

CHAPTER 6

RELIGIOUS PLURALISM AND THE TRANSFORMATION OF AMERICAN CULTURE

Charles H. Lippy

Pluralism has long been a hallmark of U.S. religious life, although precisely what pluralism denotes has shifted over time. This chapter explores the expanding understanding of pluralism before examining the intricate ties to pluralism of ethnicity and immigration. It then looks more closely at the effect on American religious life of the heavy immigration from Latin America in recent years and also of the steady increase in the number of immigrants identifying with strands of the Hindu, Buddhist, and Muslim traditions. The concluding section addresses some long-term implications of the ways pluralism is transforming U.S. culture.

INTRODUCTION

In recent years, students of American religious life have evinced a new fascination with the phenomenon of pluralism. For some, religious pluralism, or the extent of religious diversity in the United States, represents one key to understanding U.S. religious history. William Hutchison, in his book *Religious Pluralism in America* (2003), argued that such pluralism was a founding ideal, albeit one with a "contentious history." Even so, Hutchison demonstrated that religious pluralism has had different nuances of meaning over the course of American history. The term denoted a reluctant and selective tolerance of others in the colonial period and then a struggle for inclusion in the 19th and early 20th centuries; by the dawn of the 21st century, it had come to mean something more like a "symphony" of discrete, diverse elements constituting a whole.

Others have noted that what religious pluralism embraces has also shifted over time. When the term was first used to describe American religious life, it tended to refer almost exclusively to the variety of Protestant bodies that had staked out a place for themselves on American soil. By the mid-20th century, when Will Herberg published his now-classic Protestant, Catholic, Jew (1955), "religious pluralism" suggested primarily the social equivalence of three major biblical traditions in providing a moral compass that directed the lives of good citizens. To be sure, religious pluralism even then did not mean the absence of religious prejudice or a popular conviction that all religions somehow had a claim to being true in any absolute sense. To others, the 20th century witnessed a proliferation and diffusion of religious pluralism, not only as religious bodies outside the orbit of Herberg's triad became increasingly evident in American life, but also as individuals began more and more to craft idiosyncratic, personal worlds of religious meaning that might draw on multiple religious heritages in their own quest to make sense out of life.[1]

A cursory reading of the annual Yearbook of American and Canadian Churches (National Council of the Churches of Christ, annual) or the index to a work such as J. Gordon Melton's *Encyclopedia of American Religions* (1990) reveals one facet of religious pluralism: namely, that thousands of different organized religious communities somehow manage to coexist in the United States. Those involved over the last decade or so with the Pluralism Project at Harvard University, under the direction of Professor Diana Eck, have mapped this variety in a different fashion, as associates around the nation sought to pinpoint all the different religious institutions in various local communities. The project overall has sometimes tended to minimize the continuing prevalence of "old-line" religious groups and seems to have been more interested in the hundreds of very small, often newer religious groups that frequently go unnoticed by casual observers.[2] Some of that is captured in Eck's *A New Religious America* (2001).

ETHNICITY AND IMMIGRATION

Regardless of how one defines or describes religious pluralism, its story is intertwined with two related phenomena: ethnicity and immigration. Three historical examples highlight this connection. It is impossible to track Lutheran life in the United States without examining the convoluted relationships among German Lutherans, Swedish Lutherans, Finnish Lutherans, Norwegian Lutherans, and a score of others. As the labels suggest, the strands of the Lutheran heritage are tied to places of origin of adherents, before those adherents came to the United States. Nor can one appreciate the internal history of the Roman Catholic tradition in the United States without taking into account the impact of the Irish Catholic migration to North American from 1830 to 1860 and the later immigration of Italian Catholics, Polish Catholics, and hosts of others. All these erected parishes in neighborhoods that were centers of ethnic life as well as religious life, even while Irish Catholics dominated the top ranks of leadership of the church in America.

Similarly, one cannot unravel the development of American Judaism without looking closely at the impact of German immigration in the middle two-thirds of the 19th century. For a time, this influx made it appear that Reform would dominate American Jewish experience. However, the massive immigration of Jews from southern, central, and eastern Europe that occurred between the close of the Civil War and the outbreak of World War I brought a richness to the story, and added ethnic dimensions that still prompt conversation among scholars as to whether being Jewish or claiming a Jewish identity is primarily a religious issue or an ethnic one.

These historical connections between ethnicity and immigration, and their impact on religious pluralism, illustrate how factors that at first glance might not seem related to religion have had extraordinary influence on religious life. Indeed, many years ago the historian Martin E. Marty referred to ethnicity as the "skeleton" of religion in America (Marty, 1972).[3] Careful consideration of the changing character of religious pluralism over the last four decades or so provides fresh evidence for the conviction that religion, ethnicity, and immigration are delicately intertwined.

Several forces set the stage for analysis of the current situation. One of the most important is the passage by the U.S. Congress of the Immigration Act of 1965.[4] That law effectively undid the immigration quotas, based on nation of origin, that had been in place since passage of the National Origins Act of 1924 and were basically reaffirmed by the McCarran-Walter Act of 1952.[5] The system of quotas had greatly favored nations in western and northern Europe, especially privileging those areas that had provided the Euro-American immigrant stock predominant in the years prior to the close of the Civil War. Immigrants from these countries would also likely be Protestants of one stripe or another (with some exceptions). Hence, both the 1924 and 1952 laws in effect bolstered the broad evangelical-Protestant dominance of American religion. Although the laws were never as narrow as they appeared when it came to finding exceptions, they did create barriers for those of Roman Catholic, Eastern Orthodox, and Jewish persuasions, whose adherents accounted for the bulk of immigrants in the half-century before quotas became law.

In addition, at least through World War II, rather strict enforcement of quotas virtually eliminated immigration from Asia; most Asian nations, for example, were held to quotas of around 100 immigrants per year. The 1924 legislation also prohibited Asians from becoming naturalized citizens, because of longstanding ethnic prejudice and also covert hostility to the religious traditions favored by Asians. The 1952 law eased this ban in part to make it possible for refugees from China to immigrate as the People's Republic of China was emerging, and to accommodate the large number of "war brides" who married American military personnel serving in Asia from World War II through the Korean conflict.

Several shifts in U.S. culture made a revamping of the law appropriate. By 1965 the major gains of the civil rights movement had raised the issue of whether it was appropriate to discriminate against immigrants on the basis of their place of origin; was not such discrimination of a piece with the former legal disabilities, directed against African Americans, which were being dismantled by the civil rights laws? In other words, eliminating quotas was seen as simply a matter of consistency and justice. Then, too, by the mid-1960s the Vietnam conflict had raised new concern about restricting immigration from Asia. Although earlier legislation provided for the legal immigration of refugees from time to time, there was a fresh concern that provisions should be made for Asians who were allies of the United States to enter the country as refugees. What made this concern somewhat overstated was the relatively small number of actual immigrants from Asia or elsewhere claiming refugee status in the 1960s.[6]

The quota system, even when enforced, had some loopholes, as exceptions existed for people who had family members in the United States who were already citizens. Indeed, before passage of the 1965 law, more Asian immigrants entered on that basis than under the low quota numbers. On balance, then, changes in the law at the time simply seemed a matter of course. President Lyndon Johnson, who signed the legislation during the same year that Congress also created Medicare and passed the Voting Rights Act, commented that the Immigration Act of 1965 would "not affect the lives of millions. It will not reshape the structure of our daily lives" (Johnson, 1967; as cited in Daniels, 2004, p. 226). Johnson, at least that time, was far off target in his assessment. In retrospect, it is clear that the Immigration Act of 1965 has played a major role in the changing shape of religious pluralism in the United States.

Once the law changed, the number of immigrants increased dramatically. By the 1990s, the total was approaching nearly 1 million a year, roughly the same number as in the decade immediately preceding World War I when immigration was at its zenith. The difference, of course, was that the total population by the 1990s was around 285 million, rather than just under 100 million as in 1914. Hence, the proportion of the population that was "foreign-born," as the census folks put it, was smaller. Still, the numbers indicated that daily lives were being affected, despite President Johnson's assessment at the time the old quota system was jettisoned.

Since the changes in immigration law 40 years ago, the bulk of immigrants have come from Latin America, Asia, and the Near East, with significant gains (though relatively small numbers) as well in immigration from nations in Africa. By far, Latin Americans have constituted the largest clusters. The Bureau of the Census in 2000 reported that fully 51.7 percent of all those foreign-born then living in the United States came from Latin America; more than half of those (57 percent) came from Mexico. Another 26.4 percent came from Asia, just 15.8 percent from Europe, and 2.8 percent from Africa.[7] The majority of those who have come from Latin America have identified with the Christian tradition in some form, and estimates suggest that more than half of the "post-1965 Asian immigrants are Christian" as well as "most Filipinos are Catholics, and the majority of Korean immigrants are Protestant" (Lawrence, 2002, p. 7). However, many of those coming from Asia, the Near East, and Africa are not Christian, but Muslim, Buddhist, and Hindu. Regardless, this immigration has had a tremendous impact on American religious life and has the potential to transform the religious landscape on levels from neighborhood to national.

LATIN AMERICAN IMMIGRATION AND THE TRANSFORMATION OF RELIGION
In the United States, the Latin American presence began to be felt even before the surge of immigration began to transform Christian religious life.[8] In areas like south-

ern Florida, Cuban immigrants, many of whom arrived when Castro came to power in the 1950s, had planted a Hispanic presence in religious life. Thomas Tweed has documented how Cuban immigrants, for example, reconstituted a Cuban shrine to Our Lady of Charity in Miami as a place of pilgrimage that sustains both Catholic piety and Cuban nationalism (Tweed, 1997b). In places like New York City, U.S. citizens coming from the Commonwealth of Puerto Rico, although often popularly perceived as immigrants, transformed areas of Harlem that had once been home to European ethnic communities to such an extent that popular parlance dubbed one area "Spanish Harlem." Until the upsurge in immigration after 1965, when religious analysts talked about Latin American immigrants, they tended to mean either Cubans or Puerto Ricans—except perhaps when they were talking about the southwest, from Texas to California. There the shared border with Mexico had long allowed for a spiritual presence that defied national boundaries, and captured as well the history of the area as Mexican territory until after the Mexican-American war of the mid-19th century.

The Mexican immigrants who have come in more recent decades, and the millions from other areas of Central and South America, have added several important dimensions to Latin American influence on American religious life. One such influence results from the geographic diffusion of this immigration. It is by no means limited to, or even concentrated in, areas that share a border with Mexico, or to urban centers where industry presumably seeks cheap labor and therefore offers abundant jobs. In the 1990s the largest proportional increase in Latin American immigration came in the Sun Belt, particularly in parts of the Bible Belt where evangelical Protestantism had exercised a religious (if not cultural) hegemony for more than a century and a half.

Georgia, the state of peaches and Scarlett O'Hara, provides stunning evidence of this Hispanic influence. For example, between 1990 and 1998, 25 Georgia counties reported an increase in immigration of more than 50 percent, a larger number than any other state. Although not all of this immigration originated from Latin America (in the Atlanta metropolitan area, a significant number of immigrants were of Asian origin), for Whitfield County, the 2000 census showed that almost a majority of the population was Hispanic and that more than half of the students enrolled in the elementary grades of the county's public schools were Hispanic.[9] The most obvious consequence is the number of congregations, both Roman Catholic and Protestant, that hold at least one Sunday service in Spanish or that have added at least one Spanish-speaking minister or priest to the staff. In some communities, even in the deep South, congregations from a particular denomination have banded together to fund ministries to the Spanish-speaking population. One challenge that many congregations have confronted, however, is the range of colloquial differences in the spoken Spanish of immigrant communities; Guatemalan Spanish is by no means the same as Mexican Spanish, for example. Communication in Spanish is not necessarily easily accomplished.

A second consequence has to do with the ambiance of Latin American Christianity and how it is transforming the religious culture where immigrant communities have formed. Although the majority of Latin American immigrants are Roman Catholic, the religious style of Latin American Christians, whether Catholic or Protestant, is decidedly more syncretistic and enthusiastic than that of most of their U.S. counterparts. Among Protestants, a Pentecostal flavor pervades Christian worship. Among Catholics, worship often includes exuberant dance that seems far removed especially from the staid Latin Mass of pre-Vatican II Catholicism, and festivals readily fuse Catholic dimensions with celebratory elements echoing pre-Christian Native American and African tribal observances. Even apart from Hispanic immigration, Pentecostal approaches to Christianity have been attracting increasing numbers of followers for at least the last four decades, with Pentecostal denominations such as the Church of God (Cleveland, Tennessee) and the Assemblies of God growing at a rate far exceeding that of the population as a whole. For such groups, the Pentecostal flavor that many Protestant Hispanic immigrants cherish has reinforced the sense of legitimacy of Pentecostalism and brought it closer to the "mainstream" of Protestant expression. For Catholics, the Hispanic presence has augmented the vitality of lived religion by adding to already established practice an array of new popular festivals and devotion to different clusters of patron saints, which were part of the religious tradition that these immigrants, like those who went before them, brought with them when they came to the United States.

A third consequence of Hispanic immigration is somewhat more difficult to isolate at this point, although many analysts feel that it will become more pronounced over the next decade or two. Most U.S. Christian bodies in recent years have confronted an awkward diversity when it comes to matters of theology and social practice. Particularly challenging have been debates over issues such as abortion and birth control and over a host of matters related to homosexuality: whether homosexuality itself is a sin; whether the churches should bless same-gender unions; and whether to admit practicing gay men, lesbians, bisexuals, and transgender people to the ranks of professional clergy. These issues have compounded discussion that was already divisive among Roman Catholics and many Pentecostals related to concerns rooted in second-wave feminism, such as the use of inclusive language in the church and the ordination of female clergy. Although all generalizations admit of exceptions, it seems that Hispanic immigrant Christians, like the rank and file back home in Latin America, are of a decidedly conservative bent on such matters, seeing even the postures that most Euro-Americans regard as moderate as too liberal and often as undermining the authority of scripture. Hence, the increasing importance of Hispanic Americans within denominations in which such matters are most contested seems likely to cause dissension to escalate, rather than help to resolve it.[10]

A fourth and final summons to change emerging from Hispanic immigration is seen most readily at the local, neighborhood level in the nation's cities. A generation ago, those who monitored urban life called attention to white flight to the suburbs; hundreds of downtown churches across the nation either closed when their congregants abandoned the inner city or moved with them to the suburbs. One perhaps unintended result of the civil rights movement, which paralleled changes in the immigration laws historically, has been African American flight from the core of cities to the rings of suburbs surrounding them. At the same time, although many civil rights advocates have called for churches to become more racially inclusive, few flourishing congregations contain a significant mix of Euro-Americans and African Americans. At the peak of his career, civil rights advocate Martin Luther King, Jr., repeatedly called attention to the observation of Benjamin E. Mays, made half a century earlier, that Sunday mornings from 11:00 to noon (the traditional hour of worship, particularly for American Protestants) was the most segregated hour of the week.

In many cases, if one looks comparatively at census data, one finds that Hispanic immigrants are moving into urban neighborhoods that a generation ago were the heart of the black ghetto. One result is that many congregations that were historically populated by African Americans are now located in neighborhoods where Hispanic Americans form the bulk of the residents. Those churches confront a rather different variation on the segregated worship hour. Current demographic trends suggest that there is a greater possibility for ethnic inclusivity to embrace Hispanic Americans and African Americans within single congregations than there is for inclusivity to bring Black and White together in racially mixed congregations.[11] The Pentecostal worship style favored by Hispanic Americans also resonates in many cases with the more exuberant modes historically associated with African American worship. It is, however, too early to tell whether Hispanic Americans and African Americans will on any large scale come together to fashion flourishing multi-ethnic congregations.

TURNING EASTWARD: PLURALISM'S MUSLIM, BUDDHIST, AND HINDU FACES
The 2000 census estimates cited earlier indicate that at the close of the 20th century, just over a quarter of all foreign-born people living in the United States were Asians (see also Reeves & Bennett, 2004). In this context, Asia includes most of what is popularly called the Middle East (which technically is westernmost Asia). As they make their way in a new and often very different cultural setting, immigrants coming from Asia share with immigrants across the ages the desire to draw on the religious beliefs and practices that shaped their lives in the past. Unlike many earlier generations of immigrants, those coming from some areas of Asia, such as India, are more likely to have an educational and professional orientation that surpasses what most who are already citizens possess. For example, Roger Daniels has documented that since at least "sometime in the 1980s," Asian immigrants "have been much more likely to have doctorates than are native-born Americans" (Daniels, 2004, p. 225). The story is rather different with those coming from Asia to the United States as refugees. Many of these Asians have confronted a far

greater struggle to succeed in the American environment and to plant their own social and cultural institutions, including religious ones, on U.S. soil.

The diverse religious backgrounds of these immigrants also set them apart. Earlier generations of immigrants, with those forced to come from Africa as slaves representing the largest exception, were most likely to look to one of the biblical traditions: Christianity in one of its many Protestant forms or its Roman Catholic and Eastern Orthodox manifestations and Judaism. However, even if a majority of Asian immigrants are Christians, thousands look instead to Islam, Buddhism, or Hinduism for their religious worlds of meaning. Their increasingly visible presence has added new dimensions to the pluralism that characterizes religion in American life.

Statistics from the Census Bureau again illustrate the dramatic growth of these bodies since the 1965 change in the immigration laws. Estimates indicate that between 1970 and 2000, the number of practicing Buddhists in the United States grew tenfold, from 200,000 to 2 million. There were approximately 800,000 Muslims in the United States in 1970, excluding those who identified with the Nation of Islam or Black Muslims. By 2000 that figure stood at 3,950,000, and some analysts believed that figure too low.[12] Hinduism has always been the smallest of these three, perhaps because historically Hinduism has never been a proselytizing religion and is so intertwined with (Asian) Indian ethnic identity that many of its practices are unlikely to be attractive to converts, even those who may find Hindu philosophy appealing.[13] In 1970 there were only around 100,000 Hindus in the United States, and by 2000, around 950,000. That increase was almost entirely the result of immigration from India (Lippy, 2004; U.S. Census Bureau, 2000).

In the United States as in India, Hindus have been inveterate temple builders, although in some cases in the United States, structures originally built for other purposes have been converted into temples for the Indian immigrant community. In India, where somewhere around 80 percent to 85 percent of the population identifies with some strand of the Hindu tradition, upper-caste men especially are likely to have little contact with temples on a regular basis. Nevertheless, the prevalence of temples in the cities and villages serves as a subliminal reminder of the plausibility of Hindu modes of being, and the way the aura of Hinduism pervades all of Indian culture. This means that despite modernization, a Hindu presence is simply "in the air" to sustain an abiding identity with the larger tradition. Indeed, regular attendance at temple functions has never been a barometer of Hindu faithfulness the way pollsters look at church attendance to measure the devotion of Christians. For Hindus, what transpires in the home is far more vital to Hindu identity than what goes on in the temple. Families in even the most modest circumstances will maintain an altar where *puja* or devotion may be celebrated; the more well-to-do may set aside an entire room in their abodes as a puja room.

Things are different in the United States. Temples serve, of course, as places where the devout may come to make an offering or to receive a blessing from a priest (often one trained in India). Significantly, the temples are also places for nourishing an Indian ethnic identity. Hindu temples in the United States are thus as much cultural centers as they are religious centers. Consequently, even those (especially men) who are from upper-caste backgrounds, and in India might be disinclined to take part in activities centered in the temples, assume responsibility for the construction and maintenance of temples in the United States. Without a temple, the props buttressing a cultural uniqueness would vanish. At the same time, non-Hindus might readily overlook even the presence of a temple, particularly if it is a building originally erected for another purpose. The Hindu temple in Chattanooga, Tennessee, for example, was built to house a Southern Baptist congregation, which sold the building when the congregation's own growth necessitated relocation to a site where a larger structure could be erected. Without any passion for seeking converts, Hinduism in the United States remains likely to be intimately linked with the expanding Indian immigrant community.[14]

Historically, Buddhism has been more inclined to seek converts than has Hinduism. In the United States, interest in things Buddhist antedates the upswing in immigration after 1965. On an intellectual level, some trace the roots of this interest to the Transcendentalists of the 19th century, some to the formation of societies following the World's Parliament of Religions held in Chicago in 1893, some to early immigration from Asia to the west coast before the 1924 quotas, some to spouses brought home by those who served in the military in Asia during World War II, and some to the fascination with Zen evinced by writers of the "Beat generation." As a result, Buddhism already had a presence in U.S. intellectual and religious circles before the post-1965 rise in Asian immigration began to swell its ranks. Nevertheless, with the exception of descendants of 19th-century immigrants, spouses of military personnel, and a handful of refugees, most of those who identified as Buddhists before that immigration were converts. Tassajara, a monastic center in California rooted in the Zen tradition, symbolizes that prevalent convert-based Buddhism.[15]

Some strands of Buddhism have continued to attract converts. In recent years, for example, the Dalai Lama has personified Buddhism for many westerners, thanks in part to his many lecture tours and media appearances. He represents one particular strand of Buddhism, that which developed in Tibet. Virtually no Tibetan Buddhists have immigrated to the United States or elsewhere, given the control the People's Republic of China exerts over Tibetan life. The popularity of Tibetan Buddhism has soared also because well-known personalities, such as actor Richard Gere, have made much of their own affiliation with that tradition in interviews and other media reports. Zen centers (often still found primarily in university towns) and retreat centers that are not affiliated with any single strand of the Buddhist heritage (such as the Southern Dharma Retreat Center in the North Carolina mountains near Asheville) likewise continue to draw primarily from a clientele of Euro-Americans interested in Buddhism. The surge in a highly individualized spirituality in recent years has meant that in many cases individuals who meditate at local Zen centers or spend a weekend at a place like the Southern Dharma Retreat Center do not necessarily see themselves as Buddhists. Rather, they draw on dimensions of Buddhist practice, most often some approach to meditation, and add it to other idiosyncratic practices to craft a personal religious world of meaning. Their numbers make it difficult to assess accurately how many Euro-Americans are actually practicing Buddhists or converts to Buddhism. Many centers talk about a core group of practitioners, but also interact with a much larger group who on occasion avail themselves of the religious services offered.

Harder to locate, but in some ways more indicative of the growth of Buddhism in the United States, are those centers that serve primarily immigrant communities. The numbers of immigrants to the United States from Vietnam, Thailand, Laos, Cambodia, and other Buddhist countries have grown steadily since 1965, and these immigrants have brought with them an array of expressions of Buddhism that, like the temples serving Hindu immigrant communities, are often as much centers for preserving the ethnic culture of the particular immigrant community as centers for nurturing religious life (see, for example, Lau, 2000). In some larger metropolitan areas, such as Los Angeles and New York, Buddhist immigrant communities from places such as Thailand and Vietnam have had the numerical base and financial resources to erect temples, some substantial in size and others rather modest. Elsewhere, as in the southeast, few of these Buddhist ethnic groups are poised to construct their own buildings; fewer yet advertise their presence even by signs. For example, in 2000 the North Carolina Buddhism Project sought to identify as many of the Buddhist temples and centers in that state as could be located. Some 33 were identified, although a few more have been located since the project published its guide in 2001 (Tweed & Buddhism in North Carolina Project, 2001). Just under two-thirds drew their core membership from Euro-Americans; nine served very distinct ethnic immigrant communities and often met in homes or in residences that had been refurbished to function as Buddhist temples. Sometimes these temples had no identifying markings, signs, or other indicators that would inform passers-by of the religious nature of the building. The local immigrant community simply passed on by word of mouth where the community gathered. In some cases, then, there were temples that were indistinguishable from the homes in the neighborhood that still functioned as family residences.

These ethnic-based temples were also least likely to engage in any kind of proselytizing activity. Their orientation was so focused on that delicate fusion of ethnic culture and religious expression that converts whose ethnic backgrounds were different would have been hard pressed to feel a sense of belonging. What seems likely is that the steadily increasing influx of immigrants from Buddhist countries in Asia means that what I have here called "ethnic-based Buddhism" will continue to grow at a rate exceeding that of convert-based Buddhism. As that growth occurs, the presence of scores of Buddhist temples, now almost lost to the casual observer, will become ever more prominent.

It is also not easy to calculate with any precision the size of the Muslim community in the United States.[16] One reason is that strong business and economic ties between the United States and any number of Muslim nations, in both Africa and Asia, mean that thousands of foreign nationals who are practicing Muslims live in the United States at any given moment. These people may, however, return to their nations of origin when their business or diplomatic work requires. The presence of a significant number of such transient Muslims makes accurate counting impossible. A second transient group consists of Muslim students from places such as Egypt, Saudi Arabia, Pakistan, Bangladesh, and middle eastern nations such as Iraq and Iran, who come to the United States intending to stay only until they complete their degree programs, but with some frequency later endeavor to gain immigrant status because of employment opportunities, greater political freedom, or marriage while in the United States.

Another challenge to determining just how many Muslims there are in the United States concerns the relationship of American Muslims to a mosque, the center for prayer life traditionally associated with Islam. Although the faithful, especially the men, are encouraged to attend Friday services of prayer that may include exposition of a section of the Quran, many analysts insist that the majority of American Muslims remains "unmosqued." Some believe, though, that like many Christian congregations, mosques may overstate the level of participation so as to bolster their standing. In contrast, John L. Esposito has argued that earlier generations of Muslim immigrants hesitated to build mosques because mosques would draw attention to an alien immigrant population that was struggling to assimilate and survive economically, and thus could bring latent prejudice to life (Esposito, 2000). Regardless, by the dawn of the 21st century, there were more than a thousand mosques scattered across the nation.

Islam, like Christianity and some strands of Buddhism, has historically been a religion eager to gain converts, because of an inner conviction that its truth is both absolute and final. In the United States, however, Muslims have been less aggressive in seeking converts than has been true elsewhere, particularly in earlier epochs. One reason is that Christianity, which remains the dominant tradition in the United States, has historically approached Islam with suspicion and hostility, since at least the early Middle Ages. Because Islam is as fervently monotheistic as Christianity, it appears as dangerous competition. Enhancing this competition are Islam's ties to Judaism, ties shared with Christianity although somewhat more indirect, and Islam's willingness to acknowledge Jesus as a prophet, albeit not a divine-human being as in the orthodox Christian claim.

Even before the attacks on the World Trade Center in September 2001, popular perception in the United States linked Islam with violence. Some of that association goes back to the calls for violent response to white racism characteristic of the predominantly African American Nation of Islam, at the peak of the civil rights movement in the early 1960s. This perception persists even though some "mainstream" Muslims see the Nation of Islam as something of an aberrant sect, and even though its best-known leader at the time, Malcolm X, repudiated the call for violence and separated from the Nation of Islam before his assassination in 1965.

In 1979, when the Iranian revolution brought the Ayatollah Khomeini to power and Americans there were held hostage for more than a year, links between Islam and terrorism became more firmly established. The events of September 11, 2001, cemented the image of Islam as a religion of terror in the minds of millions of Americans. For example, a survey conducted by the Pew Research Center found the largest number of respondents—44 percent—agreeing with a statement that the Islamic religion was more likely than others to encourage violence among its followers (Pew Research Center, 2003). Consequently, Muslim immigrants have been less inclined to proselytize in the United States, although there is a small but steady number of converts. A majority of these converts are African Americans who perhaps continue to see Christianity as a religion of oppression, given the history of slavery in this country. The other primary source of converts is those who marry Muslims, especially Euro-American women who marry Muslim men.

Like other immigrant communities, the two-thirds of American Muslims who are themselves immigrants, or descendants of immigrant families who have been in the United States perhaps only a generation or two, have tended to form tight-knit clusters based as much on ethnicity as religion. Non-Muslims have found it easy to ignore such ethnic enclaves, or have failed to recognize that they are centers of Muslim life. In turn, most non-Muslims, who may take for granted the presence of hundreds of different Protestant groups, remain ignorant of the tremendous variety of sects and traditions within Islam itself. Additional factors that perpetuate misunderstanding of Islam and impede its movement from the margins of public life to a posture of greater acceptance include such basic matters as the failure of schools to recognize holidays integral to Islam, the difficulty Muslims confront in employment when religious obligations require stopping for prayer during working hours and attending mosque services on Friday, and Muslim avoidance of social events centered around consumption of alcohol and foods that are taboo. The last, of course, is shared with Orthodox Jews, but accommodation of kosher dietary practice for Jews has gained a social acceptability that accommodation of Muslim dietary practice has not. Most of these struggles go unheralded by the media; more attention has been paid to calls for Muslim chaplains in the military and in the nation's prisons and to that day in 1991 when, for the first time, a Muslim religious leader offered prayer to open a session of the U.S. Congress.

IMPLICATIONS OF THE NEW PLURALISM

The rapid rise in the number of Muslims, Buddhists, and Hindus in the United States has at least four ramifications for the unfolding story of religious pluralism. First, the presence of these traditions requires recasting the image of a tripartite religious pluralism fixed in the American mind for half a century or more. It was around the time that

Herberg offered his *Protestant, Catholic, Jew* (1955) that commentators also began to speak of a Judeo-Christian heritage. That nomenclature has wedded popular perceptions of religious pluralism to the families of religions identified with the Bible. Careful analysis requires abandonment of that image. In actuality, it has no historical foundation; there are interlocking histories, but not a single tradition. There are many ways of being Protestant, not quite so many ways of being Catholic, and perhaps even fewer ways of being Jewish. However, that formulation usually omits the Eastern Orthodox traditions entirely and presumes that all who carry a Protestant, Catholic, or Jewish label affirm the same history. The recent influx of Hispanic immigrants, Filipino Catholics, and Korean Protestants suggests that we may now be dealing with many more Christianities than before. In addition, the sheer number of Muslims, Buddhists, and Hindus requires us to jettison the image, for religious pluralism now must extend its parameters to include ways of being religious that are not informed by the biblical traditions.

As well, there are signs that the number of Americans who eschew formal religious affiliation is also multiplying. They, too, are part of the story of an expanding religious pluralism, albeit one whose telling must await another study. One recent survey proclaimed that the "unchurched" U.S. population has grown from about one out of five in 1991 to more than one of three in 2004 (note the use of a Christian-based designation that reinforces the dominance of Christian traditions over the course of American history).[17] Historians remind us that traditional categories, including membership, have never captured the full range of religious orientations in American religious culture (Fuller, 2001); nor can we even be certain about what membership means. For nearly a generation, it has been fashionable to recognize those who are "spiritual" but not "religious," as a way of identifying the millions who stand outside formal religious institutions and traditions, yet see themselves as having a religious worldview. If we include these people within our purview, then the boundaries of religious pluralism get pushed almost to infinity.

Closer attention also should be directed to religious communities that defy easy classification. One such, which is among the larger single groups in American life and whose rolls are swelling at an impressive rate, is the Church of Jesus Christ of Latter-day Saints. The Mormons, as the LDS adherents are familiarly known, emerged on the margins of Protestant life in the 19th century and sought to develop a history on the borders of the country with their theocratic experiment in Utah. Over time they have become quintessentially American in terms of their fusion of perceived public values with religious beliefs, and now number in the "top ten" of religious bodies in terms of reported membership.

Second, recent trends have revitalized the connections between ethnicity and religion. Over the generations, Euro-Americans married across ethic lines with increasing frequency, even if Protestants tended to marry other Protestants (sometimes from a different denomination), Catholics to marry other Catholics (sometimes from a different ethnic community), and Jews to marry other Jews. Since the close of World War II, the rate of intermarriage across traditions has exploded. One result is the obscuring or at least diminishing of the ethnic dimensions that once sustained many congregations, whether Protestant, Catholic, or Jewish. Nevertheless, one cannot separate being Hindu from being Indian—at least not yet. Also, the many Buddhist centers that serve as focal points for nurturing mores associated with ways of being Laotian or Thai or Cambodian or Vietnamese beckon us to reaffirm the intricate and enduring pattern that weaves together religion and ethnicity. Much the same holds for the Muslim communities in cities across the nation, where American Syrian, Iranian, Iraqi, Saudi, Egyptian, Turkish, and clusters with roots in other Muslim cultures are held together by different ways of being Muslim—some of it centered around a mosque, but much of it centered around an almost tribal sense of ethnicity.

More complicated, and worth inquiry and analysis in its own right, is the resurgence of ethnic pride and heritage among Native American cultures since the last third of the 20th century. Missionaries, both Protestant and Catholic, established a powerful presence for their respective brands of Christianity among many tribal societies and actively sought converts. Frequently their presence received a boost from the role these religious bodies played in organizing government-supported schools on many reservations. Despite these efforts, though, they never snuffed out all indigenous practice. In the 21st century, it is not unusual to find quite an array of religious expression within these indigenous cultures, some fusing Christian elements with aspects of tribal religiosity, some celebrating revitalized native religious forms, and others crafting something new and distinct that defies categorization in any of the received traditions.

Third, these "newer" ethnic communities, while seeking to fit into American life economically, politically, and socially, are less inclined to abandon their religion or to jettison religious practices and beliefs that seem counter to prevailing ways. In this context, William Hutchison's image of a symphonic religious pluralism has particular power. Rather than adjust or abandon key features of a religious identity, recent immigrants—whether from Latin America, Asia, Africa, or the Near East—assume that their ways of being religious have an inherent legitimacy and integrity. They understand religious pluralism to mean that they have a voice equal to that of the Protestant-Catholic-Jewish triad, and that they thus should not be expected to repudiate what has endowed their lives with meaning merely to blend into the larger religious culture. No doubt there will be some accommodation to America; the United States, after all, is not Cambodia, India, Mexico, or Saudi Arabia. The accommodation, though, will be evolutionary rather than the result of yielding to pressure.

Finally, the expansive religious pluralism of the last half-century makes it problematic to speak of a common religious core to American culture. In 1967, just two years after the landmark changes in immigration law were enacted, sociologist Robert Bellah published his now classic essay, "Civil Religion in America." Drawing his title concept from

Jean-Jacques Rousseau, Bellah wrote with a passion for the nation emerging not from new immigration, but from division over American military engagement in Vietnam and elsewhere in southeast Asia. He argued that alongside more organized and formal religious systems and institutions, a core of beliefs and practices broadly grounded in the biblical traditions endowed the American enterprise with sacred meaning. Trained as a scholar of Japanese culture, Bellah also reflected in his essay his appreciation of the role of Shinto as a cohesive force in that society.

Both the civil rights movement and second-wave feminism began to undermine Bellah's insistence that the American civil religion echoes biblical notions filtered largely through a white-male, mostly Euro-American prism. The exploding religious pluralism that has characterized American common life in the decades since renders his contentions even more problematic. Simply put, symbols of social cohesion rooted in some fusion of Judaism and Christianity cannot speak to the lived experience of Muslim, Buddhist, and Hindu Americans, and may speak to the lived experience of Hispanic Americans only obliquely. This reality has significant implications for the politically fashionable discussion of all sorts of faith-based initiatives, particularly those that involve channeling government funds to religious communities. One must ask whether such faith-based initiatives can include the radically pluralistic understandings of what faith itself denotes, and whether such initiatives naively presume that there remains some vague American "culture" religion rooted in the Judeo-Christian tradition—whatever that is—to which all specific religions give lip service, even those removed from that amorphous heritage. Similar dilemmas emerge from the lived experience of those who identify with faith communities, but find themselves pushed to the periphery because of matters such as gender or sexual orientation.

Of course, all of these efforts to promote faith-based initiatives raise fresh issues about the separation of church and state that allowed religious pluralism to flourish. Restricting support to so-called secular endeavors managed by religious groups may prove an impossible task, for some religious communities may simply be unable to draw a neat line between what is religious and what is not. Nor may all be able to divorce overtly religious enterprises from those intended to serve the common good.

The burden of the 21st century thus becomes whether Americans can craft a symbolic configuration of symbols and associated practices that will support a common identity for all the peoples called American and grant them social cohesion. If not, the possibility lurks of a 21st-century tribalism developing in the United States: a tribalism that could cause division and discord that would make the civil upheaval of the mid-19th century seem like little more than a blip on the historical radar screen.

END NOTES
1. This is the burden of my book *Pluralism Comes of Age* (2000).
2. The work of the Pluralism Project may be examined at its Web site: http:// www.pluralism. org

3. In recent years, the work of Robert Orsi has probed these connections in provocative ways, especially as they relate to the urban setting. See Orsi (1999); more generally, see Becker (1988).

4. A good survey of a wide range of issues regarding immigration throughout the 20th century is Daniels (2004).

5. Although the McCarran-Walter Act retained national-origin quotas, it did reduce the racial and ethnic restrictions that were part of the 1924 legislation.

6. Daniels (2004, p. 227), suggests that refugee status reached its largest proportion of immigrants in the half-decade after the close of World War II (1946–1950), when the figure was 24.7 percent of the total. In the Cold War years of the 1950s, the figure was 19.8 percent, and in the 1970s, 12.0 percent. For the 1960s, though, it was just 6.4 percent.

7. Percentages are based on numbers in Table 3 of Malone, Balluja, Costanza, & Davis (2003, p. 6).

8. See Maldonado, Jr. (2000). For a general overview, see Gonzalez (2000).

9. Several articles appearing in the Chattanooga Times Free Press within a few weeks of one another help document this transformation in Georgia and in the South more generally. There were two front-page stories: Turner (2003), and one based on wire service and staff reports, "Hispanic Population Continues to Surge" (2003). The Whitfield County school census is the focus of a piece that appeared in the newspaper's "Metro" section (Baydala, 2003).

10. The conservative theological character of Third World Christianity in general, not just Latin American Christianity, is a major theme of Jenkins (2002). Jenkins points out that if demographic trends in place at the start of the 21st century remain constant, within 50 years the majority of the world's Christians will live south of the equator.

11. The issues in the preceding two paragraphs are discussed at somewhat greater length in my unpublished paper, *The Eleven o'Clock Hour on Sunday Morning* (2002).

12. Esposito (2000) believed the number was closer to 5 million, although he included in his figure those who are part of the Nation of Islam. He also claimed, as do others, that by 2020 there will be more Muslims than Jews in the United States.

13. The parallels with the Jewish immigrant experience in the later 19th and early 20th centuries are patent.

14. Relatively little has been written about Hinduism in the United States for the period since 1965. In addition to Eck (2001, pp. 80–141), see Larson (2000, pp. 125–141).

15. Helpful for this discussion have been Seager (1999), Prebish (1999), Eckel (2000, pp. 143–153), Eck (2001, pp. 142–221), Tweed (1997a), and Tweed & Buddhism in North Carolina Project (2001).

16. My understanding of Islam in America has been shaped especially by Smith (1999), Lawrence (2002), Haddad (1997), Esposito (2000), and Eck (2001, pp. 222–293).

17. The figures of 21 percent for 1991 and 34 percent for 2004 come from the Barna Group and were reported in "Ratio of 'Unchurched' Up Sharply Since 1991" (2004).

REFERENCES

Baydala, K. (2003, August 19). Immigration changes face of Dalton schools. *Chattanooga Times Free Press*. Retrieved October 20, 2005, from http://www.timesfreepress.com/archive

Becker, L. L. (1988). Ethnicity and religion. In C.H. Lippy & P. W. Williams (Eds.), *Encyclopedia of the American religious experience* (Vol. 3, pp. 1477–1491). New York: Scribners.

Bellah, R. N. (1967, Winter). Civil religion in America. *Daedalus 96*, 1–21.

Daniels, R. (2004). Immigration. In S. J. Whitfield (Ed.), *A companion to 20th-century America* (Blackwell Companions to American History, pp. 215–232). Oxford, England: Blackwell.

Eck, D. L. (2001). *A new religious America: How a "Christian country" has become the world's most religiously diverse nation.* San Francisco: HarperSanFrancisco.

Eckel, M. D. (2000). Buddhism in the world and in America. In J. Neusner (Ed.), *World religions in America* (pp. 143–153). Louisville, KY: Westminster John Knox Press.

Esposito, J. L. (2000). Islam in the world and in America. In J. Neusner (Ed.), *World religions in America* (pp. 173–183). Louisville, KY: Westminster John Knox Press.

Fuller, R. C. (2001). *Spiritual but not religious: Understanding unchurched America.* New York: Oxford University Press.

Gonzalez, J. L. (2000). The religious world of Hispanic Americans. In J. Neusner (Ed.), *World religions in America* (rev. ed., pp. 78–91). Louisville, KY: Westminster John Knox Press.

Haddad, Y. Y. (1997). Make room for the Muslims? In W. H. Conser, Jr., & S. B. Twiss (Eds.), *Religious diversity and American religious history: Studies in traditions and cultures* (pp. 218–261). Athens: University of Georgia Press.

Herberg, W. (1955). *Protestant, Catholic, Jew: An essay in American religious sociology.* Garden City, NY: Doubleday.

Hispanic population continues to surge. (2003, September 18). *Chattanooga Times Free Press*, p. 1.

Hutchison, W. R. (2003). *Religious pluralism in America: The contentious history of a founding ideal.* New Haven, CT: Yale University Press.

Immigration Act of 1965, P.L. 89-236, 79 Stat. 911 (1965).

Jenkins, P. (2002). *The next Christendom: The coming of global Christianity.* New York: Oxford University Press.

Johnson, L. B. (1967). *Public papers, 1965* (Vol. 2). Washington, DC: U.S. Government Printing Office.

Larson, G. J. (2000). Hinduism in India and in America. In J. Neusner (Ed.), *World religions in America* (pp. 125–141). Louisville, KY: Westminster John Knox Press.

Lau, B. (2000). *The temple provides the way: Cambodian identity and festival in Greensboro, North Carolina.* Master's thesis, Curriculum in Folklore, University of North Carolina, Chapel Hill.

Lawrence, B. B. (2002). *New faiths, old fears: Muslims and other Asian immigrants in American religious life.* New York: Columbia University Press.

Lippy, C. H. (2000). *Pluralism comes of age: American religious culture in the twentieth century.* Armonk, NY: M.E. Sharpe.

Lippy, C. H. (2002, September 26). *The eleven o'clock hour on Sunday morning: Separate churches for black people and white people.* Paper presented at the Fall Forum, Center for Religion in the South, Lutheran Theological Southern Seminary, Columbia, SC.

Lippy, C. H. (2004). Christian nation or pluralistic culture: Religion in American life. In J. A. Banks & C. A. McGee Banks (Eds.), *Multicultural education: Issues and perspectives* (5th ed., pp. 127–128). Hoboken, NJ: John Wiley & Sons.

Maldonado, D., Jr. (2000). The changing religious practices of Hispanics. In P.S.J. Cafferty & D. W. Engstrom (Eds.), *Hispanics in the United States: An agenda for the twenty-first century* (pp. 97–121). New Brunswick, NJ: Transaction.

Malone, N., Balluja, K. F., Costanza, J. M., & Davis, C. J. (2003, December). *In The foreign-born population: 2000* (Census 2000 Brief, Table 3, p. 6). Washington, DC: U.S. Department of Commerce, Economics and Statistics Administration, U.S. Census Bureau.

Marty, M. E. (1972, March). Ethnicity: The skeleton of religion in America. *Church History, 41*(7), 5–21.

McCarran-Walter Act of 1952. P.L. 82-414, 66 Stat. 163.

Melton, J. G. (1990). *Encyclopedia of American religions* (3d ed.). Detroit: Gale Research.

National Council of the Churches of Christ. (Annual). *The yearbook of American and Canadian churches.* Nashville, TN: Abingdon Press.

National Origins Act of 1924. 43 Stat. 153.

Orsi, R. A. (Ed.). (1999). *Gods of the city: Religion and the American urban landscape.* Bloomington: Indiana University Press.

Pew Research Center for the People and the Press. (2003). Telephone poll conducted 24 June–8 July. Retrieved January 3, 2005, from http://80-poll.orspub.com.libraryproxy.sdsu.edu/poll/lptext.dll/ors/i/islam

Prebish, C. (1999). *Luminous passage: The practice and study of Buddhism in America.* Berkeley: University of California Press.

Ratio of "unchurched" up sharply since 1991. (2004, June 1). *Christian Century*, p. 15.

Reeves, T. J., & Bennett, C. E. (2004, December). *We the people: Asians in the United States* (Census 2000 Special Reports). Washington, DC: U.S. Department of Commerce, Economics and Statistics Administration, U.S. Census Bureau.

Seager, R. H. (1999). *Buddhism in America.* New York: Columbia University Press.

Smith, J. I. (1999). *Islam in America* (Columbia Contemporary American Religion Series). New York: Columbia University Press.

Turner, D. (2003, August 17). The changing South. *Chattanooga Times Free Press*, p. 1.

Tweed, T. A. (1997a). Asian religions in the United States: Reflections on an emerging subfield. In W. H. Conser, Jr., & S. B. Twiss (Eds.), *Religious diversity and American religious history: Studies in traditions and cultures* (pp. 189–217). Athens: University of Georgia Press.

Tweed, T. A. (1997b). *Our Lady of the Exile: Diasporic religion at a Cuban Catholic shrine in Miami.* New York: Oxford University Press.

Tweed, T. A., & Buddhism in North Carolina Project. (2001). *Buddhism and barbecue: A guide to Buddhist temples in North Carolina.* Chapel Hill: University of North Carolina, Buddhism in North Carolina Project.

U.S. Census Bureau. (2000). *Statistical abstract of the United States.* Available at www.census.gov/statab

CHAPTER 7

UNDERSTANDING DIVERSITY
IN SCHOOLS

Nora L. Ishibashi and Noriko Ishibashi Martinez

If . . . an established system [of national education] were adopted, however judicious its arrangements might be—notwithstanding it might endeavor to promote liberality and independence of thought, it must eventually produce a general one-sidedness and similarity of character; and inasmuch as it did this, it would dry up the grand source of that spirit of agitation and inquiry, so essential as a stimulus to the improvement of the moral and intellectual man.
—*Herbert Spencer* (1843/1982)

For in these matters we must not believe the many, who say that free people only ought to be educated, but we should rather believe the philosophers who say that the educated only are free.
—*Epictetus, The Discourses*

INTRODUCTION

Educational institutions are major conduits of values and beliefs. Schools are the institutions where children spend the most time outside of home, and therefore schools are important environments where children experience the transformation of family norms toward societal norms (Filmer, 2003; Rodriguez, 2000). Hence, education is one of the essential building blocks of society. As the two epigraphs to this chapter illustrate, it is difficult to attain a balance between education as an emancipator and education as an oppressor. The stakes are high, however, because education is what shapes citizens for full participation in society.

By the middle of the 21st century, the total proportion of racial and ethnic minority youth in the United States will exceed that of the white population (de Anda, 2002). Changing demographics alone will require that schools evolve rapidly to create learning contexts that support the success of all students. As a major building block of society, educational institutions play an important role for all members of society, and any failures have large repercussions. Current failures in the education system are well recognized. Some problems include achievement gaps between white students and students in other racial/ethnic groups, dropout rates, school violence, and inequitable distribution of financial resources among school districts. Gaps in standardized test scores were persistent among fourth- and eighth-grade students as recently as 2003 (NCES, 2004), and those gaps extend through the SAT scores of 12th-graders. The U.S. Department of Education (2004) reported that "on average, African-American and Hispanic students in the 12th grade score four years behind White 12th-graders in both reading and mathematics."

Education is fundamental to social and economic mobility (Roderick, 2000) and represents a key to greater social power. The difference in academic achievement can therefore have long-term effects. Consequently, an argument can be made that education is not just a building block of society, but also the entrée into society. Educational attainment determines the segment of society in which one will live out one's life, thereby affecting other social benefits such as whether one will live in a safe neighborhood, have adequate housing, and enjoy access to health care and other social institutions.

This chapter explores how the structure of educational institutions shapes the educational experiences of a diverse student population with diverse needs and, conversely, how that diversity modifies educational institutions. In this chapter we examine the role of larger social ideas in shaping education, the role of educational institutions in shaping the experience of children and families, and the role of families and communities in the child's experience of education.

SOCIETY

Education plays a weighty role in the shaping of future society. By contributing to the socialization and development of children, including the development of their social identity and the ways in which they respond to diversity, schools are second only to primary caregivers in their lasting influence on children. Because of this influence, it is incumbent upon schools to form partnerships with parents. Where these partnerships are forged, children benefit from the educational resources available within two systems, the family and the school. Where these partnerships are neglected or undermined, children encounter obstacles to accessing these two reservoirs of care and information. Education is a universal social welfare program available to all children, including children without citizenship or legal immigration status. Even so, there is significant social ambivalence and disagreement about how to make the education system accessible in an equitable way. These issues continue debates that began at the very inception of public education, so it is clear that these questions do not have simple answers, and they are complicated by the ideological stance that each side represents.

Since the civil rights movement of the 1960s and 1970s, dialogue about diversity has grown in volume and complexity. In spite of this, social segregation persists in the form of greater poverty, greater risk of health problems, and lower academic achievement among many racial and ethnic groups. Segregation remains in education as well, with minority students graduating less and achieving less than their mainstream counterparts (Garcia, 2002).

A comprehensive description of the historical roots of social segregation in education is beyond the scope of this chapter; however, the current context can be seen as an outgrowth of earlier tensions arising from the popularity of the eugenics and Americanization movements. The eugenics movement was linked with the idea of a unilinear ranking of intelligence, which was considered an inherited quality. The "feeble-minded," as those ranked low on the IQ scale were called, were deported, institutionalized, and, by the mid-1920s, in 30 states eventually faced compulsory sterilization (Gould, 1996; Whitaker, 2002). If one believes that "feeble-mindedness" is innate and immutable, then it follows that education must respond differently and have different expectations of the "feeble-minded" student.

The eugenics movement is easily paired with the nationalist Americanization movement, which both enticed and forced immigrants into conformity (Higham, 1955). Education was used as a tool to expedite the transformation of immigrants into Americans, always struggling against the pessimism of contemporary science. The popularity of this idea of the innate and immutable character of intelligence 100 years ago justified a decision like the Supreme Court's 1896 holding in *Plessy v. Ferguson*,[1] which upheld the model of "separate but equal" for various social institutions—including education. This decision, which may be seen as based on the "scientific" notion that some people are biologically limited and beyond the reach of the Americanization ideal, institutionalized the mechanisms of segregation that remain in education today.

Social segregation is no longer popularly justified on biological grounds, and in 1954 the Supreme Court overturned the "separate but equal" model in *Brown v. Board of Education*.[2] However, the effect of Brown was diminished by later Supreme Court rulings that allowed segregation if it was not intended by the defendant school boards, but was simply a product of residential patterns.[3] The Supreme Court also ruled that unequal funding of schools due to differences in local property taxes—that is, segregation by socioeconomic status or class—did not violate the Equal Protection Clause of the Fourteenth Amendment[4]; this decision allowed the vast inequalities of resources now manifest in schools based on their geographic locations.

Essentially, these rulings have allowed segregation in schools to remain, and in fact there has been a trend toward greater segregation in the last 10 years, particularly for Latino students and in densely populated urban areas (Orfield & Lee, 2004). The de facto segregation that is allowed in the educational system reflects the social segregation present in society: neighborhood segregation by ethnicity, culture, and socioeconomic status is directly reflected in the funding of and enrollment in schools. Although Supreme Court rulings do not necessarily reflect the opinion of the larger society, social acceptance of those rulings and increasing segregation indicate that desegregation is no longer a priority.

These swings toward and away from desegregation have taken place in the context of an overall social and historical commitment to education and recognition of education as a common good, because of its capacity to create good citizens and protect democracy. Before the late 19th century, education was available, but not necessarily free and certainly not mandatory. By the end of the 19th century, however, elementary school education was free and available to all children. The creation of a national system of education, the expression of the hope of Americanization, was matched by the issuance of the separate-but-equal *Plessy* decision, an expression of the pessimism of eugenics. In other words, "separate but equal" belies the social movement shortly following which clearly stated that some groups of people were genetically superior to other groups of people.

Another view might argue that the *Plessy* decision created the context in which the white majority would accept the idea of free and public education for all children. Though the idea of using education to inculcate a new American identity into children may have been appealing, white parents might not have supported the shift to national education if they had thought it meant that their children would be attending the same schools as black children. That is, white parents may not have been willing to accept public education with mixed-race classes. By allowing separate-but-equal education, the fear of mixed-race classrooms could be alleviated, and the move toward national education could be realized. The important point is that educational institutions were initially structured in a social context that idealized both utter conformity and the separation of the fit from the unfit, that is, from the "criminals, rapists, idiots, feeble-minded, imbeciles, lunatics, drunkards, drug fiends, epileptics, syphilitics, moral and sexual perverts, and diseased and degenerate people" (from Iowa's 1913 sterilization bill, quoted in Whitaker, 2002, p. 58).

Although ethnic and racial segregation draw much attention, the other conflicts and controversies in the current national discourse on education also have their roots in the earliest debates surrounding public education. The issue of language diversity was addressed beginning in the 1700s, when immigrants established their own schools to teach their children in their native languages. Ohio was the first state to pass a law (in 1838) allowing children to receive German–English education at their parents' request and at state expense; German bilingual education continued up until World War I, when Germans fell out of favor (Cafferty, 1981).

The fluctuation of opinion about bilingual education manifest in the changing policies concerning German-English education continues, and the issue is complex and contentious for both pedagogical and political reasons. Some argue that children will learn better in their second language if they continue to develop their first language; others contend that separate, native-language instruction ends up being inferior (this debate contains echoes of the racial segregation issue). The question of bilingual education is further complicated by the fact that there are different models of bilingual education. Moreover, the age of the child and level of acculturation also play a role in deciding the most appropriate method of instruction. These pedagogical concerns are often eclipsed by the political contention that being taught in one's native tongue is a civil right. Though the question of whether civil rights entitlements include bilingual instruction is a phenomenon of the post-civil rights era, questions of language diversity in the public schools date back to the 1700s.

Another contemporary issue that was foreshadowed in the 18th century is that of school choice and the use of vouchers to expand choice. In 1778 Adam Smith advanced the idea of giving parents money to educate their children in the way they saw fit (Public Broadcasting Services, 2001). In 1925 the Society of Sisters, a Catholic group, won a Supreme Court ruling that states could not force public schooling on children; thus, children could legally attend private schools (and receive a Catholic education).[5] The topic of school choice continues to be hotly debated in 21st-century society. Some argue that schools should operate in a free market where parents can choose the institution that would best serve their children; others feel that vouchers will be the extra incentive that causes wealthier parents to put their children in private schools, leaving the public schools with less funding and a concentration of the most disadvantaged students whose parents cannot afford to move them to another school, even with the voucher (because of the added costs of transportation, among other things; for an example of the debate, see Gewertz, 2004).

Institutional commitment to diversity in education has a somewhat shorter history. Reflecting social trends in the 1960s and 1970s, colleges began to use affirmative-action admission policies, which in turn led to lawsuits protesting reverse discrimination in education.[6] The ideal of diversity in education maintained through affirmative action remains, however, and continues to be at least narrowly upheld in the courts.[7] The commitment to diversity in education in this country is also traceable through the beginnings of the Head Start program in 1965 and federal funding for disadvantaged students (Title I funds), as well as the Supreme Court decision ensuring free, public education for undocumented immigrants.[8] These milestones all represent active attempts by the larger society, as well as specific institutions, to overcome the historical discrimination that has been embedded in the structures of education. They also are examples of how larger social movements influence and shape the structure of education.

The history of social movements affecting education provides a context for understanding the role of diversity in education; however, contemporary events also influence the educational system. Children in the post-9/11 United States are growing up in an atmosphere of uncertainty, which interferes with the stability of their educational environment (de Anda, 2002). As mentioned briefly earlier, the atmosphere surrounding World War I made German–English bilingual education unpopular; World War II made the internment of Japanese Americans acceptable. In these moments when fear dictates social policy, decision making about education moves away from the ideals of

111

emancipation and toward the forces of oppression. Historic events join social trends as contextual influences on education and its task of preparing children to assume adult status in the larger social community. These influences are reflected in the structuring of institutions and their response to diversity among students, as discussed in the following section.

INSTITUTIONS

Ultimately, the success of a school rides on "the youths' motivation to learn and their willingness to expend the requisite effort to achieve educational goals" (Portes & Rumbaut, 2001, p. 211). Motivation comes partly from students' own expectations and those of their parents. Research suggests that "high academic expectations successfully predict subsequent educational performance and occupational choice" (Portes & Rumbaut, p. 212). Even so, the schools' responses to students' expectations can substantially affect the realization of those expectations. In other words, the way the school treats its students can have an important role in the students' belief that success is possible. Educational institutions, through their formal policies and informal practices, affect the learning culture within a school. This cultural context lays the groundwork for the kinds of individual practices that the teachers can employ to foster high expectations among students and the resources available to help students realize their expectations. Within this academic culture, the school community is formed, the classroom is managed, and the students are taught.

When educational institutions respond differentially to students of different backgrounds—through segregation, holding different expectations for student achievement, or even by using mainstream cultural values as the standard around which decisions are made—they can inhibit diversity within the institution and thereby create a system of differential access to education. Even when federal funding is provided to promote achievement—such as Title I,[9] which provides funding for programming intended to benefit at-risk students and particularly those from low-income communities—schools may use the funding in a way that serves some students but not others. For example, programs successful at targeting African American children for Title I programs can still miss Latino students, so that the latter do not reap the benefits of these programs (Juhasz & Plazas, 1993).

Institutional polices and practices can also emphasize and reify the meaning of difference (Baez, 2004). The way a school approaches, understands, and responds to a diverse population has an immediate effect on students' ability to pursue their education, as well as a long-term effect on the ways children are socialized to respond to differences in a community. Although the Brown decision attempted to limit racial segregation, the de facto segregation that has occurred in urban public school systems post-Brown has tended to occur along socioeconomic lines. Ironically, many classrooms today are quite homogenous along race, ethnicity, and class lines, reflecting the concentration of poverty and social isolation of groups such as African Americans, Latinos, and Native Americans. Some of this intraschool segregation is also a result of the overrepresentation of minorities in special education programs. Given the mounting economic disparities in this country and the shrinking resources available at the state and local levels, the deleterious effects of community poverty on the provision of an equitable, free, and public education seem likely to continue. Thus, the critical role that schools play may have to be expanded or revised. Poverty in our society creates particular challenges for educators and broader problems for a democracy if we are to have a society made up of truly free citizens.

Segregation

Although many factors affect the way in which educational institutions have responded to racial and ethic differences in the student population, two broad continua can act as a quick taxonomy, each emphasizing unity or difference. The first is the continuum of segregation. Depending on the various kinds of diversity present in schools, the manner in which the schools are structured shifts along that continuum. The movement toward and away from segregation in education is reflected in policies that determine who will attend a particular school or sit in a particular classroom. One form of segregation can be characterized as "interschool segregation." This form, though unintentional, leads to a homogeneous student body. The most common occurrence of interschool segregation stems from the fact that the school one attends is determined mostly by where one lives. Housing patterns rather than intentional actions lead to interschool segregation. This form of school selection leads to homogenous classrooms, and it also leads to inequitable funding across school districts, with wealthier school districts receiving higher funding from property taxes than poor school districts. Thus, although all children have a right to a free public education, the quality of that education is determined by the community in which they live.

Other kinds of segregation are intentional and intraschool. This form of segregation is driven by the belief that education is best accomplished in classrooms in which the students are as similar as possible. For example, schools often segregate students with low or no proficiency in English into bilingual or English as a Second Language (ESL) programs. Special education has also vacillated between keeping children in mainstream classes or pulling them out; the current guideline mandates placement of children in "the least restrictive environment" in which they can still learn.[10]

Intraschool segregation aims to uphold the ideal of keeping similar children together—in many cases, this even means tracking students with similar ability levels into the same classrooms. Researchers are recognizing that this is becoming less and less feasible, for two reasons. First, the pool of U.S. adolescents is increasingly diverse; by the middle of this century, for example, white youths will be a numerical minority. Second, even within each racial/ethnic group (and within each family) there is considerable diversity as a result of variations in acculturation (de Anda, 2002). It appears, then, that segregation could become a logistical impossibility because of increasing and increasingly complex diversity.

Standardization

The other broad continuum is that of individualization versus standardization. There is a politically driven desire to accept all different kinds of learning as equal and to create classrooms where no particular kind of learning is privileged (see, for example, Tomlinson's 1999 book on differentiated teaching). Differentiated teaching is individualized education within a classroom. Individualization can also help to address some of the culturally biased practices of U.S. classrooms by integrating different approaches to disciplines (Lee, 2003) or by recognizing fundamentally different kinds of cognition (Markus, Kitayama, & Heiman, 1996). However, individualizing teaching and differentiating classrooms makes it difficult to know exactly what children are learning and whether they are being equally prepared for the responsibilities of the next grade level or life beyond school—the primary focus of the No Child Left Behind Act.[11]

It is also becoming more and more difficult to come up with a standard measure to compare different models of education and audit students' progress. This fact underlies the controversy over standards themselves. Standards can be applied either to aid or to hinder educational progress, so the real question about standards is: How are they implemented? (Futrell & Gómez, 2003). This problem is part of what motivates segregation: Increased segregation can result in both greater standardization within groups and greater individualization by separating students into similar groups.

Sameness and Difference

These two continua both emphasize sameness or difference. Accountability and standards are based on ideals of sameness; individualization is based on ideals of difference. Segregation is based more on the ideal of sameness (keeping each child in a classroom with other children who are the same), whereas integration is based more on the ideal of difference (differential teaching within each classroom). As mentioned earlier, segregation can be a way to emphasize (or attribute negative meanings to) difference. While it may seem that ideals emphasizing difference are more in keeping with modern political correctness and the celebration of diversity, the preceding examples illustrate that a focus on similarity can also be useful. The struggle in education comes out of the unchangeable fact that any classroom is bound to encompass children with different styles of learning and different backgrounds.

The issue of sameness and difference is further complicated by the fact that the desire for segregation has historically masked a desire for distance from the "other," who may be seen as alien and unwanted. The central issues facing educational institutions are not solely pedagogical; that is, there are questions not merely about how best to teach the content, but also concerning what is conveyed about political and social ideals in the method of teaching any given curriculum. As children are developing cognitively and linguistically, they are also developing socially (Garcia, 2002); it is impossible to separate the content of education from the way it is taught. Both will affect the child's development in all three areas (cognitive, linguistic, and social), in part by modeling how to interact with other people.

Research shows that children do better in diverse classrooms (Kurlaender & Yun, 2002). Insofar as educational institutions base policies on racial difference, they are giving meaning to and propagating that difference (Baez, 2004; Grindis, Park, Paul, & Burg, 2002, p. 5). When children were separated into "tracks" to better suit their different paces, children in the remedial tracks simply did not have the opportunities that children in higher tracks had (Jones, 2003), and at-risk children separated into "transition" rooms showed little improvement in achievement (Mantzicopoulos, 2003). Furthermore, students were tracked based on the eugenics idea of a unilinear intelligence by which individuals can be ranked.

In sum, educational institutions are places where children are taught important lessons about what it means to be different, and what their place is in society. The choices made in organizing institutions must balance the need to recognize differences in children, so as to be better able to teach them, with the need to avoid attribution (or the appearance of attribution) of that difference to innate qualities within the child or the child's background. The problem is that achievement gaps between minority and nonminority students can and do exist. Caring for students of diverse racial and ethnic groups is challenging, first and foremost because it is not clear how to respond to their differing needs without exacerbating the perception of difference. Educators need to treat minority students differently so that, ultimately, they will not be treated differently: This is the paradox.

FAMILIES AND COMMUNITIES

Fundamentally, all public policy (including educational policy) is enacted on the individual level (Lipsky, 1983). For the individual student, educational institutions are places where he or she can be intimately known and increasingly connected to the larger society. Schools occupy a place in the life of the child that spans both the intimacy of family life and the anonymity of the larger social and cultural community. Our experience as school social workers shows that the single most important factor in the process of children becoming part of the educational environment—and subsequently the larger society—is the child's experience of being different and the degree of alienation carried by that experience. Part of that subjective experience arises from the differences among family, community, and school cultures; part of it comes out of how the family prepares the child to understand the school and the larger society; and part of it is created by the responses of the members of that social institution to the child in it.

However distant the child may feel from the community at large, the school provides the formative basis for the child's perception of whether the community is welcoming and supportive or hostile and punitive. This perception is partly based on expectation, but becomes molded and reinforced by actual experience. An important goal of education is to help the child traverse the distance between family culture and social culture. For children who are members of ethnic or racial groups, this distance can be greater, and there may be fewer people in the institution to help guide the transition. What roles do schools have in helping families and communities in this process?

Family involvement and parental expectation are often cited as important aspects of school achievement. However, the research in this area is far from clear. Although most families feel that education is important, this does not guarantee that their children will do well in school; and though most families are actively involved with their children's schools, this involvement does not always take the form that mainstream culture expects (Boethel, 2003). In other words, mainstream researchers and educators may not recognize the kind of involvement that is characteristic of diverse families. In addition, it is difficult for parents, many of whom are working two jobs, to be active in school, and first-generation immigrants may not have the background and experience to participate actively. In the past, approaches to families have not taken the diverse strategies of family involvement into account. Rather, they "have been based on deficit conceptions of cultures and families and thus have been aimed at remedying perceived family deficiencies" (Delgado-Gaitan, 1993, p. 139). A deficit approach fails to recognize the contributions these families make, as well as the families' resilience in being involved with a school system that is not structured to facilitate their involvement (Boethel, 2003). The focus on parent expectations also fails to recognize that, for some families, expectation does not always correlate with higher achievement (for example, in African American families; see Seyfriend & Chung, 2002). A deficit approach may unfairly assign to families what is at least partially the school's responsibility.

The other issue complicating families' attempts to be involved with their children's schools is that, as children become more acculturated to the school, they may become increasingly alienated from their families. Children of immigrant families are a clear example: they come into school and may increasingly experience what Portes and Rumbaut (2001) called "dissonant acculturation," as they move away from their parents' native culture and toward the local culture. At the same time, the child feels the burden of the family's expectations and hopes (Portes & Rumbaut, 2001).

The second generation of immigrant families does as well in school as native students, but their educational aspirations decline the longer they are in this country (Portes & Rumbaut, 2001). As the children of immigrants gradually join mainstream culture, they may experience increasing conflict within the family. This is not surprising, given the greater pressure the child feels in straddling two cultures with the burden of the parents' hopes. This conflict can impede the learning process and hinder school achievement for the child (Zambrana & Zoppi, 2002). It is the same conflict that Jane Addams described in 1908:

> And yet in spite of the fact that the public school is the great savior of the immigrant district, and the one agency which inducts the children into the changed conditions of American life . . . the public school too often separates the child from his parents and widens that gulf between fathers and sons which is never so cruel and so wide as it is between the immigrants who come to this country and their children who have gone to the public school . . . . The parents are thereafter subjected to certain judgment, the judgment of the young which is . . . founded upon the most superficial standard of Americanism. And yet there is a notion of culture . . . a knowledge of those things which have long been cherished by men, the things which men have loved because thru generations they have softened and interpreted life, and have endowed it with value and meaning. Could this standard have been given rather than the things which they see about them as the test of so-called success, then we might feel that the public school has given at least the beginnings of culture which the child ought to have. (1908/1994, pp. 136–137)

Although experiences of conflict between the culture of the family and that of the school have been recognized for nearly 100 years, educators have not yet developed means of addressing the competing loyalty demands on the child. In the best-case scenarios, schools can build communities, in the sense that children become connected with each other, and then, through their children, parents are able to connect with the rest of the community (Addams, 1908/1994; Goode, Schneider, & Blanc, 1992). The central issue in envisioning educational institutions in a culture of diversity is recognizing that differences need not lead to conflict or necessitate separation. Differences in values, ideals, and life choices between families and schools do not in themselves create problems. It is when these differences are set up as either/or choices for children that the children themselves become torn between two worlds. As described by Dean (2001), the best response to diversity is to accept one's own lack of knowledge; educators can then become learners as well as teachers, listeners as well as speakers. The stance necessary for the constructive inclusion of all members of the social environment is not merely to give lip service to the importance of diversity in cultural life, but to allow that conviction to inform policy choices and allocations of resources.

The other issue that relates directly to student well-being and achievement is the level of resources available to the child. It is important to recognize that environment plays a significant role in the child's life, as, for example, in the holistic model described by Grindis et al. (2002). The child needs to have an environment that is conducive to mental health and academic achievement. This is a necessary condition, without which "even the most motivated individuals flounder, despite brave declarations to the contrary"

(Portes & Rumbaut, 2001, p. 267). A 2003 study with a Native American population found that, after the opening of a casino increased all families' annual incomes, those families whose reported income rose above the federal poverty criteria experienced an immediate decrease in child mental health problems (Costello, Compton, Keeler, & Angold, 2003). This is telling evidence of the way family financial resources can directly affect a child's ability to participate in school.

Communities and families can be valuable resources in terms of supporting both children's learning and the community's educational institutions. It is when institutions and families are set up in opposition to one another, rather than developing a willingness to adjust and appreciate the other's contributions, that diversity becomes an obstacle.

IMPLICATIONS FOR SOCIAL WORK

Current research and practice form a basis for some educational policy recommendations. First, educational institutions that serve poor people must develop effective strategies to address the environmental effects of poverty on a family's ability to support a child's academic aspirations and nurture a child's capacity to learn. Moreover, the social isolation and heightened concentration of poverty among the urban poor demand that educational institutions serving this population consider ways to expose their students to various sectors of society as part of the educational curriculum. For many of these children, school trips to local museums and other cultural institutions represent journeys into different worlds only minutes from their homes. The lack of money for transportation and for admission present formidable obstacles for many individuals, but can be overcome by institutions cooperating with one another and recognizing the value of crossing social boundaries for the benefits of social inclusion. Second, school problems, including absenteeism, learning difficulties, and lack of motivation, should be addressed early and in a nonpunitive manner. Likewise, assuring equal access to federal and other programs, such as Head Start, will be important. Research shows consistently that later achievement builds on earlier success.

The complex diversity within ethnic and racial groups, as well as the complex constellations of factors affecting each child, suggests that schools should be organized to use a variety of interventions for any child. Ultimately, children are connected to schools and feel a sense of belonging based on the relationships they form there, both with peers and with adults. Engaging diverse children in learning requires that schools put time and money into the school's response to the unique nature of each child. This means educating adults to engage with different kinds of children and making use of school social workers to engage children and bridge gaps. In addition, schools need to create healthy and supportive environments rather than targeting individual deficits; similarly, for students of different racial and ethnic groups, schools must translate cultural wealth into social capital (Zambrana & Zoppi, 2002).

Overall, Grindis and colleagues (2002) found that "adolescents are less likely to engage in risk behaviors if they have a sense of physical, emotional, and economic security, are able to make a contribution to the community, have input into decision-making and have opportunities to participate in engaging and challenging activities that build skills and competencies" (p. 5). This finding can be expanded beyond adolescents to all children: it represents an ideal of creating an environment in which each child's own natural, healthy development can be supported. This in turn will ensure their success in educational development as well.

CONCLUSION: HOW DOES CHANGE HAPPEN?

As Reynoso noted in 1988: "Change does not come easily in large part because people believe in what they are doing" (p. 109). Because educators have come through the system as it is, and they believe they are successful, they are reluctant to alter that system. Any change requires awareness and a willingness to take risks. It also requires a supportive environment in which teachers and administrators see themselves as professional colleagues who, along with parents and children, are working toward a common goal: giving children the freedom to be educated.

Working together, these partnerships can do much to provide children with an educational experience that fosters the highest ideals for maximizing human potential and undermining the most coercive effects of poverty and segregation—namely, the lowest expectations for those most marginalized from society. Such a partnership calls for teachers and administrators to pursue a wholehearted commitment to a continuity of acceptance, inclusion, and support in the face of whatever response is generated from the child or family. Policies such as "zero tolerance," under which certain kinds of infractions result in expulsion from the community, create a contingent kind of membership that works against a child's developing an investment in community involvement. For the same reasons, the No Child Left Behind Act will not help, first because it is not supported by sufficient funding, and second because it represents a simplistic view of the achievement gap and does nothing to develop educational environments that foster collective efforts of educators, administrators, and parents to ameliorate the factors that indirectly hamper children's ability to learn (Fusarelli, 2004).

The United States is changing rapidly, as is the rest of the world. To prepare an increasingly complex and diverse population to meet change and succeed in an unknown future, the educational system must adapt to new realities and make use of current research on best practices. School social workers can provide important supports for students with varying needs. By acting as facilitators of school community and individual students' experiences, school social workers are in a position to bridge home and school and to help students from diverse backgrounds find a balance between mainstream and family cultures. The continuing disparity of community resources and the current context of political turmoil have again created a moment when society may move toward fear and oppression rather than emancipation. If they are to continue to uphold the ideals of a free, public education, though, teachers and administrators will need to remain open to change and committed to their own continuous growth and learning.

END NOTES

1. 163 U.S. 537 (1896).
2. 349 U.S. 294 (1954).
3. Keyes v. Denver Sch. Dist. No. 1, 413 U.S. 921 (1973); Board of Educ. of Okla. City v. Dowell, 498 U.S. 237 (1991); Freeman v. Pitts, 503 U.S. 457 (1992).
4. San Antonio Indep. Sch. Dist. v. Rodriguez, 411 U.S. 1 (1973).
5. Pierce v. Society of Sisters of the Holy Names of Jesus & Mary, 268 U.S. 510 (1925).
6. Regents of Univ. of Cal. v. Bakke, 438 U.S. 265 (1978).
7. Grutter v. Bollinger, 539 U.S. 982 (2003).
8. Plyler v. Doe, 457 U.S. 202 (1982).
9. Elementary and Secondary Education Act, Title. I, P.L. 103-382 (1994).
10. 20 U.S.C. §1412(5).
11. No Child Left Behind Act of 2001, P.L. 107-110, 115 Stat. 1425.

REFERENCES

Addams, J. (1994). The public school and the immigrant child. In *On education.* New Brunswick, NJ: Transaction Press. (Originally published 1908, in *Journal of the Proceedings and Addresses of the National Education Association,* pp. 99–102)

Baez, B. (2004). The study of diversity: The "knowledge of difference" and the limits of science. *Journal of Higher Education, 75,* 285–306.

Boethel, M. (2003). *Diversity: School, family, and community connections* (Annual Synthesis, 2003). (Report No. ED-01-CO-0009). Austin, TX: National Center for Family and Community Connections with Schools, Southwest Educational Development Laboratory. (ERIC Document Reproduction Service No. ED483003).

Cafferty, P. S. J. (1981). *The politics of language: The dilemma of bilingual education for Puerto Ricans.* Boulder, CO: Westview Press.

Costello, E. J., Compton, S. N., Keeler, G., & Angold, A. (2003). Relationships between poverty and psychopathology: A natural experiment. *JAMA, 290,* 2023–2029.

Dean, R. G. (2001). The myth of cross-cultural competence. *Families in Society, 82,* 623–630.

de Anda, D. (2002). Preface. *Journal of Ethnic and Cultural Diversity in Social Work, 11*(1/2), xv–xx.

Delgado-Gaitan, C. (1993). Research policy in reconceptualizing family-school relationships. In P. Phelan (Ed.), *Renegotiating cultural diversity in American schools* (pp. 139–158). New York: Teachers College Press.

Filmer, A. A. (2003). African-American vernacular English: Ethics, ideology, and pedagogy in the conflict between identity and power. *World Englishes, 3,* 253–270.

Fusarelli, L. D. (2004). The potential impact of the No Child Left Behind Act on equity and diversity in American education. *Educational Policy, 18,* 71–94.

Futrell, M. H., & Gómez, J. (2003). Making it work: Conclusions regarding diversity as a unifying theme in standards, assessments, and accountability. In N. Carter (Ed.), *Convergence or divergence: Alignment of standards, assessment, and issues of diversity* (pp. 129–146). (Report No.

ED-99-CO-0007). Washington, DC: AACTE Publications. (ERIC Document Reproduction Service No. ED480849).

Garcia, E. E. (2002). Bilingualism and schooling in the United States. *International Journal of Social Language, 155/166,* 1–92.

Gewertz, C. (2004). N.J. alliance launches petition drive for school choice. *Education Week, 24*(11), 16.

Goode, J. G., Schneider, J. A., & Blanc, S. (1992). Transcending boundaries and closing ranks: How schools shape interrelations. In L. Lamphere (Ed.), *Structuring diversity: Ethnographic perspectives on the new immigration* (pp. 173–213). Chicago: University of Chicago Press.

Gould, S. J. (1996). *The mismeasure of man, revised and expanded.* New York: W.W. Norton.

Grindis, C., Park, M. J., Paul, T., & Burg, S. (2002). A profile of adolescent health: The role of race, ethnicity and gender. *Journal of Ethnic and Cultural Diversity in Social Work, 11*(1/2), 1–32.

Higham, J. (1955). *Strangers in the land: Patterns of American nativism, 1860–1925.* New Brunswick, NJ: Rutgers University Press.

Jones, D. L. (2003). Diverse practitioners and diverse student populations: Opportunities and challenges in the alignment of national standards. In N. Carter (Ed.), *Convergence or divergence: Alignment of standards, assessment, and issues of diversity* (pp. 71–78). (Report No. ED-99-CO-0007). Washington, DC: AACTE Publications. (ERIC Document Reproduction Service No. ED480849)

Juhasz, A. M., & Plazas, F. C. A. (1993). The impossible dream: Education for the integration of Hispanic families. *Marriage and Family Review, 19*(3/4), 311–323.

Kurlaender, M., & Yun, J. T. (2002). *The impact of racial and ethnic diversity on educational outcomes: Cambridge, MA school district.* Cambridge, MA: Harvard Civil Rights Project. Retrieved September 20, 2004, from http://www.civilrightsproject.harvard.edu/research/diversity/cambridge_diversity.php

Lee, O. (2003). Equity for linguistically and culturally diverse students in science education: A research agenda. *Teachers College Record, 105,* 465–489.

Lipsky, M. (1983). Street-level bureaucracy. New York: Russell Sage Foundation.

Mantzicopoulos, P. (2003). Academic and school adjustment outcomes following placement in a developmental first-grade program. *Journal of Education Research, 97,* 90–105.

Markus, H. R., Kitayama, S., & Heiman, R. J. (1996). Culture and "basic" psychological principles. In E. T. Higgins & A. W. Kruglanski (Eds.), *Social psychology: Handbook of basic principles* (pp. 857–913). New York: Guilford Press.

National Center for Education Statistics (NCES). (2004). *National assessment of education progress.* Retrieved September 20, 2004, from http://nces.ed.gov/nationsreportcard/

Orfield, G., & Lee, C. (2004). Brown *at 50: King's dream or* Plessy's *nightmare?* Cambridge, MA: Harvard University Civil Rights Project. Retrieved September 20, 2004, from http://www.civilrightsproject.harvard.edu/research/reseg04/resegregation04.php

Portes, A., & Rumbaut, R. G. (2001). *Legacies: The story of the immigrant second generation.* Berkeley: University of California Press.

Public Broadcasting Services. (2001). *School: The story of American public education.* Retrieved September 18, 2004, from http://www.pbs.org/kcet/publicschool/

Reynoso, C. (1988). Educational equity. *UCLA Law Review, 36,* 107–117.

Roderick, M. (2000). Hispanics and education. In P. S. J. Cafferty & D. W. Engstrom (Eds.), *Hispanics in the United States: An agenda for the twenty-first century* (pp. 123–174). New Brunswick, NJ: Transaction Publishers.

Rodriguez, R. (2000). Aria: A memoir of a bilingual childhood. In J. C. Oates & R. Atwan (Eds.), *The best American essays of the century* (pp. 447–466). New York: Houghton Mifflin.

Seyfriend, S. F., & Chung, I. (2002). Parent involvement as parental monitoring of student motivation and parent expectations predicting later achievement among African American and European American middle school age students. *Journal of Ethnic and Cultural Diversity in Social Work, 11*(1/2), 109–131.

Spencer, H. (1982). The man versus the state. Indianapolis, IN: LibertyClassics. (Original work published 1843)

Tomlinson, C. A. (1999). *The differentiated classroom: Responding to the needs of all learners.* Alexandria, VA: Association for Supervision and Curriculum Development.

U.S. Department of Education, Office for Civil Rights. (2004). *Achieving diversity: Race-neutral alternatives in American education.* Retrieved September 1, 2004 from http://www.ed.gov/about/offices/list/ocr/edlite-raceneutralreport2.html

Whitaker, R. (2002). *Mad in America: Bad science, bad medicine, and the enduring mistreatment of the mentally ill.* Cambridge, MA: Perseus Publishing.

Zambrana, R. E., & Zoppi, R. M. (2002). Latina students: Translating cultural wealth into social capital to improve academic success. *Journal of Ethnic and Cultural Diversity in Social Work, 11*(1/2), 33–54.

PART III

ACCESS TO INSTITUTIONS IN

A DIVERSE SOCIETY

CHAPTER 8

IMPRISONMENT AND ITS AFTERMATH: RACE AND ETHNICITY IN PRISON AND BEYOND

Damian J. Martinez

INTRODUCTION

The U.S. criminal justice system has two major goals: ensuring the safety of citizens and punishing those who engage in harmful behavior. Importantly, this system is charged with carrying out its public-safety obligation in a fair and nondiscriminatory fashion. Nevertheless, the historical record indicates that the many interlocking components of the criminal justice system often have promoted injustice, unfairness, or disproportionate punishment of some citizens, whether purposely or unintentionally.

This chapter examines the ways in which individuals from diverse racial and ethnic groups have experienced incarceration, and explores the thesis that the causal factors leading to racial disproportionality in imprisonment can best be understood and addressed by examining social institutions outside of the criminal justice system. It is not enough simply to reveal that the criminal justice system has differentially punished certain racial or ethnic groups, or that it has contributed to the devastation of impoverished communities; racial and ethnic disproportionality in incarceration rates cannot be explained simply by institutional injustice within the criminal justice system. Although the identification of differential treatment is important, it is even more important to examine this phenomenon in a way that both provides insight into causal processes and informs social action and social change efforts.

SOCIETY

Punishment and Incarceration in the United States

Of all countries in the world, the United States currently incarcerates more people (2,212,475 in 2003) (Harrison & Beck, 2004), and has the highest imprisonment rate (701 per 100,000) (Walmsley, 2003). Strangely, the U.S. reliance on incarceration that is indicated by these dramatic statistics is a recent development.

During the 1970s, incarceration policies focused on the rehabilitation of offenders, as well as on punishment. Compared with other countries in the Western world, the

United States was among the nations where incarceration was used most infrequently (Tonry, 2004b). After the 1970s the imprisoned population steadily rose from approximately 100 prisoners per 100,000 U.S. residents (at its lowest point) to 445 inmates per 100,000 in 1997 (Blumstein & Beck, 1999).

In 1979, approximately 6 percent of the incarcerated population was there for drug offenses (Blumstein, 2004), whereas by 2002 that percentage had jumped to 20 percent (Harrison & Beck, 2003). This increase often is attributed largely to the harsh penalties imposed upon drug offenders (Blumstein & Beck, 1999). The larger factor, however—of which harsh drug policies were a part—was the rise of law-and-order, "get tough with criminals" perspectives and policies on the part of politicians and citizens.

The data regarding all people who either are in prison or are former prisoners show a nearly 4-million-person increase from 1974 through 2001. The total number of individuals ever incarcerated (for all offenses) in 1974 was 1,819,000 (149 current inmates and 1,102 former prisoners per 100,000 adult U.S. residents); by 2001, these numbers had grown to 5,618,000 (628 current inmates and 2,045 former prisoners per 100,000 residents) (Bonczar, 2003). Clearly, there has been a massive increase in the number of current and former prisoners since the 1970s.

Explaining Incarceration: Differing Views

It is important to note the various perspectives on, and explanations of, incarceration. A naive citizen might suppose that high or low rates of imprisonment directly reflect the number of crimes committed. Indeed, that citizen might assume that incarceration is a directly proportional response to crime: If crime increases (or, alternatively, if it decreases), so does the number of imprisoned people. Those who commit crimes are identified, arrested, tried, convicted, and sentenced to prison (so goes the simple crime-to-incarceration view).

The reality is that levels of crime in this country do not in any simple or direct way affect the policies of punishment or the rates of imprisonment. Instead, governmental policymakers make decisions to increase or decrease the use of incarceration and, in many instances, they do so largely independent of crime levels (Blumstein & Beck, 1999; Sorensen & Stemen, 2002; Tonry, 1995, 2004b). If incarceration policies are not simply or mainly a response to crime rates, then what other factors inform these policies, and what has contributed to the increase in these rates?

Several explanations have been offered for the increase in incarceration since the 1980s, including public concern over seemingly pervasive drug use, particularly among the young; an increased media focus on crime; and politicians' concern about not appearing "soft on crime" (Blumstein, 2004). The intertwining of public opinion, media reporting, and political decision making is central to understanding incarceration policies. In other words, emphasis on crime by politicians and the media strongly influences public perceptions of crime and citizens' concerns over what to do about it (Tonry, 2004b).

Changes in parole and sentencing policies, rather than in crime rates, have also been offered as reasons for the increase in incarceration rates and numbers (Tonry & Petersilia, 1999). An example of such a sentencing-policy change can be seen in murder cases. From 1980 to 1996, the average sentence length for murder increased from five years to 11 years: parole boards became increasingly concerned about releasing murderers, judges were more likely to resentence murderers to prison for parole violations, and judges handed down longer sentences for murder (Blumstein & Beck, 1999).

Other factors include "three-strikes" policies,[1] "truth-in-sentencing" mandates,[2] and "zero-tolerance" policing[3] in the United States. Crime rates in the United States and in every other Western nation were declining at the same time that three-strikes, truth-in-sentencing, and zero-tolerance policing policies were being adopted (Tonry, 2004b). Some scholars have argued that states with three-strikes laws do not incarcerate more individuals per arrests for violent crimes than do the states without such laws; nevertheless, in the main, such laws have disproportionately affected drug offenders. Truth-in-sentencing policies seem to have had little effect on the rate of incarceration (Sorensen & Stemen, 2002). Also, the increased recommitment of parolees has been a major factor in the recent growth of the U.S. prison population (Blumstein, 2004).

As a result of these influences, incarceration has become the penultimate punishment (the ultimate is death) and, often, the preferred penalty to be inflicted upon those who commit crimes. For a very long time, incarceration has been the primary method of dealing with those who commit crimes in the United States.

Although incarceration rates and numbers vary by jurisdiction, and the growth of the incarceration rate has recently slowed (U.S. Department of Justice, 2003), the national prison population has increased from nearly 1.6 million in 1995 to more than 2 million in 2003. During that same time period, the incarceration rate increased from 601 to 714 prison and jail inmates per 100,000 U.S. residents (Harrison & Beck, 2004). Clearly, reliance on incarceration is heavily offender-centered, with little concern for victims; incarceration has been described as an experiment in punishing as harshly as possible (Mauer & Chesney-Lind, 2002).

Unfortunately, racial and ethnic minorities are disproportionately affected by these sentencing and imprisonment trends. The following discussion examines the literature on, and arguments about, racial disproportionality in penal institutions.

INSTITUTIONS: RACE AND IMPRISONMENT

Some criminologists have had a long-standing interest in the tangled relationships between racial and ethnic variations in offenders, differential enforcement practices, sentencing, and imprisonment rates. Much of the research on race, ethnicity, and imprisonment has centered on three major points of inquiry: (1) agents of the criminal justice system who intentionally engage in discrimination, (2) criminal justice policies that have unintentionally differential effects on racial minorities, and (3) the disproportionate levels of crime committed by different races that have led to disproportionate involvement with the criminal justice system (Blumstein, 2001; Coker, 2003; D'Alessio & Stolzenberg, 2003; Kennedy, 1997; Ruth & Reitz, 2003; Sorensen, Hope, & Stemen, 2003; Tonry, 1995, 2004b; Zatz, 2000).

It is clear that intentional and historically legal discrimination has existed and has resulted in racial disproportionality in incarceration (Kennedy, 2001). It is incontrovertible that U.S. legislators and policymakers have used punishment to discriminate against African Americans (overprotection) more than to bring about crime reduction (underprotection). Historically, legal authorities have been reluctant to protect African Americans because they were either unwilling or unable to defend African Americans or to punish white offenders (Kennedy, 1997). Although the existence of racially motivated acts of violence in the post-Civil War era influenced the construction and passage of the Fourteenth and Fifteenth Amendments and the development of Department of Justice policies, after the 1870s, Congress rarely (if ever) considered further legislation promoting the protection of African Americans (Kennedy, 1997).

The occurrence of disproportionate prosecution and conviction has affected African American families and communities by contributing to racial disproportionality in incarceration. Punishment and incarceration of African Americans, as a means of social control, arose from the institutions of slavery, Jim Crow policies, and deprived socioeconomic conditions of the urban ghetto (Wacquant, 2001). In particular, individuals in African American communities have experienced overprotection (discriminatory enforcement) in policing, prosecution, and imprisonment, in part because law enforcement and the judicial system have been unprepared to fight against underprotection (lack of crime reduction efforts) in these communities (Kennedy, 1997). Not until the 1960s were the treatment of prisoners, racial inequalities in prisons, and abuses of power by prison administrators scrutinized by the judiciary (Kennedy, 1997). This brief overview of the legacy of discrimination against African Americans provides some insight into the fact that intentional and legal acts of discrimination have historically been a part of our nation's criminal justice practices.

The question of whether historic, discriminatory criminal justice practices have been continued or preserved in current incarceration policies is of major concern to some scholars. The policy that has most often been identified as leading to increased, rather than reduced, racial disproportionality is the so-called War on Drugs, which was "officially" declared during the 1980s (Berndt, 2003; Blumstein & Beck, 1999; Coker, 2003; Jensen, Gerber, & Mosher, 2004; Kennedy, 1997; Rubinstein & Mukamal, 2002; Ruth & Reitz, 2003; Tonry, 1995, 2004b; Travis, 2002; Zatz, 2000).

The federal Anti-Drug Abuse Act of 1986 provides that a person who is caught, with intent to sell, possessing 50 grams or more of "crack" cocaine must be incarcerated for at least 10 years. For powder cocaine, the offender receives a similar sentence only if he or she possesses 5,000 or more grams—100 times more than the amount legislatively set for crack (Zatz, 2000). Further, the federal Anti-Drug Abuse Act of 1988 requires that a person serve a sentence of at least five years in prison if he or she possesses one to five grams of crack cocaine (Zatz, 2000).

Policies that differentiate crack cocaine from powder cocaine have been the most controversial because of the different punishments established. Though the policies per se are facially neutral, the result of these policies has been that African American crack users and dealers have been targeted for drug enforcement under both federal and many state laws, and have received much harsher punishments than people convicted of possessing powder cocaine (Berndt, 2003; Jensen, Gerber, & Mosher, 2004). More specifically, early in the 1990s, approximately 4 percent of African Americans, 2 percent of Hispanics/Latinos, and 1.5 percent of white individuals reported using crack (Kennedy, 1997). In raw numbers, however, white crack users outnumbered African American users by more than 60,000 and Hispanic/Latino users by 170,000 (Lockwood, Pottieger, & Inciardi, 1995). Furthermore, at around the same time, more than 90 percent of convictions for crack offenses involved African Americans, whereas white citizens were more than twice as likely as African Americans to be convicted for powder cocaine offenses (Cole, 1999; Tonry, 1995). Although drug use in the 1980s was declining overall, among the most disadvantaged, poverty-stricken areas it was not (Tonry, 1995).

The War on Drugs originated from legislators' concerns about claims that crack inflicted more harm than powder cocaine, because it was more addictive, more associated with violence, more detrimental to health, and easier to purchase—despite the fact that crack and powder cocaine have the same pharmacological base (Kennedy, 1997). Their concerns were not entirely unfounded: although the physiological and psychoactive effects of crack and powder cocaine are similar, individuals who smoked or injected crack (because it was cheaper) had much more violent criminal histories than did powder cocaine users (Hatsukami & Fischman, 1996). Even with this evidence and the decision to support and enforce the crack-cocaine differential, the greater frequency of drug abuse by racial and ethnic minorities is insufficient to account for or to justify the racial and ethnic disparities in incarceration (Berndt, 2003; Ruth & Reitz, 2003). In fact, it turns out that illegal drug use was declining markedly years before the War on Drugs was declared (Jensen, Gerber, & Mosher, 2004; Tonry, 1995).

When there is a general intolerance of drug use, racial and ethnic minorities are more likely to be viewed as depraved and deviant drug users than are members of the majority classes (Tonry, 1995, 2004b). Further, evaluations of anti-drug policing strategies for dealing with crack cocaine use have shown that law enforcement officers have specifically and disproportionately targeted street-level, inner-city dealers, who predominantly are African American. Because of such targeting, African Americans have been more likely to be incarcerated for drug offenses (Tonry, 2004b; Zatz, 2000).

As noted, some people assume that disproportionate incarceration of African Americans is due mainly to their more frequent involvement in crime. It may also be that African

Americans are more likely to be arrested than are white individuals who are apprehended for similar crimes. Some evidence exists both of disproportionate criminal involvement and disproportionate arrest rates of African Americans. It has been documented, for example, that racial disparities in imprisonment most likely arise from differential treatment by law enforcement officers, who are more likely to stop and search African Americans (Coker, 2003), than from differential involvement (Sorensen, Hope, & Stemen, 2003; Tonry, 1995).

It also has been revealed that the primary reason for the increase in the incarceration rates of African Americans is because the crimes they commit are more likely to result in incarceration (Tonry, 1995). More specifically, African Americans and Hispanics/Latinos are more heavily involved than white individuals in certain drug-related and violent crimes—particularly murder, rape, and robbery—that draw both convictions and lengthy prison sentences (Tonry, 2004b).

Similarly, researchers who analyzed African American-vs.-white crime commission rates found that the odds of arrest vary for different crimes. These researchers, however, also cautioned that the relationship between race and the probability of arrest, particularly for drug and property crime, requires further study (D'Alessio & Stolzenberg, 2003).

Whatever the reason for the high incarceration rates of African Americans, Hispanics/Latinos, and other racial and ethnic minorities, highly questionable assumptions about differing rates of criminal activity among these groups have played a major role in formation and adoption of crime policies (Mauer & Chesney-Lind, 2002). Despite the lack of consensus on explanations for the disproportionate incarceration of racial and ethnic minorities, the fact is that African Americans, in particular, are overly represented in prisons. This is indicated by a rate of incarceration of 3,405 African American prisoners per 100,000 U.S. residents—nearly three times the rate of Hispanics/Latinos, and more than seven times that of white people (Harrison & Beck, 2004). If, as the literature suggests, historical conditions and contemporary penal policies have (either intentionally or inadvertently) targeted racial and ethnic minorities, the criminal justice system has failed to adjudicate and imprison under nondiscriminatory circumstances.

Imprisonment also indirectly affects prisoners' families and communities by depriving them of the prisoners' participation. That these communities and community members tend to be socially and economically deprived raises the question of whether racial disproportionality in incarceration may be the result of social and economic injustice that occurs outside of the criminal justice system. This question is addressed in the next section.

FAMILIES AND COMMUNITIES: THE NOT-SO-INVISIBLE EFFECTS OF INCARCERATION

When individuals are incarcerated, they inevitably disappear physically, and at times psychologically, from their families and their communities. It is impossible to identify all the contributions (tangible or intangible) that someone makes to his or her family or community before entering prison, because there is no way of knowing who will commit a crime that will result in incarceration. We cannot measure these phenomena with great accuracy for anyone, prisoners or otherwise; when we do send someone to prison, we have an even tougher job in gauging what might have been. In other words, what would have happened if that person had never been sent to prison?

Social control initiatives have been part of social welfare policies and programs that have been immeasurably harmful both to those who are incarcerated and to their families. Take, for example, the Personal Responsibility and Work Opportunity Reconciliation Act of 1996, designed to require work by individuals who receive time-limited governmental assistance. The Act's purpose statement (Section 401) asserts that the legislation seeks to: assist families in need so that their children will remain in, and be cared for by, their families; promote job preparation, work, and marriage that ends dependence on governmental benefits; avert or decrease out-of-wedlock pregnancies; and encourage the creation and preservation of two-parent families.

At first glance, it might seem that such a policy would not intentionally deprive prisoners, former prisoners, or their families of assistance, but further review of the legislation suggests otherwise. In particular, four sections of the federal legislation warrant attention. Section 408(a)(9) of the act mandates that individuals be denied assistance if they violate a condition of probation or parole. Section 115 stipulates that anyone convicted of a felony offense for drug possession, use, or distribution is ineligible for any state assistance or federal- or state-funded food stamp program. Further, this section prohibits convicted offenders from being counted as members of the household eligible to receive benefits. However, their income and resources are counted as part of the household income,[4] which reduces the level of assistance provided to the rest of the family. Section 202(5) specifies that if an individual flees from prosecution, custody, or confinement, or violates a condition of probation or parole under federal or state law, he or she will be denied Supplemental Security Income (SSI).[5] Finally, section 203(a) prohibits individuals from receiving any SSI benefits while incarcerated.

How do these particular sections of the statute affect prisoners' families and communities? Once released from prison, former prisoners are eligible for and can qualify for assistance under the welfare legislation discussed earlier if they committed any crime other than a felony drug offense (Rubinstein & Mukamal, 2002). We know, for example, that within their respective incarcerated groups, African Americans (25 percent) and Hispanics/Latinos (23 percent) are more likely than white individuals (14 percent) to be incarcerated in state prisons for a drug offense (although the types of drug offenses are unspecified) (Harrison & Beck, 2003). Thus, it is likely that African Americans and Hispanics/Latinos will be disproportionately affected by these policies.

Furthermore, if former prisoners violate a condition of parole or probation, they can be denied a wide variety of benefits. What is particularly worrisome is that parole

131

revocations have increased over the years and have more frequently resulted in rein-carceration (Blumstein, 2004), and not always for a new criminal offense. Even so, as Section 115 of the act requires, parole revocations are factored into determinations about a family's earnings and earning potential and, in the end, will reduce the family's benefits. Therefore, withholding welfare benefits from individuals who are released from prison after serving time affects the ability of those individuals to contribute to their families and households.

Those who are incarcerated often come from areas in urban communities where most of the residents are not white (Clear, 2002). In New York City, for example, incarcerated individuals most often were residents of the city's poorest communities. A breakdown of the incarcerated population in New York City shows that more than 50 percent is African American and more than 40 percent is Hispanic/Latino, despite the fact that together these two groups constitute only about 25 percent of the total nonincarcerated population of New York City (Fagan, 2004). It has been suggested that high rates of imprisonment are common in communities characterized by racial segregation, high poverty, and high percentages of nonwhite citizens (Fagan, 2004).

Before incarceration, many of the criminally involved individuals who come from the most socially deprived communities may have contributed much-needed resources to the families they have perforce left behind (Clear, 2002). Accordingly, when drug-enforcement efforts are targeted at nonwhite communities, the consequences further intensify the poverty and social disorganization in those communities (Coker, 2003).

Use of the criminal justice system to address a widespread drug problem is only one possible course of action that society may choose. It is interesting to note that the same communities that are most targeted for law enforcement attention also are those that lack viable employment alternatives, substance abuse treatment services, and antipoverty efforts to combat community problems such as inadequate housing, unemployment, and lack of education opportunities.

Incarceration of large numbers of people and particularly of adult males, many of whom also happen to be parents, may well have the unintended consequence of further exacerbating the conditions that led to the incarcerated people's law-breaking in the first place. For example, prison officials deal with prisoners and their families in ways that are designed to bring order to prisons—but these restrictions also have negative effects on the prisoners, their families, and their communities (Rosen, 2001). In a 2001 National Institute of Corrections study of 48 state departments of corrections, 38 of the agencies studied indicated that although they were in the process of creating policies or programs designed to assist inmates in maintaining supportive family or parent-child relationships, less than half had implemented these policies agency-wide or had actu-ally provided family visitation assistance (National Institute of Corrections, 2002). Although fewer than half of all prisoners in the study had resided with their children before incarceration (the rates vary by gender and by prison), most of the prisoners did have contact with their children—through telephone, mail, or personal visits—while incarcerated (Mumola, 2000). Additionally, from 1986 to 1997 the rate per 1,000 children who had a parent in state or federal prison doubled; and in 1997 the number of mothers and fathers who indicated that they had lived with their children prior to incarceration was lower than for 1986 (Johnson & Waldfogel, 2002).

Data from the federal government's criminal justice data collection agency paints a bleak picture for the nation's ethnic minority children. African American children were more than eight times more likely, and Hispanics/Latinos more than three times more likely, than white children to have incarcerated parents (Mumola, 2000). In state prisons, of those prisoners who had minor children, nearly half were African Americans, fewer than a third were white, and nearly a fifth were Hispanics/Latinos. In federal prisons, of those prisoners who had minor children, 44 percent were African Americans, 30 percent were Hispanics/Latinos, and 22 percent were white people (Mumola, 2000).

Despite these racial differences, all children who are left without a parent because of incarceration are casualties of the criminal justice system. Society has an obligation to provide additional support and economic resources to these children and their remaining caregivers.[6]

IMPLICATIONS FOR SOCIAL WORK
Probing the Complexities of Racial Disproportionality in Prisons
The discussion thus far of racial disproportionality in the penal system has been limited by the fact that much of what we know about race and the criminal justice system—particularly with regard to incarceration—comes from comparisons of African Americans to white people. Some researchers have argued that the African American-white experience can be extrapolated to that of other racial groups within the criminal justice system (see, for example, Kennedy, 2001), but this is a mistake. The experiences of African Americans cannot be substituted for the experiences of members of other racial and ethnic groups.

In addition, in existing studies, race has been conceptualized narrowly in a way that excludes ethnicity. In short, it is unwise and inaccurate to suggest that categorization into the popular groupings of white, African American, Hispanic/Latino, and so on can adequately or accurately reflect the complexity and variety of racial and ethnic groupings, societal perceptions of those groups, and the behavior patterns or specific views and perspectives regarding the social order of those groups.

Attempting to explain racial disproportionality in prisons by making generalizations is problematic, because we may not be aware of the complexities of the various socioeconomic environments of racial, ethnic, and multiracial and multiethnic communities. Equally troublesome is the fact that our ability to identify and understand imprisonment and the racial disproportionality that follows is limited by poor or nonexistent data. In particular, governmental data on groups other than white people and African

Americans, such as Hispanics/Latinos, were not adequately collected until the 1980s (Beck et al., 1993; Beck & Shipley, 1997; Holman, 2001; Langan, 1991); national data on various other racial and ethnic groups have yet to be collected in a comprehensive, comparative fashion.

Given the complexity of racial disproportionality, it is not surprising that the question of how to reduce this problem has not been adequately addressed. An extensive body of literature exists that describes current conditions, explores their causes, and concludes that racial disproportionality in incarceration is a crucial, primary problem that the United States must address (Blumstein, 2001; Coker, 2003; Everett & Wojtkiewicz, 2002; Kennedy, 2001; Ruth & Reitz, 2003; Wacquant, 2001; Zatz, 2000). Nevertheless, little attention has been given to approaches other than social control methods. Although racial disproportionality in prisons imparts a strong sense of unfairness and injustice to those who are overrepresented in incarceration (Blumstein, 2001), racial disproportionality in prisons is not a problem solely of the prison system. To the contrary, this phenomenon is fueled by the socioeconomic conditions in deprived communities. Incarceration policies only highlight and exacerbate other existing problems.

Although incarceration policies have clearly affected African American communities, principally through enforcement efforts in the War on Drugs, it is the socioeconomic deprivation in these communities that is the root cause or central problem. Penal racial disproportionality is the outcome of a legacy of injustice, which includes, but is by no means limited to, the faults and unfairness of the criminal justice system (Tonry, 1995). The criminal justice system, for all the reasons stated in this chapter, may need overhauling, but to assume that a faulty criminal justice system is the sole or even main cause of disproportionate punishment is inaccurate. The criminal justice system has fostered and aggravated the preincarceration conditions that contribute to racial disproportionality in prisons.

In essence, most aspects of the criminal justice system are designed to punish offenders, so trying to correct penal racial disproportionality by reducing and lessening punitive actions runs counter to the main intent of incarceration (that is, to punish). By focusing on racially disproportionate punishment and the role of the criminal justice system in this problem, we overlook social injustices that occur in other institutional arenas and also contribute to criminal behavior, criminalization, and imprisonment. If social control strategies are inadequate, because they focus on penal racial disproportionality as a primary problem for intervention, we must discover what perspectives and actions are appropriate.

Some Paths to Racial and Ethnic Disparity in Incarceration
It is more important to analyze major inequalities in preincarceration experiences than mere racial disproportionality in incarceration. Racial and ethnic inequalities become

apparent from analyses of income and poverty issues. In particular, Hispanics/Latinos and African Americans earn less than white people and Asian Americans. Specifically, the median income of Hispanics/Latinos in 2003 was 69 percent of that of white people, and that of African Americans was 62 percent of that of white people; in contrast, Asian Americans had a median income 117 percent of that of white people (DeNavas-Walt, Proctor, & Mills, 2004).

The official poverty numbers and rates have risen from 31.6 million and 11.3 percent in 2000 to 35.9 million and 12.5 percent in 2003. The actual number of white people living in poverty is larger than that of any other racial or ethnic group (DeNavas-Walt, Proctor, & Mills, 2004). In terms of the poverty rate, however, African Americans, Native Americans/American Indians, and Alaskan Natives are more than twice as likely, and Hispanics/Latinos nearly twice as likely, to be living in poverty as Asian Americans or white people (DeNavas-Walt, Proctor, & Mills, 2004). This brief review of income and poverty inequality lends credence to the contention that disparate conditions before incarceration should be the focus of action, rather than emphasizing a limited social control solution to racial disproportionality.

Furthermore, some racial and ethnic communities are geographically and economically isolated and segregated in residential terms. For example, Hispanics/Latinos, both in the aggregate and in each ethnic group, are more geographically concentrated and more likely to live in central cities in metropolitan areas than are white people (Ramirez & de la Cruz, 2003). In addition, in the aggregate and for each ethnic group, Hispanics/Latinos are more likely to be unemployed than are white people (Ramirez & de la Cruz, 2003). For example, Brownsville, Texas, had the highest poverty rate (36 percent) and Miami the fifth highest in the United States in 1999 (Bishaw & Iceland, 2003); Hispanics/Latinos made up more than 90 percent of the population of Brownsville and 65 percent of that of Miami (Guzmán, 2001). The eighth highest poverty rate in the United States for a city with a population of 100,000 or more was found in New Orleans (Bishaw & Iceland, 2003), which had an African American population of more than 67 percent (McKinnon, 2001).

These examples highlight complex social conditions that affect racial and ethnic groups, and even white populations, in ways that are not easily changed or fixed by curing penal racial disparities. More complicated issues of poverty and other associated problems, and the lack of policy and practice interventions in poor and deprived communities, are of utmost concern.

The Shift from Social Control to Social Consciousness

There is an urgent need to shift our focus from social control solutions to thinking about how to address social ills within our most desperate communities. Certainly, we should acknowledge that the prison system is just one of many potential systems of punishment, and that, currently, while offenders are being punished, their imprisonment and recidivism affect their partners, their families, and their communities. If we do recognize these facts, then we must shift the agenda and simultaneously begin examining the consequences of incarceration before, during, and after the prison term (Tonry, 2004a). The unequal justice meted out by various agents of the criminal justice system (police, courts, correctional institutions, etc.) is only partially responsible for racial disproportionality. Scholars have neglected to critically examine community dysfunction, increased crime, and victimization (Ruth & Reitz, 2003). If racial disproportionalities in incarceration actually reflect racial disproportionalities in commission of crimes, we should focus our efforts on understanding and fighting the causes of crime in poor, urban, minority communities (Ruth & Reitz, 2003).

Social workers can help address these problems. Whereas correctional practices center on control and supervision, social work models of treatment emphasize support and service provision; assessment of clients' needs; and connection of clients to a wide range of services, such as employment assistance, medical care, various types of therapy, housing, education, and others (McNeece & Roberts, 2001). Efforts involving early intervention, comprehensive education programs, and juvenile offender treatment programs have been shown to be effective at diverting both juvenile and adult criminal offenders from entering the penal system (McNeece & Roberts, 2001; Tonry, 1995).

As a society, we must move toward interventions directed at the economic, social, structural, psychological, and ecological forces that contribute to inequality, because the racial and ethnic inequalities in the criminal justice system reflect our social failures in these other domains (Hawkins, 2001). An analysis based on the National Longitudinal Survey of Youth found that persistent poverty (either in length or percentage of time spent in poverty) was a significant predictor of delinquency in later life (specifically violence and property offenses); however, the analysis also found that this relationship was mediated (and weakened) in particular by the quality of supervision by the mother, the influence of peer pressure, cognitive stimulation, and family interaction and structure (Jarjoura, Triplett, & Brinker, 2002). Clearly, racial disproportionality in imprisonment distracts us from more pressing issues that necessitate immediate attention and action: concentrated poverty; unequal enforcement, underenforcement, and overenforcement of the law; disparate education; poor and inadequate public services; minimal employment opportunities; and the unequal criminalization of drug use.

The argument in this chapter is by no means unique. On the contrary, social and civil rights activists, academics, researchers, scholars, and laypeople for centuries have advocated for social and economic justice for the disenfranchised. This chapter, however, examines the implications of current criminal justice perspectives on aspects of contemporary social welfare policies and their detrimental effects on certain segments of the populace, and advocates for a serious analytical deconstruction of the ways in which we think about criminal justice and social welfare policies. By focusing on and advocating for a change in the precursors of and contributors to racial and ethnic disproportionality in imprisonment, we can assist and guide our neediest citizens toward the goal of socioeconomic inclusion.

END NOTES

1. In California, for example, these laws require that sentences be doubled for a second felony conviction; with a third "strike" (conviction), the punishment is a lengthy prison sentence of 25 years to life (King & Mauer, 2001).
2. Through the Violent Crime Control and Law Enforcement Act of 1994, incentives were created to encourage state-operated prisons to create truth-in-sentencing programs. These programs require a prisoner to serve a substantial portion of his or her sentence before becoming eligible for release, so as to reduce the discrepancy between the sentence imposed and the time actually served in prison (Ditton & Wilson, 1999).
3. Zero-tolerance policing "is meant to impose order through the literal interpretation and strict enforcement of rules" (Ismaili, 2003).
4. Individual states have the right to opt out of some of the federal Act's provisions. Regardless of whether individuals have been convicted of felony drug offenses, however, they will not be denied emergency medical services, emergency disaster relief (noncash, in-kind), public health aid for immunizations and diseases, prenatal care, job training, or access to substance abuse treatment programs.
5. This program pays benefits to people who have limited incomes and resources and who are disabled, blind (children and adults), and/or more than 65 years old.
6. There is some light at the end of the tunnel. The Promoting Safe and Stable Families Amendments of 2001, § 439, enables the provision of competitive grants to state, local, or tribal governments; faith-based organizations; and community-based organizations that serve areas where considerable numbers of children of prisoners reside. This program, however, is subject to annual appropriation only through 2006.

REFERENCES

Anti-Drug Abuse Act of 1986, P.L. 99-570, 100 Stat. 3207.

Anti-Drug Abuse Act of 1988, P.L. 100-690, 102 Stat. 4181.

Beck, A., Gilliard, D., Greenfeld, L., Harlow, C., Hester, T., Jankowski, L., et al. (1993). *Survey of state prison inmates, 1991* (NCJ 136949). Washington, DC: Bureau of Justice Statistics.

Beck, A., & Shipley, B. E. (1997). *Recidivism of prisoners released in 1983* (NCJ 116261). Washington, DC: Bureau of Justice Statistics.

Berndt, B. (2003). Ritual and racism: A social-historical analysis of the crack sentencing guidelines. *Crime, Law and Social Change, 39,* 175–192.

Bishaw, A., & Iceland, J. (2003). *Poverty: 1999* (No. C2KBR-19). Washington, DC: U.S. Government Printing Office.

Blumstein, A. (2001). Race and criminal justice. In N. J. Smelser, W. J. Wilson, & F. Mitchell (Eds.), *America becoming: Racial trends and their consequences* (Vol. 2, pp. 21–31). Washington, DC: National Academy Press.

Blumstein, A. (2004). Restoring rationality in punishment policy. In M. Tonry (Ed.), *The future of imprisonment* (pp. 61–80). New York: Oxford University Press.

Blumstein, A., & Beck, A. J. (1999). Population growth in U.S. prisons, 1980–1996. In M. Tonry & J. Petersilia (Eds.), *Prisons* (pp. 17–61). Chicago: University of Chicago Press.

Bonczar, T. P. (2003). *Prevalence of imprisonment in the U.S. population, 1974–2001* (NCJ 197976). Washington, DC: Bureau of Justice Statistics.

Clear, T. R. (2002). The problem with "addition by subtraction": The prison-crime relationship in low-income communities. In M. Mauer & M. Chesney-Lind (Eds.), *Invisible punishment: The collateral consequences of mass imprisonment* (pp. 181–193). New York: New Press.

Coker, D. (2003). Foreword: Addressing the real world of racial injustice in the criminal justice system. *Journal of Criminal Law & Criminology, 93*, 827–879.

Cole, D. (1999). *No equal justice: Race and class in the American criminal justice system.* New York: New Press.

D'Alessio, S. J., & Stolzenberg, L. (2003). Race and the probability of arrest. *Social Forces, 81*, 1381–1397.

DeNavas-Walt, C., Proctor, B. D., & Mills, R. J. (2004). *Income, poverty, and health insurance coverage in the United States: 2003* (No. P60-226). Washington, DC: U.S. Government Printing Office.

Ditton, P. M., & Wilson, D. J. (1999). *Truth in sentencing in state prisons* (NCJ 170032). Washington, DC: Bureau of Justice Statistics.

Everett, R. S., & Wojtkiewicz, R. A. (2002). Difference, disparity, and race/ethnic bias in federal sentencing. *Journal of Quantitative Criminology, 18*, 189–211.

Fagan, J. (2004). Crime, law, and the community: Dynamics of incarceration in New York City. In M. Tonry (Ed.), *The future of imprisonment* (pp. 27–59). New York: Oxford University Press.

Guzmán, B. (2001). *The Hispanic population* (No. C2KBR/01-3). Washington, DC: U.S. Government Printing Office.

Harrison, P. M., & Beck, A. J. (2003). *Prisoners in 2002* (NCJ 200248). Washington, DC: Bureau of Justice Statistics.

Harrison, P. M., & Beck, A. J. (2004). *Prisoners in 2003* (NCJ 205335). Washington, DC: Bureau of Justice Statistics.

Hatsukami, D. K., & Fischman, M. W. (1996). Crack cocaine and cocaine hydrochloride: Are the differences myth or reality? *JAMA, 276*, 1580–1588.

Hawkins, D. F. (2001). Commentary on Randall Kennedy's overview of the justice system. In N. J. Smelser, W. J. Wilson, & F. Mitchell (Eds.), *America becoming: Racial trends and their consequences* (Vol. 2, pp. 32–51). Washington, DC: National Academies Press.

Holman, B. (2001). *Masking the divide: How officially reported prison statistics distort the racial and ethnic realities of prison growth.* Alexandria, VA: National Center on Institutions and Alternatives.

Ismaili, K. (2003). Explaining the cultural and symbolic resonance of zero tolerance in contemporary criminal justice. *Contemporary Justice Review, 6*, 255–264.

Jarjoura, G. R., Triplett, R. A., & Brinker, G. P. (2002). Growing up poor: Examining the link between persistent childhood poverty and delinquency. *Journal of Quantitative Criminology, 18*, 159–187.

Jensen, E. L., Gerber, J., & Mosher, C. (2004). Social consequences of the War on Drugs: The legacy of failed policy. *Criminal Justice Policy Review, 15*(1), 100–121.

Johnson, E. I., & Waldfogel, J. (2002). Parental incarceration: Recent trends and implications for child welfare. *Social Service Review, 76*, 460–479.

Kennedy, R. (1997). *Race, crime, and the law.* New York: Vintage Books.

Kennedy, R. (2001). Racial trends in the administration of criminal justice. In N. J. Smelser, W. J. Wilson, & F. Mitchell (Eds.), *America becoming: Racial trends and their consequences* (Vol. 2, pp. 1–20). Washington, DC: National Academies Press.

King, R. S., & Mauer, M. (2001). *Aging behind bars: "Three strikes" seven years later.* Washington, DC: The Sentencing Project.

Langan, P. (1991). *Race of prisoners admitted to state and federal institutions, 1926–1986* (NCJ 125618). Washington, DC: Bureau of Justice Statistics.

Lockwood, D., Pottieger, A. E., & Inciardi, J. A. (1995). Crack use, crime by crack users, and ethnicity. In D. F. Hawkins (Ed.), *Ethnicity, race, and crime: Perspectives across time and place* (pp. 212–234). Albany: State University of New York Press.

Mauer, M., & Chesney-Lind, M. (2002). Introduction. In M. Mauer & M. Chesney-Lind (Eds.), *Invisible punishment: The collateral consequences of mass imprisonment* (pp. 1–12). New York: New Press.

McKinnon, J. (2001). *The black population: 2000* (No. C2KBR/01-5). Washington, DC: U.S. Department of Justice.

McNeece, C. A., & Roberts, A. R. (2001). Adult corrections. In A. Gitterman (Ed.), *Handbook of social work practice with vulnerable and resilient populations* (pp. 342–366). New York: Columbia University Press.

Mumola, C. J. (2000). *Incarcerated parents and their children* (NCJ 182335). Washington, DC: Bureau of Justice Statistics.

National Institute of Corrections. (2002). *Services for families of prison inmates.* Longmont, CO: National Institute of Corrections Information Center.

Personal Responsibility and Work Opportunity Reconciliation Act of 1996, P.L. 104-193, 110 Stat. 2105.

Promoting Safe and Stable Families Amendments of 2001, P.L. 107-133, 115 Stat. 2413.

Ramirez, R. R., & de la Cruz, G. P. (2003). *The Hispanic population in the United States: March 2002* (No. P20-545). Washington, DC: U.S. Census Bureau.

Rosen, D. M. (2001). Mass imprisonment and the family: A legal perspective. *Marriage & Family Review, 32*(3/4), 63–82.

Rubinstein, G., & Mukamal, D. (2002). Welfare and housing—Denial of benefits to drug offenders. In M. Mauer & M. Chesney-Lind (Eds.), *Invisible punishment: The collateral consequences of mass imprisonment* (pp. 37–49). New York: New Press.

Ruth, H., & Reitz, K. R. (2003). *The challenge of crime: Rethinking our response.* Cambridge, MA: Harvard University Press.

Sorensen, J., Hope, R., & Stemen, D. (2003). Racial disproportionality in state prison admissions: Can regional variation be explained by differential arrest rates? *Journal of Criminal Justice, 31*(1), 73–84.

Sorensen, J., & Stemen, D. (2002). The effect of state sentencing policies on incarceration rates. *Crime & Delinquency, 48,* 456–475.

Tonry, M. (1995). *Malign neglect: Race, crime, and punishment in America.* New York: Oxford University Press.

Tonry, M. (2004a). Has the prison a future? In M. Tonry (Ed.), *The future of imprisonment* (pp. 3–24). Oxford, England: Oxford University Press.

Tonry, M. (2004b). *Thinking about crime: Sense and sensibility in American penal culture.* New York: Oxford University Press.

Tonry, M., & Petersilia, J. (1999). American prisons at the beginning of the twenty-first century. In M. Tonry & J. Petersilia (Eds.), *Prisons* (pp. 1–16). Chicago: University of Chicago Press.

Travis, J. (2002). Invisible punishment. In M. Mauer & M. Chesney-Lind (Eds.), *Invisible punishment: The collateral consequences of mass imprisonment* (pp. 15–36). New York: New Press.

U.S. Department of Justice. (2003, July 27). *Incarceration rate, 1980–2002.* Retrieved May 28, 2005, from http://www.ojp.usdoj.gov/bjs/glance/tables/incrttab.htm

Violent Crime Control and Law Enforcement Act of 1994, P.L. 103-322, 108 Stat. 1796.

Wacquant, L. (2001). Deadly symbiosis: When ghetto and prison meet and mesh. *Punishment & Society, 3,* 95–133.

Walmsley, R. (2003). *World prison population list* (5th ed., No. 234). London: Home Office.

Zatz, M. (2000). The convergence of race, ethnicity, gender, and class on court decisionmaking: Looking toward the 21st century. In *Criminal Justice 2000* (NIJ Publication, pp. 503–552). Washington, DC: U.S. Department of Justice.

CHAPTER 9

WORKPLACE AND WORKFORCE CONSIDERATIONS IN ACCESS TO EMPLOYMENT OPPORTUNITY

Anna Haley-Lock and Sarah K. Bruch

INTRODUCTION

This chapter reviews the domains of society, institutions, families, and communities as central forces affecting individuals' experiences in the U.S. labor market. We first consider the role of society, in the forms of government policies and programs that constitute promotion of work by our "welfare state"; dominant cultural norms about work, personal responsibility, and individualism on which the U.S. version of the welfare state is largely based; and demographic trends among the working-age population that affect the demand for and availability of labor. We then turn to institutions, our examination of which includes pre-labor market forces that shape subsequent labor market opportunity, access to education, and the determinative role of employers' workplace policies and practices in distributing labor market opportunity. We turn finally to families and communities, investigating central sources of workers, work supports, and need and obligation, the demands of which workers juggle with the demands of their jobs.

The perspective we take here, informed by research on firm-level labor markets and work-life balance, is that individuals' outcomes with respect to employment are substantially shaped by the institutions in which those individuals are situated. These institutions range from the macro to the micro level, spanning federal, state, and local governmental systems; workplaces located across diverse industries and sectors; communities of geography and identity; and both nuclear and extended families. Workers navigate through all these domains en route to attaining security, status, and satisfaction in their jobs, as well as personal and familial well-being. It is during this structurally bounded navigation that pressing inequalities in employment outcomes emerge across race, ethnicity, and class.

The orientation we adopt extends the study of these inequalities away from primarily individual-level accounts—for example, the effects of a worker's below-average skills on her job acquisition and mobility. This is not to suggest that human capital is not implicated in employment marginalization; indeed, we review that research briefly here. We believe, however, that the story of the workplace as a key stratifier of access to employment opportunity is underexamined. Following Reskin's (2003) call for greater attention to the mechanisms that produce inequality, we focus instead on what we know, and what has yet to be learned, about how social policymakers and organizational administrators act as key allocators of employment-related resources for the working poor, and for minority racial and ethnic group members.

We consider, for example, how characteristics of the U.S. welfare state and variations in both American workplace and familial structures may interact to facilitate—or largely prohibit—an individual's entry into the labor force and advancement at work, and how these interdependencies can place disproportionate burdens on workers of color and those with low incomes. Attention to the structural drivers of American employment success is, in some recent lines of research, beginning to help us think about how the benefits of work can become "racialized" apart from overtly prejudicial, interpersonal acts (Glass, 1999). We believe this knowledge is critical for informing socially just social work practice that advances labor market opportunities for workers of diverse identities and means.

The chapter begins with a review of key characteristics of the U.S. sociopolitical context of work: notably, its strong individualism, the outlines of which are reflected in a work ethic of mythological proportions and what Noble (1997) termed the United States' "market conformism." These characteristics have yielded a set of distinctly American governmental institutions that promote entrepreneurial employment activity and grant U.S. employers wide discretion in contracting with individuals for paid employment. Their practices—the provision of what we and others have termed "workplace opportunity" (Haley-Lock, 2003, in press; Lambert & Haley-Lock, 2004)—have important implications for workers' job retention, advancement, and work-life balance that disproportionately disadvantage socioeconomically marginalized workers.

These examinations of the U.S. welfare state and workplace help us better grasp the role of families and communities in work, and the effects of work on these other spheres of personal and civic life. Although research from the work-life field has, to date, offered few direct investigations of race or ethnicity, it has revealed the particular struggles of workers occupying lower-skill, low-wage jobs (Kossek, Huber-Yoder, Castellino, & Lerner, 1997; Lambert & Haley-Lock, 2004; Lambert, Waxman, & Haley-Lock, 2002). Findings from this nascent area of scholarship warn of the exponentially negative effects employment can have on family, as well as the limited success workers can look forward to when they and their families are required to adjust to fixed, taxing work conditions. We conclude the chapter by discussing the roles that social work researchers and practitioners have to play in advancing workplace opportunity in light of this multidomain assessment.

SOCIETY

> The American welfare state is often characterized as laggard in cross-national terms. The United States does far less than many similarly rich countries to redistribute and equalize income or to actively manage labor markets. We also do much less to socialize the costs of caregiving—through government policies that redistribute income to families with children, public services that reduce employment penalties associated with devoting time to caregiving, or labor market regulations that protect parents' time with children. (Gornick & Meyers, 2003, p. 8)

Shaping the Employment Contract: The U.S. Welfare State
As Gordon (1994) described in her history of U.S. welfare policy, a "welfare state" represents more than the sum of social service and income support programs provided to those in need. Its design and operation define the role of a government in assuring the basic well-being of its people, including their socioeconomic and political status, their civic rights, and the life opportunities to which they have access. Labor force preparation, entry, and participation are in turn shaped by this expansive symbol, operationalized through a web of policies and programs that directly regulate employment (for example, minimum wage and workers' compensation laws, the Earned Income Tax Credit), address domains of life that are preludes to work (for example, educational programs such as Head Start or federal Pell grants for college), and support labor force participation peripherally (for example, health insurance and child care subsidies for low-income parents).

In cross-national comparisons, scholars have characterized the U.S. welfare state as "laggard," providing minimal social welfare benefits in comparison to other Western, industrialized nations (for example, Gornick & Meyers, 2003; Noble, 1997). In his typology of welfare states, Esping-Andersen (1990) characterized the U.S. model as the least supportive, following a market-supporting approach that provides public services according to narrowly defined need rather than universal entitlement. This stands in contrast to countries like France, where welfare assistance is relatively generous and state-operated, though not redistributive; and Sweden, where fairly universal state services are oriented to preventing as well as remedying structural barriers to opportunity. Lieberman (2005) tied cross-national contrasts in welfare provisions to variation in racial and ethnic heterogeneity (the relatively diverse United States and France, for example, versus homogeneous Scandinavia). He noted that countries with considerable population diversity have created welfare states "that deviated in important respects from the solidaristic, social democratic model, which entails generous universal benefits .... [They] restrict access to social benefits in significant ways, whether through the labor market or through other means of stratification, with important consequences for minority incorporation" (Lieberman, 2005, pp. 16–17).

The 1996 passage of the Personal Responsibility and Work Opportunity Reconciliation Act (PRWORA), which transitioned U.S. welfare policy from Aid to Families with Dependent Children (AFDC) to Temporary Assistance to Needy Families (TANF), embodied this market-supporting quality (Gilbert, 2002). It also reflected the deeply held American cultural sensibility of rugged individualism, romanticizing the notion that with sufficient will—captured in Horatio Alger's (1868) famous image of pulling oneself up by the bootstraps—personal dreams can be fulfilled despite awesome obstacles. TANF eliminated needs-based entitlement to welfare benefits and made receipt of assistance contingent on parents' working. This condition of welfare receipt, in tandem with a program for offering tax credits to employers who hire TANF recipients, exemplifies the "carrot-and-stick" approach to work support in the United States. The carrot offered to the employer is an incentive for charitable employment practices, such as hiring from particular classes of workers or locating in designated empowerment zones (Internal Revenue Service, 1999). The stick, or sanction, is applied to the worker, whose modest welfare benefits depend upon successful work effort and are terminated after five years, or sooner if work activities are found to be insufficient.

In the United States, then, there exist particularly strong social, political, and economic orientations toward requiring workers, rather than employers or government, to adapt to the demands of the market, as a matter of personal responsibility. Not coincidentally perhaps, business as an organized political interest group has been far more successful than the labor movement in advancing its concerns onto the U.S. public agenda. For workers whose labor contributions are historically undervalued in the open market because of persistent discrimination, or who face little or no market for their work qualifications (as in inner cities facing rapid job loss), this prevailing ethic bears little relevance to their experiences with employment.

Government Supports for Labor Force Participation
In the United States, the legitimate role of government in employment matters has been constructed as one of encouraging entrepreneurial behavior by both business and worker, rather than assuring that workplaces sufficiently support individual effort by regulating all private employers or broadly providing supplemental public services.

Government as Employer Regulator. The government engages in limited regulation of the workplace and of employers through laws that establish a minimum wage, collective bargaining rights for employees, health and safety standards, equal employment opportunity (EEO) protections for certain groups of workers, and job-protected extended leave for specified family and medical reasons. Numerous studies have shown that when effectively enforced, affirmative action policies and equal employment legal protections have clear, positive effects for workers of color in both public and private employment settings, including greater access to managerial and professional jobs

(Badgett, 1999; Carrington, McCue, & Pierce, 2000; Chay, 1998; Heckman & Payner, 1989; Reskin, 1998).

The implementation of such legislation has sometimes been more symbolic than real, however. In the case of EEO law, organizations have been found to adopt changes that assure merely legal compliance—thus minimizing employers' exposure to risk—while only minimally addressing the employer behaviors that influence the legal goals of equality for protected groups of workers (Dobbin, Sutton, Meyer, & Scott, 1993; Edelman, 1992; Edelman & Petterson, 1999). In the case of the Family and Medical Leave Act (FMLA), a wide swath of firms and jobs were exempted from this benefit based on size (fewer than 50 employees) and number of hours that employees work (less than 1 year and 1,250 hours). Legislation directly targeting workplaces and employment has, further, been unable to protect marginalized workers against "legitimate" forms of labor market marginalization that reflect premarket discrimination in access to qualifying education and job experience (Glass, 1999).

Government as Employer. Government also directly supports labor force participation by serving as an employer, or by contracting with private firms to provide goods or services; the latter is increasingly common in certain social service fields (for example, privatization of child protective and child welfare services). As will be discussed in more detail in the next section, past research has revealed that jobs in the public sector frequently provide higher levels of employment benefits, including wages and access to upward mobility, for women and people of color (Bernhardt & Dresser, 2002). This mechanism represents one way in which government promotes a relatively progressive distribution of workplace opportunity—one that flies under the radar of a national culture antagonistic to overt market regulation: the design of high-quality public work.

SOCIETAL BARRIERS TO LABOR FORCE PREPARATION AND ENTRY

Sociopolitical forces of racial, ethnic, and class marginalization are implicated not only in individuals' experiences in the workplace, but also in how those individuals are sorted into jobs as a result of their premarket human and social capital development. These same forces also act on the sheer availability of high-quality, local jobs.

In the case of education, continuing residential and school segregation stratify youth via unequal school choices. The problems of dilapidated facilities, large class sizes, and inexperienced and less educated teachers have historically been concentrated among schools and districts with the economically poorest student bodies, and those with the highest percentages of racial and ethnic minority students. These same schools receive disproportionately low state and local funding (Jencks & Phillips, 1998; Phillips & Chin, 2004). These inequalities translate into below-average instructional attention (time spent in school, class size), instructional resources (advanced placement and "gifted" classes), instructional materials and computers, and teacher quality. In a review of the extent of school-based disparities, Phillips and Chin (2004) noted that some aspects of school quality, such as teacher experience and education, grew more unequal between the late 1980s and late 1990s, particularly between schools with majority white students and those with a majority of students of color.

Revealing some of the long-term effects of such disparities, Johnson and Neal (1998) found that a "skills gap" accounts for most of the disparity in wages between black and white workers. Such an obstacle both compresses workers' range of opportunity before they enter the workplace and limits chances for mobility thereafter. As will be discussed later in this section, these stratifying conditions are magnified in American workplaces through the declining quality of low-wage, low-skill jobs (Jencks, Perman, & Rainwater, 1988; Kalleberg, Reskin, & Hudson, 2000; Reskin, McBrier, & Kmec, 1999).

Difficulties that people of color disproportionately face in geographic access to quality work also systematically disadvantage their future employment prospects (Heckman, 1998; Neal & Johnson, 1996; Tienda & Stier, 1996). Years ago, Wilson (1987) described the impact on black inner-city residents of spatial dislocation, or the increasing separation of urban resident workers from jobs that were moving out to the suburbs. In an extension of this effect, the trend of internationalization of labor means that the demand for labor in industrialized countries that even modestly protect labor rights (such as the United States) is likely to decline as firms shift capital to countries with even lower-cost labor. As a result, employment conditions are likely to decline for entry-level service jobs sited in distant suburbs, as jobs in the inner cities disappear altogether (Hendrickson, 2000; Mishra, 1999; Wilson, 1996).

THE CHANGING AMERICAN LABOR FORCE

The evolving racial and ethnic composition of the American workforce is also changing the employer–employee interface, particularly at lower levels of employment. The U.S. Bureau of Labor Statistics projected that although the proportion of working, non-Hispanic white people will dip from 73 percent in 2000 to 53 percent in 2050, representation of Hispanics will jump from 11 percent to 24 percent, of Asians from 5 percent to 11 percent, and of black people from 12 percent to 14 percent in the same time period (Toossi, 2002). This expansion of workforce diversity is due primarily to immigration, predominantly among Hispanics and Asians (Nightingale & Fix, 2004; Toossi, 2002). Though in 2002 immigrants constituted 11 percent of the U.S. population, they made up 14 percent of the workforce, an increase from 6 percent in 1960 (Capps, Fix, Passel, Ost, & Perez-Lopez, 2003; Hagan, 2004). Recent immigrants have tended to have higher fertility rates than native-born residents (Toossi, 2002), further speeding workforce diversification.

These more recently arrived workers have also been younger, with lower levels of educational attainment and English fluency than previous groups (Capps et al., 2003; Hagan, 2004; Nightingale & Fix, 2004). They, like native-born ethnic minority workers, are significantly overrepresented in poorly compensated and low-mobility employment, including service occupations (primarily women) and transportation, material-moving, and agricultural work (mostly men). They constitute 20 percent of the U.S. low-wage workforce (Capps et al., 2003). Occupational segregation into dead-end employment, combined with increasing numbers of single-parent and dual-earner households and (for some immigrant groups) above-average fertility rates, intensifies the challenges of balancing work and family responsibilities (Nightingale & Fix, 2004).

INSTITUTIONS: THE WORKPLACE

The characteristics of U.S. society that shape the provision of employment supports for individuals have by now been well examined by an array of scholars. We now consider a more rarely told story: the role of workplace structures in stratifying individuals' experiences with employment by race, ethnicity, and class. The structural features of workplaces, including the benefits extended to specific jobs, should be of great concern to scholars and practitioners who seek to address racial, ethnic, and class disparities in employment outcomes. Even without direct discrimination against socially marginalized workers, the ways in which work and workplaces are arranged and rewarded may disproportionately and negatively affect such workers (Glass, 1999). Research that looks primarily at either societal- or individual-level explanations for race-based labor market inequality, and does not investigate the distribution of opportunity within employing organizations, falls short of capturing this complete story (Haley-Lock, 2003, in press; Lambert & Haley-Lock, 2004). The complex constellations of organizational policies regarding job design and benefits, as well as discrepancies between official policy and de facto practice, function as many points of potential disparate impact on racial and ethnic minorities in the workplace. They are, in other words, pivotal mechanisms of social stratification.

The firm-level labor market perspective provides a helpful framework for understanding the effect of organizations on individuals' employment experiences through the opportunity infrastructures these organizations establish in the form of human resource policies and practices (Althauser & Kalleberg, 1981; Baron, Davis-Blake, & Bielby, 1986; Doeringer & Piore, 1985). An internal labor market (ILM) is comprised of the benefits an employer attaches to jobs as a workforce recruitment and retention strategy (Althauser & Kalleberg, 1981; Baron, Davis-Blake, & Bielby, 1986; Doeringer & Piore, 1985; Jacobs, 1994). Such strategies have been alternately termed "high road" or "high commitment" for their focus on developing human resources, rather than strictly minimizing labor costs, as a means of achieving organizational performance (Appelbaum & Batt, 1994; Kochan & Osterman, 1994; Osterman, 1994; Tsui, Pearce, Porter, & Tripoli, 1997).

Although ILMs have traditionally been conceptualized as including promotion ladders, competitive wages, and training (Baron, Davis-Blake, & Bielby, 1986), recent research has expanded this framing to incorporate management initiatives concerned with employees' work-life balance. Within the nonprofit human services sector, and in low-wage, low-skill jobs in for-profit settings, Haley-Lock (2003, in press) and Lambert and Haley-Lock (2004; Lambert, Waxman, & Haley-Lock, 2002) have investigated the range of availability of full-time status; paid days off and extended leave; health insurance for employees and their dependents; and scheduling flexibility and stability, as well as wages, promotion ladders, and training. These researchers also considered how organizations implement such benefits through their policies on waiting periods, accrual rates, and employer contribution levels (to insurance and retirement plans), in an effort to reveal the true accessibility of benefits.

The trend among U.S. employers toward increasing use of part-time and otherwise contingent jobs provides one example of such variation. In some cases, the offer of a part-time job is a human resource management strategy, designed to attract certain highly desired candidates who prefer fewer than full-time hours but expect benefits: namely, professional working mothers seeking to balance work-life demands (Tilly, 1996b). At the other end of the wage and skill spectrums, part-time and contingent work at the front lines offers minimal opportunity, reward, or job security (Barsky, 2004; Hipple & Stewart, 1996; Kalleberg, 2003; Kalleberg, Reskin, & Hudson, 2000; Tilly, 1996b) and is disproportionately occupied by Black people and Hispanics (Presser, 2003; U.S. Bureau of Labor Statistics, 2005). Employers undertake these internal labor market-devolving arrangements primarily to contain costs (Moss, Salzman, & Tilly, 1998).

Notably, though, this vein of research has found that the degree to which work is embedded in opportunity varies substantially even among jobs at the same level, within the same industry, and within the same local economic conditions (Haley-Lock, 2003; Hunter, 2000; Lambert & Haley-Lock, 2004; Lambert, Waxman, & Haley-Lock, 2002; Moss, Salzman, & Tilly, 1998; Tilly, 1996a). These disparities have profound implications for workers' employment outcomes, as Haley-Lock (2003) has reported. They suggest that employment opportunity within an organizational context is not a given, and is not merely a product of external market forces or technical imperatives imposed by the nature of work tasks. Opportunities are, instead, products of choices made by employers that significantly influence individuals' job prosperity.

Scholarship on employment benefits has further identified a set of broad organizational characteristics that tend to be associated with jobs offering more generous compensation and other employment supports. The industry in which an employer is located, as well as employer size, appears to be decisive for the generosity of benefits. Goods-producing firms that are relatively large offer more than their services-producing, smaller counterparts (Barsky, 2004; Burke & Morton, 1990).

At the sectoral level, some studies suggest that employment in public and nonprofit agencies is better in this sense than in for-profit firms. The U.S. Congressional Budget Office (1998) found that the federal employment system offers more, and more generous, benefits (for example, paid vacation days and disability insurance, retiree health insurance and retirement plans) than the private sector. Moore and Newman's (1991) study of the Houston Metropolitan Transit Authority similarly revealed that workers received wages and fringe benefits 31 to 83 percent higher in value than their private-sector equivalents. Miller (1996) found that front-line state and local government jobs also offered better pay than those with private employers. It is not surprising, then, that government work at federal, state, and local levels disproportionately attracts people of color and women (Bernhardt & Dresser, 2002; Blank, 1985). In the nonprofit sector, Haley-Lock and Kruzich (2005) found that the entry-level nursing assistant job, within both nonprofit and public-sector nursing homes, carried better benefits than in for-profit facilities. As Gonyea (1999) noted, however, far less research on employment benefits has been conducted in these settings (Haley-Lock, 2003 and in press, though not cross-sectoral comparisons, are two exceptions).

From this review we can appreciate how variations in the structured opportunities provided to jobs, exacerbated by persistent inequalities in the American education system and their consequent occupational sorting effects, may racialize employment outcomes. Our next discussion of families and communities critically complements our treatment of workplace as a mechanism of stratification. We now turn to considering the racially, ethnically, and economically disparate implications for individuals of the interdependence of work and life.

FAMILIES AND COMMUNITIES

There is considerable variation in what people need from work: some need a lot, others very little. Families and communities, for example, greatly influence individuals' likelihood of needing a job. For some workers, families include a spouse who securely earns the primary household income in a job that offers low- or no-cost access to health insurance for dependents. Many children have no pressing problems related to health or well-being and are comfortably ensconced in a local, high-quality and affordable child care center or school. Elderly parents are in equally good health and actively support their adult children, or, if frail, are well cared for in a nearby, high-quality care setting. Similarly, some workers depart for work from neighborhoods where they enjoy kind and capable neighbors who volunteer to help out when unexpected events challenge this otherwise well-oiled system; vibrant community institutions, such as churches and temples, parent-teacher associations, and youth centers, cultivate and in turn benefit from their members' social and human capital (Duncan & Raudenbush, 1999; Putnam, 1995). In addition, a wide variety of competitively priced goods and services are available outside of work hours. All these resources promote an individual's ability to obtain a good job, to be flexible in fulfilling the responsibilities thereof, and therefore to thrive in it.

These circumstances, however, are not shared by all, or even most, individuals seeking to participate and prosper in the U.S. labor force. Some need more from their employment because their families and communities are in no position to compensate for poor working conditions. Loved ones may be numerous, emotionally or physically demanding, unable to work themselves, or have unpredictable or intense needs for care. As Galinksy, Hughes, and David (1990), and more recently Heymann (2000), have observed, the mismatch between families in need of supportive workplaces and workplaces that support families appears to be increasing: "Employees least likely to work for companies with more supportive policies may, in fact, be the employees who need it most—the working poor and women who work for middle size and small employers" (Heymann, 2000, p. 88). Communities, moreover, may not offer excellent opportunities for work or schooling, or medical or child care, within their boundaries.

A product of the societal forces (reviewed earlier), employment contracts in the United States ignore much of the impact of workers' lives upon their jobs—and are even less responsive to how jobs affect the rest of life. The prevalent normative assumption in the United States is that workplace conditions are largely fixed, and that it is the responsibility of individual workers to adapt to them. Nevertheless, the domains of work, family, and communities are of course interdependent, and when workers' level of need for employment accommodation correlates with their societal marginalization by race, ethnicity, nativity, or class, the "work-family-community" interplay (Barnett & Morgan, 2003) inevitably exacerbates these inequalities.

EMPLOYMENT-BASED HEALTH INSURANCE

Although programs such as Medicare, Medicaid, and the public Children's Health Insurance Program (SCHIP) provide safety-net coverage for the elderly, low-income families, and children with American citizenship status, the primary vehicle of access to health insurance in the United States remains individual adult employment. However, only 63 percent of adult Americans, and 56 percent of children, had employer-provided health care in 2004 (Hoffman, Carbaugh, Moore, & Cook, 2005). Such statistics reveal a considerable shortfall in employment as an effective source of health insurance protection for individuals and families, and this gap has enlarged over the last several years (Boushey & Murray Diaz, 2004). Employees are also increasingly paying more for their employer-sponsored insurance plans. From 1989 to 2003, the proportion of workers making a contribution to their monthly plan premiums rose from 66 to 92 percent, and in that time the average premium rates jumped by 11 percent for single workers and 43 percent for dependents (Boushey & Murray Diaz, 2004). The trend appears to be that while work remains an important source for protecting Americans' health, that protection is decreasingly accessible.

Hispanics suffer disproportionately from barriers to obtaining this employment benefit. In 2003, 60 percent of Americans (including 66 percent of white people), but just 42 percent of Hispanics, had employer-provided health insurance (DeNavas-Walt, Proctor, & Mills, 2004). This is in large part explained by the fact that Hispanic workers are more likely to work in sectors that do not provide health coverage to any workers (for example, agriculture), or in low-wage jobs that are specifically excluded from eligibility (for example, part-time, contingent, entry-level) (Quinn, 2000; Schur & Feldman, 2001). In this respect, the decline in the quality of low-level jobs, as employers increasingly turn to cost-containing labor practices like part-time, outsourced, and contingent work arrangements, as discussed earlier, has affected Hispanic workers particularly harshly.

As with native-born workers of color, immigrants—both documented and undocumented, a group significantly comprised of Hispanics—also experience obstacles to receiving employer-based health insurance for themselves and their families. According to the U.S. Census Bureau, in 2000, 55 percent of native-born residents, but only 45 percent of foreign-born, had employer-provided health insurance. Further, for immigrants residing in the United States for fewer than 10 years and for undocumented residents, the rates of job-based coverage were just 36 and 38 percent, respectively (Schmidley, 2001). The effect of this lack of job-based coverage is magnified for undocumented residents, who are ineligible for public health insurance. Even families with U.S.-born children and immigrant adults often face difficulties in securing this benefit for their documented children (Harrell & Carrasquillo, 2003; Holcomb, Tumlin, Koralek, Capps, & Zuberi, 2003).

The employment benefit of health insurance coverage can promote the health and well-being of both workers and their families. Absent a governmentally overseen, universal system of access, or a requirement that employers insure all their workers, however, health insurance is often not available to workers, or requires a substantial monetary contribution by employees. As a result, many go without. The implications for racial and ethnic minorities and immigrants, who disproportionately work at the lower wage levels of the labor force, are significant.

EXTENDED FAMILY AND MEDICAL LEAVE FROM WORK

The availability of job-protected leave for workers to care for a new child or ill family member, or to recover from their own medical conditions, has emerged as critically important to promoting women's labor force participation and minimizing the negative effects of work on family and community life (Gerstel & McGonagle, 1999; Gornick & Meyers, 2003; Heymann, 2000; Lovell, 2004; Spilerman & Schrank, 1991). In an important piece that extends insights from Stack's seminal 1974 ethnography of African American family structures, Gerstel and McGonagle (1999) examined workers' use of extended leave following passage of the Family and Medical Leave Act in 1993. One of their main findings was that while black employees reported needing leave significantly more often than workers of other races, they were not more likely to take it. The authors offered several explanatory factors. First, black people have been documented as suffering disproportionately from health problems, which creates greater need for leave, but have disproportionately limited ability to afford leave that is unpaid. The FMLA does not provide wage replacement, and only a handful of states have complemented the federal law with state programs offering partial wages to workers who are on leave.

Most striking from the standpoint of work's effect on family life, Gerstel and McGonagle (1999) found that the types of leave black workers often needed (to provide care for extended family members such as in-laws, aunts and uncles, and grandparents) do not qualify for FMLA protection, as these types of kin do not constitute family under the legislation. This has the effect of requiring workers to make difficult choices between caring for loved ones and possibly losing both wages and also job security. If workers of color, on average, count extended family members as part of their core kinship ties (per Stack's observations), the result is a racialization of government employment policy, and disproportionate sacrifice by minority workers of their work and familial well-being. Given the overlap between family and neighborhood networks among many minority groups, this void in leave protection can be expected to affect health at a larger community level.

CHILD CARE

The availability, affordability, and quality of child care are important not only for enabling workers' labor force participation, but also for ensuring children's positive development in the short and long terms. Children placed in nonparental care have been found to do better emotionally, cognitively, linguistically, and socially when their caregivers interact positively with them, when child-provider ratios are low, when the physical setting of care is engaging and safe, and when activities are age-appropriate, among other factors (see Vandell & Wolfe, 2000, for a review of this literature). Having reliable, good child care arrangements is also favorably correlated with parents' work performance and retention (Lee, 2004; Meyers, 1993; Ross & Paulsell, 1998; Vandell & Wolfe, 2000).

As we reviewed in an earlier section, employers significantly shape the challenges their employees face in balancing work and childrearing responsibilities. In addition to supporting some workers by offering on-site child care, subsidies for care, or contracts with child care referral and finder agencies, firms' approaches to employee work scheduling determine their workers' capacity to plan for—or themselves engage in—child care (Lambert & Haley-Lock, 2004; Lambert, Waxman, & Haley-Lock, 2002). Flexible work arrangements, including compressed work weeks, telecommuting, and fluctuating in and out of part-time hours, help parents to care for their own children. Stability and predictability of work hours—for example, being guaranteed a minimum number of hours weekly (if a worker is not salaried) and knowing in advance the specific hours or shifts to be worked—support the stability of arrangements made with child care providers.

Here again, in both scheduling flexibility and stability, it is workers at the lower levels, who disproportionately are from minority racial and ethnic groups, who are at a particular disadvantage. Low-wage, low-skill jobs are more likely to involve inflexible and unstable scheduling and offer workers limited input over the hours they work (Lambert & Haley-Lock, 2004; Lambert, Waxman, & Haley-Lock, 2002). Such employment practices can mean that a part-time worker must enlist and pay for nearly full-time child care to cover work shifts that cannot be anticipated in advance; risk placing children in less dependable or lower-quality, ad hoc care arrangements; or miss work to care for children (Lambert & Haley-Lock, 2004).

Inaccessibility of institutional child care further exacerbates this work-life conflict for many, disproportionately so for workers and families of color. In a 2003 focus group study of child care conditions in Chicago, Hispanic mothers reported a lack of availability of center-based child care in their communities; the services that did exist were difficult to reach by public transit, unaffordable, or had long waiting lists (Illinois Facilities Fund, 2003b). A separate Illinois Facility Fund assessment of child care need by Chicago community area found that 12 of the 30 highest-need areas in the city had a majority of Hispanic residents, with four additional high-need areas featuring large and growing Hispanic populations. Compared to those that were predominantly white or black, Hispanic neighborhoods were most underserved by licensed child care facilities (Illinois Facilities Fund, 2003a). Other studies have found that low-income and Hispanic parents are often unaware of their eligibility for government child care subsidies, created as part of the PRWORA welfare reform of 1996, or face perceived or real barriers to use of these subsidies (Illinois Facilities Fund, 2003b; Shlay, Weinraub, Harmon, & Tran, 2003).

In the United States, families and communities are held significantly responsible for facilitating the work efforts of their adult members, and for adapting to workplace conditions presented by the free market. For workers from families and communities with ample social and economic assets, such a charge does not generally imperil labor force entry and success. For families and communities at the margins, however, such demands may be untenable, or accommodated only at a disturbing cost. In such situations, employees and employers each face constrained choice. Individuals must select from a limited range of jobs and workplaces that are, for them, adequately supportive. Organizations, in turn, have access to a restricted pool of labor: those candidates whose resources outside of work are sufficient to sustain unsupportive employment.

IMPLICATIONS FOR SOCIAL WORK

The field of social work has important roles in both promoting the understanding of and influencing individuals' labor market experiences. Its adoption of a "person-in-environment" lens (NASW, 1999) further suggests that its members readily grasp the significance of societal and workplace factors for workers' performance and well-being. Through the endeavors of scholarly research, policy analysis and advocacy, organizational administration, and counseling and case management, social workers are actively engaged in shaping the interplay between work and life. They serve as gatekeepers to employment opportunity (as, for example, case managers in public welfare offices and job trainers in welfare-to-work programs), and as those who hold the gatekeepers accountable (as program evaluators and lobbyists, to name two relevant positions). When providing therapeutic services, social workers are themselves greatly affected by their clients' navigations between the domains of employment, family, and community.

Bringing Structure Back into Social Workers' Consideration of Work
Social work scholars and practitioners have shortchanged their ability to explain and reduce employment-based inequalities, however, because they have tended to use limited tools. Too often, we have attempted to address problems of the workplace by focusing on the workforce. Scholarship directed at our own human services organizations has sometimes reflected this. For example, we have sought to identify causes of worker turnover (the core of a "workforce crisis" in child protective services in particular) by considering employees' level of commitment, emotional stability, and time management skills. These approaches have yielded recommendations for greater professionalization of the social services workforce and more refined candidate selection procedures (Alwon & Reitz, 2000; Ellis & Westbrook, 2004; Reagh, 1994; Rycraft, 1994). Social work research and practice related to employment have thus displayed a noticeable bias toward individual—rather than structural-level accounts of worker turnover, retention, and advancement. By focusing mainly on individuals—workers, rather than the resource-allocating employers (Reskin, 2003)—we learn relatively little about how employment-related inequality is produced through the larger systems of organizational policy and practice, and we may consequently hamper the effectiveness of our social change efforts.

Attending to the Intersection of Work, Family, and Community
The profession has also attended too little to the interactions between work, family, and community, often concentrating its investigations, diagnoses, and interventions on one of these realms in isolation. It is by examining the intersections of these three domains that we may best understand how the delivery of employment opportunity is institutionally "racialized" (Glass, 1999) and identify points of leverage for engaging in effective change.

The chronic lamentation of many nonprofit human service agencies about their lack of staff diversity represents another telling example of this oversight. Interpersonal staff dynamics that perpetuate homogeneity may partially explain why predominantly white, middle-class workers often wind up serving largely poor clientele from racial and ethnic minority groups. Nevertheless, the role of workplace and job design and compensation in whether an individual can afford—as much as want—to enter or stay in a human services job remains largely an investigative "black box" within social work management and scholarship.

The field's central contribution to these concerns can be the promotion of new research that simultaneously incorporates structural and individual perspectives in the study of individuals' labor force experiences, and embraces the unavoidable interdependence of the spheres of the workplace, family, and community in conceptualization, measurement, and analysis. We can also better assure that we train future administrators, employment assistance professionals, caseworkers, and job trainers in the specific tools of workplace diagnosis and intervention. Our professional schools would do well to reinvest in and reinvigorate the practice area of "occupational social work," now rare in curricula.

Influencing the Public Agenda Regarding Work
As Rayman and Bookman (1999) observed, attention to this interplay of the workplace, family, and community has only recently permeated the realm of public policy. As noted earlier, government presently puts to relatively conservative use the employment-promoting tools of private employer regulation, direct public employment, and provision of peripheral supports to working individuals and families. As social and economic disparities increase, however, they challenge us to reconsider whether employment should provide a minimum floor of opportunity, discounting no qualified candidate on the basis of her particular family's or community's capacity to support her work effort. Similarly, it pushes us to revise our decisions regarding the proper allocation of responsibility, across government, employers, families, and communities, for making employment accessible and sustainable. This compels us to begin treating productive engagement in the labor force, within families, and in the civic arena as joint goods that produce both public and private benefits. Social workers should be actively involved in this effort.

REFERENCES
Alger, H. (1868). *Ragged Dick; or, Street life in New York with the boot-black people.* Boston: Loring.
Althauser, R., & Kalleberg, A. (1981). Firms, occupations, and the structure of labor markets. In I. Berg (Ed.), *Sociological perspectives on labor markets* (pp. 119–149). New York: Academic Press.
Alwon, F., & Reitz, A. (2000). *The workforce crisis in child welfare.* Washington, DC: Child Welfare League of America.
Appelbaum, E., & Batt, R. (1994). *The new American workplace.* Ithaca, NY: ILR Press.
Badgett, M. V. L. (1999). The impact of affirmative action on public-sector employment in California, 1970–1990. In Paul Ong (Ed.), *Impacts of affirmative action: Policies & consequences in California* (pp. 83–102). Walnut Creek, CA: AltaMira Press.
Barnett, R. C., & Morgan, C. (2003). *Community: A critical missing link in work-family research.* Paper presented at the Workforce/Workplace Mismatch: Work, Family, Health, and Well-being Conference, Washington, DC, June 16–18.
Baron, J. N., Davis-Blake, A., & Bielby, W. T. (1986). The structure of opportunity: How promotion ladders vary within and among organizations. *Administrative Science Quarterly, 31,* 248–273.

Barsky, C. B. (2004). Incidence benefits measures in the National Compensation Survey. *Monthly Labor Review, 127*(8), 21–28.

Bernhardt, A., & Dresser, L. (2002). *Why privatizing government services would hurt women workers.* Washington, DC: Institute for Women's Policy Research.

Blank, R. M. (1985). An analysis of workers' choice between employment in the public and private sectors. *Industrial and Labor Relations Review, 38,* 211–224.

Boushey, H., & Murray Diaz, M. (2004). *Improving access to health insurance* (Health Insurance Data Briefs No. 1). Washington, DC: Center for Economic and Policy Research.

Burke, T. P., & Morton, J. D. (1990). How firm size and industry affect employee benefits. *Monthly Labor Review, 113*(12), 35–43.

Capps, R., Fix, M., Passel, J. S., Ost, J., & Perez-Lopez, D. (2003). A profile of the low-wage immigrant workforce: Immigrant families and workers—Facts and perspectives (Brief No. 4). Washington, DC: Urban Institute.

Carrington, W. J., McCue, K., & Pierce, B. (2000). Using establishment size to measure the impact of Title VII and affirmative action. *Journal of Human Resources, 35,* 503–523.

Chay, K. Y. (1998). The impact of federal civil rights policy on black economic progress: Evidence from the Equal Employment Opportunity Act of 1972. *Industrial and Labor Relations Review, 51,* 608–632.

DeNavas-Walt, C., Proctor, B. D., & Mills, R. J. (2004, August). *Income, poverty, and health insurance coverage in the United States: 2003.* Washington, DC: U.S. Department of Commerce, Census Bureau, Economics and Statistics Administration.

Dobbin, F., Sutton, J. R., Meyer, J. W., & Scott, W. R. (1993). Equal opportunity law and the construction of internal labor markets. *American Journal of Sociology, 99,* 396–427.

Doeringer, P., & Piore, M. (1985). *Internal labor markets and manpower analysis.* New York: M. E. Sharpe.

Duncan, G. J., & Raudenbush, S. W. (1999). Assessing the effects of context in studies of child and youth development. *Educational Psychologist, 34*(1), 29–41.

Edelman, L. B. (1992). Legal ambiguity and symbolic structures: Organizational mediation of civil rights law. *American Journal of Sociology, 97,* 1531–1576.

Edelman, L. B., & Petterson, S. M. (1999). Symbols and substance in organizational response to civil rights law. *Research in Social Stratification and Mobility, 17,* 107–135.

Ellis, J., & Westbrook, T. M. (2004, January 16). *Retention of child welfare staff: What can we learn from committed survivors?* Paper presented at the annual meeting of the Society for Social Work and Research, New Orleans.

Esping-Andersen, G. (1990). *Three worlds of welfare capitalism.* Princeton, NJ: Princeton University Press.

Galinksy, E., Hughes, D., & David, J. (1990). Trends in corporate family-supportive policies. *Marriage and Family Review, 15*(3/4), 75–94.

Gerstel, N., & McGonagle, K. (1999). Job leaves and the limits of the Family and Medical Leave Act. *Work and Occupations, 26,* 510–534.

Gilbert, N. (2002). *The transformation of the welfare state: The silent surrender of public responsibility.* Oxford, England: Oxford University Press.

Glass, J. (1999). The tangled web we weave. *Work and Occupations, 26,* 415–421.

Gonyea, J. G. (1999). The nonprofit sector's responsiveness to work-family issues. *Annals of the American Academy of Political and Social Science, 562,* 127–142.

Gordon, L. (1994). *Pitied but not entitled: Single mothers and the history of welfare.* Cambridge, MA: Harvard University Press.

Gornick, J. C., & Meyers, M. K. (2003). *Families that work: Policies for reconciling parenthood and employment.* New York: Russell Sage Foundation.

Hagan, J. M. (2004). Contextualizing immigrant labor market incorporation. *Work and Occupations, 31,* 407–423.

Haley-Lock, A. (2003). *Advancing in one's calling: The roles of internal labor markets and social capital in human services career plateauing.* Unpublished doctoral dissertation, University of Chicago, School of Social Service Administration.

Haley-Lock, A. (in press). A workforce or workplace conflict?: Applying an organizational perspective to the study of human services employment. *Administration in Social Work, 31*(1).

Haley-Lock, A., & Kruzich, J. (2005). *The roles of organizational ownership, chain affiliation and performance in front-line job benefits: The case of nursing assistants.* Unpublished manuscript, University of Washington, School of Social Work.

Harrell, J., & Carrasquillo, O. (2003). The Latino disparity in health coverage. *JAMA, 289,* 1167.

Heckman, J. J. (1998). Detecting discrimination. *Journal of Economic Perspectives, 12,* 101–116.

Heckman, J. J., & Payner, B. S. (1989). Determining the impact of federal antidiscrimination policy on the economic status of black people: A study of South Carolina. *American Economic Review, 79,* 138–177.

Hendrickson, G. A. (2000). *Globalization and its impact across sectors: Developmental effects and public sector implication in the United States.* Paper presented at the 41st annual convention of the International Studies Association, Los Angeles, March 14–18. Retrieved December 14, 2004, from http://www.ciaonet.org/isa/heg01/

Heymann, J. (2000). *The widening gap.* New York: Basic Books.

Hipple, S., & Stewart, J. (1996). Earnings and benefits of workers in alternative work arrangements. *Monthly Labor Review, 119*(10), 46–54.

Hoffman, C., Carbaugh, A., Moore, H., & Cook, A. (2005). *Health insurance coverage in America: 2004 data update.* Kaiser Commission on Medicaid and the Uninsured. Retrieved November 21, 2005, from http://www.kff.org/uninsured/upload/Health-Coverage-in-America-2004-Data-Update-Report.pdf

Holcomb, P. A., Tumlin, K., Koralek, R., Capps, R., & Zuberi, A. (2003). *The application process for TANF, Food Stamps, Medicaid and SCHIP: Issues for agencies and applicants, including immigrants and limited English speakers.* (Report prepared by the Urban Institute for the U.S. Department of Health and Human Services, Office of the Secretary, Office of the Assistant Secretary for Planning and Evaluation.) Washington, DC: Urban Institute.

Hunter, L. W. (2000). What determines job quality in nursing homes? *Industrial and Labor Relations Review, 53,* 463–481.

Illinois Facilities Fund. (2003a). *Moving towards a system: The community profiles fact book* (Illinois Early Childhood Care and Education, Statewide Needs Assessment). Chicago: Illinois Facilities Fund.

Illinois Facilities Fund. (2003b). *We need more day care centers: Latino families and child care preferences in Metropolitan Chicago.* Retrieved February 11, 2005, from http://www.iff.org/resources/content/3/6/documents/iff_latino_study.pdf

Internal Revenue Service. (1999). *Tax incentives for empowerment zones and other distressed communities* (Pub. 954). Washington, DC: U.S. Department of the Treasury.

Jacobs, D. (1994). Organizational theory and dualism: Some sociological determinants of spot and internal labor markets. *Research in Social Stratification and Mobility, 13,* 203–235.

Jencks, C., Perman, L., & Rainwater, L. (1988). What is a good job? A new measure of labor market success. *American Journal of Sociology, 93,* 1322–1357.

Jencks, C., & Phillips, M. (1998). The black–white test score gap: An introduction. In C. Jencks & M. Phillips (Eds.), *The black–white test score gap* (pp. 1–51). Washington, DC: Brookings Institution Press.

Johnson, W. R., & Neal, D. (1998). Basic skills and the black–white earnings gap. In C. Jencks & M. Phillips (Eds.), *The black–white test score gap* (pp. 480–500). Washington, DC: Brookings Institution Press.

Kalleberg, A. L. (2003). Flexible firms and labor market segmentation: Effects of workplace restructuring on jobs and workers. *Work and Occupations, 30*, 154–175.

Kalleberg, A. L., Reskin, B. F., & Hudson, K. (2000). Bad jobs in America: Standard and nonstandard employment relations and job quality in the United States. *American Sociological Review, 65*, 256–278.

Kochan, T. A., & Osterman, P. (1994). *The mutual gains enterprise: Forging a winning partnership among labor, management, and government.* Boston: Harvard Business School Press.

Kossek, E., Huber-Yoder, M., Castellino, D., & Lerner, J. (1997). The working poor: Locked out of careers and the organizational mainstream? *Academy of Management Executives, 11*(1), 76–92.

Lambert, S., & Haley-Lock, A. (2004). The organizational stratification of opportunities for work-life balance: Addressing issues of equality and social justice in the workplace. *Community, Work and Family, 7*(2), 179–195.

Lambert, S., Waxman, R. E., & Haley-Lock, A. (2002). *Against the odds: A study of sources of instability in lower-skilled jobs* (Working paper of The Project on the Public Economy of Work). Chicago: University of Chicago, School of Social Service Administration.

Lee, S. (2004). *Women's work supports, job retention, and job mobility: Child care and employer-provided health insurance help women stay on the job* (No. B244). Washington, DC: Institute for Women's Policy Research.

Lieberman, R. C. (2005). *Shaping race policy: The United States in comparative perspective.* Princeton, NJ: Princeton University Press.

Lovell, V. (2004). *No time to be sick: Why everyone suffers when workers don't have paid sick leave.* Washington, DC: Institute for Women's Policy Research.

Meyers, M. (1993). Child care in JOBS employment and training programs: What difference does quality make? *Journal of Marriage and the Family, 55*, 767–783.

Miller, M. A. (1996). The public-private pay debate: What do the data show? *Monthly Labor Review, 119*(5), 18–29.

Mishra, R. (1999). *Globalization and the welfare state.* Northampton, MA: Edward Elgan Publishing.

Moore, W. J., & Newman, R. J. (1991). Government wage differentials in a municipal labor market: The case of Houston Metropolitan Transit workers. *Industrial and Labor Relations Review, 45*, 145–153.

Moss, P., Salzman, H., & Tilly, C. (1998). *Rising from the ashes? The reconstruction of internal labor markets in the wake of corporate restructuring.* Paper prepared for presentation at the National Bureau of Economic Research Summer Institute, Center for Industrial Competitiveness and Department of Regional Economic and Social Development, University of Massachusetts at Lowell.

National Association of Social Workers. (1999). *Code of Ethics of the National Association of Social Workers.* Washington, DC: Author.

Neal, D., & Johnson, W. R. (1996). The role of premarket factors in black–white wage differences. *Journal of Political Economy, 104*, 869–895.

Nightingale, D. S., & Fix, M. (2004). Economic and labor market trends. *Future of Children, 14*(2), 49–59.

Noble, C. (1997). *Welfare as we knew it: A political history of the American welfare state.* New York: Oxford University Press.

Osterman, P. (1994). How common is workplace transformation and who adopts it? *Industrial and Labor Relations Review, 47,* 173–188.

Phillips, M., & Chin, T. (2004). School inequality: What do we know? In K. M. Neckerman (Ed.), *Social inequality* (pp. 467–520). New York: Russell Sage Foundation Press.

Presser, H. B. (2003). Race-ethnic and gender differences in nonstandard work shifts. *Work and Occupations, 30,* 412–439.

Putnam, R. (1995). Bowling alone: America's declining social capital. *Journal of Democracy, 6*(1), 65–78.

Quinn, K. (2000). *Working without benefits: The health insurance crisis confronting Hispanic Americans* (Pub. 370). New York: Commonwealth Fund, Task Force on the Future of Health Insurance for Working Americans.

Rayman, P. M., & Bookman, A. (1999). Policy perspectives: Creating a research and public policy agenda for work, family, and community. *Annals of the American Academy of Political and Social Science, 562,* 191–211.

Reagh, R. (1994). Public child welfare professionals: Those who stay. *Journal of Sociology and Social Welfare, 21*(3), 69–78.

Reskin, B. F. (1998). *The realities of affirmative action in employment.* Washington, DC: American Sociological Association.

Reskin, B. F. (2003). Including mechanisms in our models of ascriptive inequality. *American Sociological Review, 68,* 1–21.

Reskin, B. F., McBrier, D. B., & Kmec, J. A. (1999). The determinants and consequences of workplace sex and race composition. *Annual Review of Sociology, 25,* 335–361.

Ross, C., & Paulsell, D. (1998). *Sustaining employment among low-income parents: The role of quality in child care—A research review* (Final report). Princeton, NJ: MPR.

Rycraft, J. (1994). The party isn't over: The agency role in the retention of public child welfare caseworkers. *Social Work, 39,* 75–80.

Schmidley, A. D. (2001). *Profile of the foreign-born population in the United States: 2000* (Current Population Reports, Series P23-206, U.S. Census Bureau). Washington, DC: U.S. Government Printing Office.

Schur, C., & Feldman, J. (2001). *Running in place: How job characteristics, immigrant status, and family structure keep Hispanics uninsured* (Pub. 453). New York: Commonwealth Fund.

Shlay, A. B., Weinraub, M., Harmon, M., & Tran, H. (2003). *Barriers to subsidies: Reasons why low-income families do not use child care subsidies.* Philadelphia: Temple University, Center for Public Policy. Retrieved February 11, 2005, from http://www.temple.edu/cpp/content/reports/barriersfinaltosocialscienceresearch.pdf

Spilerman, S., & Schrank, H. (1991). Responses to the intrusion of family responsibilities into the workplace. *Research in Social Stratification and Mobility, 10,* 27–61.

Stack, C. (1974). *All our kin: Strategies for survival in a black community.* New York: Harper & Row.

Tienda, M., & Stier, H. (1996). Generating labor market inequality: Employment opportunities and the accumulation of disadvantage. *Social Problems, 43,* 147–165.

Tilly, C. (1996a). *The good, the bad, and the ugly: Good and bad jobs in the United States at the millennium.* Unpublished working paper of the Russell Sage Foundation.

Tilly, C. (1996b). *Half a job: Bad and good part-time jobs in a changing labor market.* Philadelphia: Temple University Press.

Toossi, M. (2002, May). A century of change: The U.S. labor force, 1950–2050. *Monthly Labor Review, 125*(5), 15–28.

Tsui, A. S., Pearce, J. L., Porter, L.W., & Tripoli, A. M. (1997). Alternative approaches to the employee-organization relationship: Does investment in employees pay off? *Academy of Management Journal, 40,* 1089–1121.

U.S. Bureau of Labor Statistics. (2005, February). *Contingent and alternative employment arrangements* [Press release]. Retrieved October 14, 2005, from http://www.bls.gov/news.release/conemp.nr0.htm

U.S. Congressional Budget Office. (1998, August). *Comparing federal employee benefits with those in the private sector* (Memorandum). Washington, DC: Author.

Vandell, D. L., & Wolfe, B. (2000). *Child care quality: Does it matter and does it need to be improved?* Madison: University of Wisconsin, Madison, Institute for Research on Poverty. Retrieved February 11, 2005, from http://aspe.hhs.gov/hsp/ccquality00/ccqual.htm

Wilson, W. J. (1987). *The truly disadvantaged.* Chicago: University of Chicago Press.

Wilson, W. J. (1996). *When work disappears: The world of the new urban poor.* New York: Alfred A. Knopf.

CHAPTER 10

DEMOCRACY AND DIVERSITY:
EXPANDING NOTIONS OF CITIZENSHIP

Maria de los Angeles Torres

Imagine a society that succeeds in sustaining a monoculture in which everyone has the same worldview, religion, language, eating habits, musical and artistic aesthetics—and then think about what kind of government would be needed to sustain this monoculture. It would have to be able to control the political and educational systems and repress any differences that might emerge; in essence, an authoritarian regime. In contrast, more open societies are characterized by some degree of tolerance toward cultural differences, and consequently have more open political systems.

The founders of the United States envisioned a society in which people of different faiths could come together to form a political community that would respect its members' differences and at the same time grant them equal rights. It was a radical project, one that created the possibility for communities to be based not on bloodlines or religious beliefs, but rather on a commitment to a set of political principles. The philosophical underpinnings of this new democracy included a belief that all men were created equal—however, not all human beings were included in this formula. Indeed, the original group was quite homogeneous. During the last two centuries, ideas about who may have a voice in public affairs have become more inclusive, even though there have been moments of retrenchment; a stubborn thread of intolerance runs throughout U.S. history. As each new group was incorporated into this country, questions about diversity and democracy were debated. This chapter looks at how ideas of inclusion have evolved throughout U.S. history and discusses what limits still circumscribe our contemporary notions of who is entitled to participate in politics.

EXPANDING NOTIONS OF WHO IS ENTITLED TO CITIZENSHIP
Modern societies are defined in part by the idea that individuals are rational and can be called upon to make decisions about their lives. In contrast to earlier societies, which insisted that only a few rulers were anointed and that the rest of the populace was subject to their power, modern societies transformed subjects into citizens who were entitled to rights, including property and voice, and were to be protected from abuses by the state. Cultural differences were relegated to the private realm, and participation in the public realm was legally defined along various dimensions, including age, class,

gender, race, and nationality. Group identity thus became a way of both including and excluding individuals. Initially, only white, property-owning males of certain ages were entitled to participate in politics. Notably, immigration status was not a detriment; indeed, one of the complaints in the Declaration of Independence was that England made difficult the encouragement of new immigrants. For a couple of decades after the War of Independence, immigrants were allowed to vote in some local and state elections, but the sentiment of openness was a fairly short-lived phenomenon. In 1798, the federalists in Congress succeeded in passing the Alien and Sedition Acts as a way of curtailing immigrant support for Thomas Jefferson. This was the first national effort to depict immigrants as a potential threat to democracy.

Although no one was immediately prosecuted under these acts, an anti-immigrant grassroots movement was organized by a secret society named the Order of the Star-Spangled Banner, better known as the "Know-Nothings" because it told its members to say, "I know nothing" if interrogated. This movement gave way to the formation of the American Party, which succeeded in getting anti-immigrant and anti-Catholic candidates elected to Congress. This party later disintegrated when its membership split on the question of whether to support slavery (Anbinder, 1992).

The nation was again redefined, and became more inclusive, as a result of the Civil War. After the emancipation of the slaves, the Constitution was amended to prohibit slavery. In 1868 the Fourteenth Amendment granted citizenship to all those born in the United States. The Fifteenth Amendment made it illegal for any state to deny a person the right to vote on account of skin color or condition of former servitude, thereby enfranchising black men. Although various states thereafter passed a host of provisions that in effect denied them the right to vote, in principle, the notion of who was entitled to participate in politics had been expanded.

Women, however, regardless of color or nationality, had no such rights until 1920, when, after decades of struggle, the Constitution was amended to extend suffrage to them. For Native Americans, the struggle for voting rights was won piecemeal. This battle has been characterized by a series of legal victories that together eventually resulted in Native Americans legally gaining voting rights. In some cases, though (for instance, the Pueblo Indians of New Mexico), voting rights did not become a reality until the 1950s (Torres & Vazquez, 2002).

COLONIZATION, IMMIGRATION, AND CITIZENSHIP

At its founding, the United States comprised people who were immigrants, those who had been forced into slavery, and Native Americans. By the mid-1800s, the groups that continued to grow were inhabitants of colonized territories and immigrants (Gabaccia, 2002). At the end of the war with Mexico in the mid-1800s, the United States annexed most of Mexico's northern territory. The Treaty of Guadalupe Hidalgo gave Mexicans in those territories the choice of becoming U.S. citizens, thus opening the door to a new national group. Like African Americans, Mexican Americans faced a series of discriminatory practices that contributed to a denial of their full voice in society.

The push west was accompanied by legislation that encouraged immigrants to settle and acquire land in the United States. The Homestead Act granted citizenship to any immigrant who settled in the West and cultivated land for five years. Lincoln advocated for laws to encourage immigration, and in 1864, Congress passed a bill providing for the appointment of a Commissioner of Immigration. However, specific immigrant groups, such as Chinese Americans, were excluded from these provisions. Anti-Chinese sentiments, in part born of competition during the Gold Rush, finally culminated in passage of the Chinese Exclusion Act of 1882, which made these people the first group in American history to be barred from entering the United States on the basis of race and class (Lee, 2003). The denial of citizenship to Chinese and other Asian Americans continued well into the next century.

From 1870 to 1900, more than 12 million immigrants, mainly from Great Britain, Russia, and western Germany, entered the United States; Scandinavian immigrants also joined this stream. From 1905 until World War I, an average of more than 1 million immigrants a year came to the United States. Italy and Ireland joined the other countries in Europe in sending emigrants to the United States, spurring concern about the "stock" of immigrants, their religions, and their political ideologies. The immigration numbers declined with the outbreak of World War I (Daniels, 2002), but the United States has always been a popular receiving country.

Concerns about immigrants manifested themselves in laws that, instead of encouraging immigration, began to set limits, particularly on the kinds of people who would be let in. By 1917, Congress had become very specific about who was allowed to enter the United States; for example, every person over the age of 16 had to be able to read. The 1924 Immigration Act set national quotas on how many immigrants could enter the United States; these quotas favored northern Europe over southern and eastern Europe.

Anti-immigrant sentiments were expressed in U.S. social relations as well. Irish and Italian immigrants were targeted in part because of their religious affiliation. From 1854 to 1929, orphan trains from New York sent out 150,000 to 200,000 children from urban areas, mainly to homes in the farming communities of the Midwest. Charles Loring Brace, the founder of the Children's Aid Society, began the orphan trains as a way to "save" poor street children by placing them with farm families. Most of these children were poor and Catholic, and many were also orphans, but others were children whose families could not afford to raise them. Catholics vehemently opposed this "emigration" plan, seeing it as a way of snatching children from their faith. Others, though, viewed the program as a way to find shelter for children and to introduce them to the Protestant work ethic (Holt, 1992; O'Connor, 2001). Similar thinking led to the establishment of Native American boarding schools, where children taken from their families were placed in the hopes of Americanizing them.

Although many thought that children could be molded into good citizens, nativists argued that immigrants in general could not be Americanized. Nativism took many forms, including struggles concerning the place of religion in public schools, antiradicalism in the workplace, and eventually the formation of political parties with anti-immigrant legislative agendas (Billington, 1938; Higham, 1988). This movement contributed to the revitalization of the Ku Klux Klan and the expansion of its platform to include the elimination of Jews and Catholics, as well as black people.

The nativist movement was fueled by the eugenics movement, which basically grew from the new science of genetics and counted among its many proponents scientists, philanthropists, and preachers (Rosen, 2004). The eugenics movement sought to curtail the reproduction of those deemed defective or less human, defined mainly by "mental" and social deficiencies (Selden, 1999).[1] In the eugenics perspective, Americans from northern Europe were thought to be genetically superior to those from southern Europe. The positivist eugenicists sought to encourage the "best" to breed while curtailing immigration from lesser countries. Negative eugenics proponents advocated institutionalization and sterilization of deficient individuals.

The eugenics movement was popularized through community lecture series, through county-fair photo contests to find the best American family, and through film (Pernick, 1996). In all, it was a movement to define a "right" American through the genetic pool and to encourage such people to procreate (Ordove, 2003). The eugenics movement also fueled tensions along the United States-Mexico border, and even succeeded in having Mexicans defined as a separate race in the U.S. census count (Stern, 1999).

In contrast, reformers such as John Dewey believed deeply in people's capacity to be educated. He and other reformers advocated public education for all people as a means to create the good citizen. For Dewey, democracy depended on the ability of a nation's citizens to act and think independently; public education was held to be the key to this endeavor. Social activists like Jane Addams further advocated for the rights of immigrants and maintained that they could indeed become Americans.

EFFECT ON POLITICS: THE URBAN ETHNIC PHENOMENON

Despite the backlash against immigrants, ethnicity continued to be a force in U.S. politics. This was particularly evident in urban areas, where foreign-born laborers contributed to radical unionization movements as well (Hirsch, 1990). Chicago, for instance, had become home to immigrants from all over the world. At the end of the 1800s, labor activism made Chicago the center of support for the eight-hour workday (Ansell & Burris, 1977). The union movement in the late 1860s and 1870s was deeply divided, though, and with the absence of a strong central labor voice, ethnic bosses, representing middle-class immigrants, moved into the role of political spokespeople for their communities. For instance, after the Great Chicago Fire of 1871, Anton Hesing led a coalition of Germans and Irish to protest Mayor Joseph Medill's ordinance that allowed only brick homes to be built. Later, he organized the successful movement against temperance laws (Jentz, 1991). Politics became a way to consolidate emerging communities, as it gave communities of new immigrants economic and political opportunities (Nelli, 1970).

One effect on local politics was the hyphenation phenomenon: immigrant groups retained a cultural allegiance to their home country, but for political purposes everyone was defined as an American. It was assumed that by the second generation, immigrants would cut their ties with their homelands. Ethnicity was relegated to the private realm, while in the public realm citizens rallied around the construction of a political American. Despite a social anti-immigrant backlash, new immigrants became an important part of the emerging Democratic Party's base in urban areas.[2]

Politicians understood the power of ethnic identification; in 1919, one of Chicago's congressional representatives declared that the party that eliminated the hyphen would eliminate itself from politics (Buenker, 1974). Debates about national immigration reform found their way into local politics, as did discussions about the role of the United States in Europe (Allswang, 1971), and ethnicity as a means to mobilize voters became part of the electoral tradition in the United States.

GLOBAL REACH AND ITS EFFECT ON NOTIONS OF ENTITLEMENT

The southwestern expansion of the United States laid the structure for the country's rise in international status and eventually the entrance of the United States into a war on European territory. This global reach was accompanied by an internal thrust to unify the nation, which resulted in narrowing the conceptual contours of who was entitled to have a voice in America—indeed, in the permissible boundaries of voice itself.

Armed with the Espionage Act of 1914 and the Sedition Act of 1917, Woodrow Wilson, the president at the time of World War I, unleashed an extensive campaign to thwart dissent and opposition to the war. Many of his targets were immigrants (Germans and Italians) who were also labor activists who supported radical economic and political change. Wilson unleashed a popular campaign to identify potential enemies of the United States and organized citizen committees that had the power to investigate suspected groups and individuals. Civil liberties were suspended during this period. The U.S. postal system was used as a means of collecting information about ethnic groups. Newspapers and mail written in non-English languages were impounded. Many states in the Midwest outlawed the use of foreign languages in public places, and ethnic newspapers were censored. Immigrants were called ethnics—at the time, a derogatory term meaning "foreign" (Murphy, 1979).

There was one exception to the trend of limiting immigration. Puerto Rico had been a colony of the United States since 1898, and activists on the island were starting to push for full independence. When the United States entered World War I, Wilson needed to send more troops abroad. At the behest of the president, Congress passed the Jones

Act, which unilaterally made all Puerto Ricans citizens of the United States, even though Puerto Rico itself retained colonial status. As citizens, Puerto Ricans could be sent to war without creating the impression that the United States was using (or endorsing the use of) foreigners as soldiers. This rather bizarre solution to the problem of individual status was one way to avoid the contradictions inherent in colonization of the island, even though it created a puzzling entanglement for the United States (Burnett & Marshall, 2001). As far as democracy went, the territory would not be incorporated; rather, its people would be included as citizens—after an intense Americanization program (Caban, 1999).

World War II brought a renewed commitment on the part of government to unify the nation. It was during World War II that patriotism became closely identified with being an American. Most states passed laws requiring schoolchildren to recite the Pledge of Allegiance at the start of the day, and mandating that U.S. flags be placed in every classroom (Tuttle, 1993). Americanism now required a collective performance.

This hyperpatriotism was accompanied by a renewed repression of immigrants and their ancestors. In effect, a national policy that demanded patriotic loyalty discouraged ethnic communities, particularly Germans, Italian, and Japanese, from maintaining ties with their respective homelands. The harshest treatment, however, was reserved for the Japanese, as racism fueled by fear contributed to mass hysteria (Creef, 2004). Between 1942 and 1946, 120,000 Japanese Americans, 70,000 of whom were citizens of the United States and most of whom were under the age of 21, were placed in concentration or internment camps. Japanese Americans lost all rights, including the right to own property, to work, and to vote. Not until after the war were they again granted the right to become citizens. It took another three decades for Congress to approve reparations and the president to issue a formal apology (Hatamiya, 1993).

THE COLD WAR: FREEDOM ABROAD, RACIAL AND ETHNIC EXCLUSION AT HOME
The United States emerged from World War II as a world leader. There was optimism in the air and a promise of freedom for the world and prosperity at home—but many African American and Latino soldiers returning from the war did not find these opportunities. Indeed, Latino families were not even allowed to bury their dead sons in the same cemeteries as white people, and returning soldiers were not allowed into the same schools as white people. The Cold War propelled the United States into an intense competition with the Soviet Union in what has classically been described as a struggle between two diametrically opposed political systems: democracy based on equality and individual freedom; and communism, under which the individual lost all freedoms. Internationally, the United States was leading a coalition against communism, but internally, many of its own citizens were oppressed and denied basic opportunities and services because of their skin color or ancestry.

These glaring contradictions fed the fire of a massive civil rights movement that questioned the very essence of this nation and the legal premise that all men were created equal. A long legal tradition that bolstered states' rights had essentially approved the construction of two separate societies, one for black people and the other for white people. In 1954, the Supreme Court overturned this practice in the landmark case of Brown v. Board of Education, in which the Court declared that the separate-but-equal idea made impossible the construction of a plural democratic society.

Despite Brown, communities organized along precisely the same identity lines that had been used to exclude their members from political participation. Thus, black people organized along race lines to demand entrance into the political system and an equitable share of public services and social benefits. After a decade of community protests, lobbying, and legal challenges, President Lyndon Johnson signed the most far-reaching civil rights legislation since the passage of the Thirteenth Amendment. The Civil Rights Act of 1964 prohibited discrimination on the basis of a person's color, race, national origin, religion, or sex, and extended this protection of rights into the workplace, voting booth, places of public accommodation (including hotels and restaurants), and other public spaces. In addition, private entities that received federal funding were also covered by the act (Hamilton, 1973).

Despite this broad- and wide-reaching legislation, the federal government had a hard time enforcing voting rights. Therefore, in 1965, after intense lobbying by civil rights organizations, Johnson signed another sweeping civil rights bill, this time intended to focus on voting rights in counties that had a history of serious violations. The Voting Rights Act suspended literacy tests, and provided for the appointment of federal examiners who could register people to vote. In addition, jurisdictions with a history of voting rights violations had to obtain preclearance from the Justice Department before making any change in voting procedures. Local groups could register their objections during a specified time period.[3]

Another obstacle to political participation was age. The government came under increased pressure to lower the voting age to 18: after all, advocates reasoned, young men of 18 were being drafted to fight in the Vietnam War, so why shouldn't they be allowed to vote? The argument resonated with the U.S. public, and in 1965, the Constitution was amended to lower the voting age to 18. (Incidentally, this was the last time to date that the Constitution has been amended.)

By the mid-1960s, the United States had succeeded in enacting laws that in effect allowed the federal government to enforce the Thirteenth, Fourteenth, and Fifteenth Amendments to the Constitution. Citizenship and an individual's right to participate in the political process thus became truly protected by government, not merely guaranteed by law.

Although the Civil Rights Act outlawed discrimination on the basis of nationality, the Voting Rights Acts was narrower in scope. During the next 10 years, Mexican Americans throughout the southwest joined in demanding voting rights. During hearings held to discuss extension of the Voting Rights Act in 1975, Latinos, Native Americans, and

Asian Americans presented testimony about voting rights violations in their communities. Because of this activism, the 1975 extension included an amendment that added these specific groups as protected language minorities. The extension also broadened the kinds of activities that would be considered voting rights. For example, the act recognized that a person's vote could be diluted by gerrymandering, annexation, adoption of at-large elections, and other structural changes.[4]

THE STRUGGLE FOR EQUALITY: IDENTITY POLITICS

During the 1970s voting rights projects throughout the south and the southwest documented instances of voting rights violations. In conjunction with the voting rights section of the Justice Department, communities advocated for redrawing of districts to maximize the number of black people and Latinos in those districts. The assumption was that when the numbers of ethnic minority groups in a district were maximized, those groups would have a better possibility of electing someone of their choice. In addition, at-large systems were replaced with single-member districts. The immediate effect was an increase in the numbers of black people and Latinos elected to city councils, school boards, and other public bodies.

By the 1980s unprecedented numbers of black people and Latinos had been elected to every level of government. In Congress, these representatives organized caucuses along ethnic and racial lines to promote common agendas. Local governments also began to reflect more closely the racial and ethnic composition of their populations. Affirmative action and equal employment opportunity plans helped increase the numbers of ethnic minorities in the public sector, higher education, professional schools, and the corporate world. Municipal governments also instituted set-aside programs to more fairly distribute city contracts to ethnic minorities and women.

The politics of the civil rights movement have been termed identity politics, because groups organized around gender, racial, and ethnic identities to leverage power. Identity politics succeeded in reasserting the rights of groups denied entrance on the basis of who they were, precisely by organizing individuals into groups. The debate in U.S. politics moved from establishment and enforcement of individual rights to the restoration of rights for groups previously denied political access. Once the question of the right of representation was raised, other issues, such as social and economic rights, also found their way into the political arena.

CULTURAL WARS

The entrance of individuals from previously excluded groups into mainstream U.S. politics and society had two effects. For many ethnic minority groups, experiences with formerly almost all-white institutions often led to a reaffirmation of their cultural heritage.

The effect on these groups' political agendas was perhaps more profound. As minorities entered boardrooms and public-sector universities, they began to demand more transformative agendas. It was not enough just to be included as the representatives of an ethnic minority group, say, on an editorial board, or in an academic department; many now began, for instance, to demand that distributive mechanisms for public goods be revamped to be more inclusive of their communities, that the ways news was covered be changed, and that the curriculums in universities be expanded.

What became known as the "culture wars" of the 1980s first erupted on college campuses. At Stanford University, a group that included an interdisciplinary and multiracial faculty began with a simple demand to include American writers in the Great Books classes. Charging that the "canon" was Eurocentric, the group continued to push to have works by all kinds of American writers included in the course. Not only did they criticize the traditional canon as exclusionary, but they also questioned the ways in which history itself was conceived and taught by those in power—particularly the methods of social analysis, which, in their view, privileged those in power (Rosaldo, 1993).

The culture wars succeeded in changing the curriculum in many U.S. universities. Curriculums were expanded to include courses about people and literatures that had formerly been excluded from or ignored by the traditional canon. Ethnic, race, and gender studies were added to university programs. These developments did not take place without resistance. Some thought that multiculturalism was a value- and agenda-laden movement that would in the long run dilute a more objective and distant canon. To some, the idea of ethnic and race studies was merely trendy. Others were uncomfortable teaching and talking about areas with which they were not familiar, and some were afraid of offending students and faculty from ethnic minority communities if they raised questions. Some accused multiculturalists of promoting intolerance and acting like "thought police" (Bernstein, 1995). Others worried that "political correctness" had simply replaced one set of prejudices with another (Ravitch, 2003).

What brought integration to a screeching halt, at least for a time, was not political correctness, but the anti-affirmative action backlash. Affirmative action had become the most effective legal mechanism in U.S. history for integration. The aims were modest: most plans adopted goals (not quotas) based on a simple formula that tried to achieve a workplace that reflected the labor force itself, not the population. The labor market statistics already reflected deep, long-standing prejudices, so using them as goals made for modest changes indeed. Nevertheless, affirmative action by educational institutions had another purpose as well: to create a diverse environment in which students could learn from each other. For service providers, employing people with ties to particular communities was a way to provide better services to those communities.

For many white Americans, though, affirmative action was seen as a way to allow unqualified members of ethnic minorities into colleges and workplaces (D'Souza, 1998). Some argued that unqualified members of ethnic minority groups were lowering educational standards, and warned that nothing less than America's greatness was at stake.

169

The Bakke case became a flashpoint. Twice denied admission to a California medical school, despite better grades and test scores than successful ethnic minority applicants, Allan Bakke sued the school, claiming that he was a victim of reverse discrimination. At the Supreme Court level, eight Justices were split evenly; the ninth brokered a compromise decision mandating that Bakke be admitted, but upholding affirmative action and recognizing that the underlying principles and goals were justified (Ball, 2000). Since then, universities and other institutions have struggled to create balanced programs under which minority students are given equal opportunities without denying nonminorities theirs.

The idea of eliminating race as a means to include previously excluded groups also affected voting rights cases. Many courts held that voting districts could not be drawn or redrawn to maximize any racial or ethnic group's chance of electing one of its own.

In addition to the obvious struggle for resources among the diverse racial and ethnic groups, a battle began over what "America" should be. Some claimed that diversity itself had been invented by the left as a way to undermine democracy, and argued that using the cultural and physical traits of a group as a means to include them in society thereby privileged them and broke the promise of equality (Wood, 2002). Others called for an end to the use of race and ethnicity as markers for group membership, advocating instead that group membership should be voluntary, not prescribed by social constructions (Hollinger, 1996). For others, multiculturalism challenged what they perceived to be the greatness of the U.S. social experiment: instead of fostering unity, it fragmented the nation (Schlesinger, 1998). The alternative model was the melting pot, into which all would go and in which all would become American (Glazer, 1997).

The goal was civic harmony among all groups. Nevertheless, none of these commentators was clear on how equality could be achieved in the face of tremendous social inequities, nor did anyone make it clear exactly how an "American" was to be defined (though on this last point it was often assumed that American did have an Anglo-Saxon, Protestant cultural construction). Some critics, however, were willing to allow immigrants to continue practicing their culture at home, as long as they did not demand that public institutions change.

In contrast, the multicultural projects emanating from ethnic minority communities proposed a way of expanding the notion of who should be considered an American. These groups were trying to find ways to guarantee their inclusion in all aspects of U.S. life.

The two visions of how the United States could become a more unified nation generated very different kinds of policies regarding the incorporation of new immigrants. Those worried about fragmentation called for an end to special bilingual programs and demanded that only English be used to conduct public business. In contrast, multiculturalists saw no danger in supporting programs aligned with immigrants' cultures, if those programs made it easier for immigrants to become part of the nation. The multiculturalists understood that the presence of new immigrants would change the United States, but perceived that change as a part of building inclusive human societies.

GLOBALIZATION: NEW IMMIGRANTS AND OLD NATIVISM

In the 1990s the U.S. population increased by more than in any other decade in its history. Although greater longevity and steady birth rates helped fuel this increase, attention focused on the unprecedented number of immigrants that accounted for most of this growth. In real numbers, more than 14 million new immigrants entered the United States from 1990 to 2000. More than two-thirds of all foreign-born reside in six states: California, New York, Florida, Texas, New Jersey, and Illinois. However, in the 1990s, increasing numbers of immigrants settled in nontraditional urban and rural receiving communities, particularly in the southern and midwestern states. For example, during the 1990s, the Hispanic population more than doubled in Arkansas, Georgia, Nebraska, Nevada, North Carolina, and Tennessee. The Mexican American Legal Defense and Educational Fund even closed one of its offices in California and opened one in Atlanta. Even in traditional receiving metropolitan areas like Chicago, the increase in new immigrants was most marked in blue-collar townships such as Cicero.

Another important difference between this immigrant wave and earlier ones in the last century was the place of origin of the foreign-born. In 2000, 25.5 percent were born in Asia, 15.3 percent were born in Europe, and the remaining 8.1 percent were born in other regions of the world; 51 percent were born in Latin America. (One-third of the foreign-born population is from Mexico or a Central American country.[5]) In 2000 white people still constituted 75 percent of the population, and Asians 3.6 percent, but the big news was the fact that Latino population made up 13 percent, in contrast to African Americans' 12 percent.

The most dramatic increases did occur in the Hispanic or Latino community, which increased by more than 50 percent from 1990, from 22 million to 35 million, compared to an increase of 13 percent for the total U.S. population. Mexicans, the largest group, constitute slightly more than half of the Latino population, at 20 million. The influx of new immigrants doubled the limited-English proficient population, from 6 percent in 1980 to 12 percent in 2000, or 25 million adults. Of foreign-born children, 40 percent have limited English proficiency, and one in five are themselves immigrants.[6]

These new numbers obviously have profound implications for the future of the United States, particularly with regard to the question of how to create a political community from a diverse linguistic, religious, and social population. Like most social movements demanding broad societal change so as to make society more inclusive and responsive to marginalized communities, immigrants have been met with a backlash, including propositions to deny them (even those who are legal residents) health and educational services. In California, this trend was embodied in ballot Proposition 186; in the 2004

171

election, a ballot initiative in Arizona basically called for an end to funding of programs for undocumented workers, even programs mandated by federal laws. Especially poignant have been the English-only initiatives: Since the mid-1980s, more than 20 states have made English the official language of the state.

There has also been a vigorous debate on the implications of immigration on the future of U.S. society. Perhaps the most prominent critic of the new immigrants, Samuel Huntington, the director of area studies at Harvard University, has warned that their presence constitutes a danger to the future of democracy, for a variety of reasons. Following a long-standing U.S. tradition of questioning the assimilation capabilities of current immigrants, he argues that the foundation of U.S. culture is Anglo-Saxon Protestantism. The new immigrants (mainly Latinos and specifically Mexicans) speak a different language and practice a different religion. Because of these cultural differences, Huntington believes that they are a threat to the very foundation of U.S. democracy (Huntington, 2004).

Although he recognizes that there have been past waves of mainly Catholic, non-English-speaking immigrants, such as Italians, Huntington suggests that the proximity to home country and the scale of immigration itself will make it difficult to assimilate Latinos. In addition, Spanish language use is reinforced by Spanish-language television and radio stations and newspapers. He points to Miami as an example of a city populated by Latinos, and says that it has become a Spanish-speaking city with corrupt politics.

Huntington's rendition of U.S. history glosses over deep divides that continue to characterize our society. He assumes that there was a painless absorption of former slaves and 19th- and early 20th-century immigrants. He also appears to hold a woefully pessimistic belief that the common political project of democracy can be sustained only when all its members share one language and have a homogenous culture to bind its community. Philosophically, in some fundamental ways, Huntington's perspective is the antithesis of the project promoted by the founders of the United States. In contrast to the Founding Fathers, who envisioned a pluralistic and possibly multilingual society with a political community in which everyone participated, Huntington sees difference as a threat to the political community.

An alternative view envisions a viable democracy that can make room for a pluralistic society; one that can redefine itself to adapt to the changing demographic realities of its political community. Such a democracy would avoid the pitfalls of Huntington's model of democracy—a democracy that cannot transform itself and results in the political marginalization of others. Although change is never easy, Huntington's model undermines the potential power of democratic ideals to achieve social justice and underestimates the goodwill of people who want to create a society in which all may participate freely.

United States history is filled with examples of anti-immigrant hysteria, particularly in election seasons and moments of expansion and inclusion. The truth is that the presence of Latinos, and other immigrants, in the United States demands new ways of thinking about how immigrants can be incorporated into society.

The impact of globalization cannot be ignored in any discussion of democracy in the world today. There is a need to think about universal human rights that are sensitive to distinct traditions and cultural practices; at the same time, certain basic universal rights should be promoted above specific cultural practices. Certain situations are illustrative. For instance, most people would probably agree that the teaching of various languages is a good thing, despite the fact that one group may be "imposing" its language on another. Learning a new language does not hurt an individual; indeed, it is something that as a society we tend to value, as witnessed by the fact that we encourage university students to learn new languages. There may also be cultural and religious practices that do not appear to harm any particular group. For example, in France, Muslim girls are not allowed to wear hijabs (headscarves) to public schools. Although wearing the hijab does introduce religious symbolism into a state-run space, no one is being physically harmed by this practice.

The human rights issue gets more complicated when we consider situations that do hold the potential for physical harm. For instance, arranged marriages of minors can be thought of as providing children for sex to adults. In the United Nation's Convention on the Rights of Children,[7] universal standards advocate that children should have the right to participate in decisions that affect their lives, including their sexuality. The same can be said for genital mutilation, a traditional cultural practice in certain societies. A universal standard that no bodily harm should be inflicted on minors may override the cultural tradition. (It is quite a different situation if an adult voluntarily decides to undergo such a procedure.) This is why some feminist groups have suggested that multiculturalism in and of itself may not always prove beneficial to women, or children for that matter (Okin, Cohen, Howard, & Nussbaum, 1999). The problem, of course, is who decides whether a standard is an imperially constructed and imposed value, or a universal right for all human beings.

Another aspect of globalization that affects people's ability to participate fully in politics is increased immigration. This fact becomes particularly relevant because politics is still organized primarily along the contours of the nation-state, and the concept of citizenship is closely related to the rise of nation-states. In today's world, though, national communities are not bound as tightly as they were 200 years ago. Economies, cultures, and people cross borders, but political institutions are still bound by geography. What happens to groups that either cross borders or have borders cross them? Today they are still considered outside the established political communities. Many countries of origin are extending all sorts of rights and services to emigrants who have left those homelands, in part recognizing the importance of the emigrants' economic contributions. At the same time, receiving countries are limiting the rights of and services to the same groups.

DEMOCRACY AND DIVERSITY

Throughout the past two and a quarter centuries, notions of who is entitled to participate in society have expanded. There are still obvious barriers to participation, particularly immigrant status and age. These hurdles, in and of themselves, do not seem insurmountable, in that the voting age could be lowered and criteria such as tax-paying or residency could become the basis of qualification for citizenship. If the concern is that immigrants may not be able to "mainstream," one way to start could be to facilitate voting and bring people into the political community. Still, there are complicated theoretical questions on how to think about diversity in the context of democracy, a system that can truly function best when its participants have some social equality along with political rights.

Notions of citizenship have expanded along the lines of gender, race, and age. In practice, although there is an implicit social promise of equality, inequalities persist along those same lines. Identity politics produced political results in that it helped mobilize communities. The danger, however, was that racial, ethnic, and gender identities could become essentialized in the struggle for inclusion. That is, the category itself, such as race, did not really provide an alternative conceptualization of what it meant to be diverse, but rather was simply a reactive binary to the original category that excluded the group.

One of the most eloquent critics of the pitfalls of essentializing race was Ralph Ellison. In his book *Invisible Man* (1995 ed.), he cautioned against simplifying notions of race because these categories could be manipulated by anyone—black or white—who was seeking personal power. The result could be both exclusion of an entire group, and also the promotion of minority power brokers and, for that matter, white liberals whose aim was to advance themselves politically rather than to empower individuals.

As long as racism and discrimination persist, group rights cannot be ignored. Some of the 2004 U.S. election results were driven by anti-immigrant sentiment that reveals the persistence of discrimination and racism in U.S. society. For example, in Long Island, New York, residents had complained: "A new wave of Hispanic immigrants had swept Long Island; they were furious about the overcrowded homes and lines of day laborers they saw in their towns. They told Mr. Levy (who was running for county executive) they wanted action" (Healy, 2004). In Lewiston, Maine, the mayor of the city published an open letter asking Somalis to stop encouraging others to move to his town (Jones, 2004).

Can we afford to do away with all racial or ethnic signifiers in the struggle to make societies more inclusive, when the disparities are so closely correlated with group membership? How can we think about inequalities that affect certain groups more than others without relying on group identities? For example, Iris Marion Young (2000) suggested that structural situations place all Latinos in vulnerable social positions: they have had uneven access to citizenship, many must cope with language differences, and they have been stereotyped and discriminated against. Calls for social justice should acknowledge and deal with social inequalities, not just present an identity agenda.

Although society still appears to support the philosophical concept that all human beings are created equal, the fact of deep social inequalities creates a major obstacle to provision and protection of individual rights. The political system itself may be a public undertaking in which all individuals are theoretically equal, but in reality disparities of wealth and access in the private realm of society give certain individuals and groups a more advantageous position from which to influence the public. There are also deep cleavages within most groups. The matrix of inequalities is complicated, but suggests that perhaps coalitions based on class position can be formed that transcend racial, ethnic, and gender lines. Nevertheless, deep-seated racism and discrimination create spatial distances that make class coalitions difficult to construct. Even coalitions among historically marginalized groups are challenging, precisely because the histories of these groups are so distinct. Still, the search for issues of commonality and discussions about common agenda and strategies could be part of a democratic society in which self-defined groups try to develop common political platforms that may lead to solution of some social problems.

One of the greatest theoretical challenges to thinking about democracy and multiculturalism is that democracy is a liberal project that emerged out of a notion of individual rights; that is, that individuals are imbued with a series of inalienable rights that cannot be usurped by the state (Taylor, 1994). However, multiculturalism promotes the protection of groups. Theorists have suggested that group rights (that is, rights accorded to certain groups) are compatible with democratic liberalism precisely because the goal of democracy is to develop a society in which all individuals are equal. They warn, however, that there is no single way of dealing with groups; great variations exist among, for instance, national minorities, diasporas, and indigenous groups, and these differences must be taken into consideration when society decides how each group's rights can be protected (Kymlicka, 1996). Feminist theorists have also contributed to conceptualizing a more democratic society. Chantal Mouffe (1993) has pointed out that because identities are socially constructed, they can also be socially deconstructed. In a more radical participatory democracy, individuals would be able to choose how they define themselves, rather than having to accept what is imposed on them. Therefore, grassroots struggles to redefine identities could potentially emerge, as identities will still be important sites for political contests (Mouffe).

Others have tried to reconcile individual rights with group oppression by offering universal human rights as the solution. They argue that claims for social justice should be based on universal rights. Even if rights are denied to an entire group, each individual within that group would still be protected by these universal rights. Therefore, rights are claimed not on the basis of group identity, but rather on the basis of human rights (Zaibert & Millan-Zaibert, 2000).

175

John Dewey promoted the idea that democracy could not be sustained without informed and educated individuals. It is this perspective that educators today say is necessary to build a multicultural democratic society, particularly in the age of globalization. New scholarship is needed so that we can understand the multiple layers embedded in notions of gender, race, and ethnicity. Some of this is being done by theorists who begin with the premise that education is political, because it is a public act through which the state and private actors struggle to influence how children are taught. As such, education is also a moral act, though it need not promote only one set of moral codes; rather, education can attempt to promote an ethical system that is part of broader public discussions. These would include discussions about questions of justice and equality in national and global terms (Torres, 1998).

Whether or not homogenous states have ever existed is debatable. As long as individuals differ from each other, diversity will continue to characterize all human societies. We have also always found ways to marginalize and create "Others," though from epoch to epoch the ways we use for marginalization have changed. Groups have often been marginalized because of their religion, gender, race, or national origin. Obviously, these are social constructions that are unique to historical periods. What is constant are the opposing human needs to marginalize and to fight against this marginalization (Kristiva, 1991).

Although under certain circumstances the foreigner has functioned to consolidate the democratic project (Honig, 2001), more often the foreigner has been feared, marginalized, oppressed, and annihilated. If marginalization is part of the human condition, is it utopic to envision a society in which we include rather than exclude people? In a way, this was the question posed to Albert Einstein and Sigmund Freud by the League of Nations, which asked these two great thinkers to correspond with each other about the question, "Why war?" Einstein saw the solution as really quite simple: war occurs when one country encroaches on another, so a world tribunal should be set up to judge and punish nations that invade other nations. To prevent warlike behavior, all people should receive universal education. Then, however, Einstein complicated his own answer by pointing out that it is usually the most educated who decide to go to war. He asked Freud whether there is something instinctual about war, which may be the ultimate act of marginalization. Freud answered that, in essence, human beings have the capacity both to hate and to love each other. He too thought that education was a key to furthering the nurturing side of human beings (Freud & Einstein, 1932). Taking Einstein and Freud together, an argument can be made that government has a central role to play in bringing out the best in us.

The history of the United States demonstrates that there have been both expansions and contractions in notions of who is entitled to participate in society. The expansions have come from creative struggles to open up society by marginalized communities and their allies. Changing notions of who is entitled to participate politically are critical, as the political arena is an important place in which new groups obtain access to public goods. There is good reason to believe that, despite contemporary obstacles, notions of who is entitled to have a voice in public affairs will continue to become more inclusive in the future. A continuing challenge is how to construct economies that can sustain some level of equality among all their members, so that political voices can be meaningful as well as representative.

END NOTES

1. For a comprehensive review of various components of the American eugenics movement, see http://www.eugenicsarchive.org/eugenics/
2. Katznelson (1981) discusses the decline of class and the rise of ethnic identification in urban areas.
3. See http://www.usdoj.gov/crt/voting/intro/intro_b.htm
4. See note 3.
5. See http://www.ncsl.org/programs/immig/issuebrief051702.htm
6. See http://www.urban.org/UploadedPDF/410654_NABEPresentation.pdf
7. The United States is one of only two countries in the world that have not signed on to this document.

REFERENCES

Allswang, J. (1971). *A house for all peoples: Ethnic politics in Chicago.* Lexington: University of Kentucky Press.

Anbinder, T. (1992). *Nativism and slavery: The northern Know Nothings and the politics of the 1850s.* New York: Oxford University Press.

Ansell, C. K., & Burris, A. L. (1977, Spring). Bosses of the city unite! Labor politics and political machine consolidation, 1870–1910. *Studies in American Political Development, 11,* 1–43.

Ball, H. (2000). *The Bakke case: Race, education and affirmative action.* Lawrence: University of Kansas Press.

Bernstein, R. (1995). *Dictatorship of virtue: How the battle over multiculturalism is reshaping our schools, our country, and our lives.* New York: Vintage.

Billington, R. A. (1938). *The Protestant crusade, 1800–1860: A study of the origins of American nativism.* New York: Times.

Buenker, J. (1974). Dynamics of ethnic politics 1900–1930. *Journal of the Illinois State Historical Society, 67*(2), 175–199.

Burnett, C. D., & Marshall, B. (2001). *Foreign in a domestic sense: Puerto Rico, American expansion, and the Constitution.* Durham, NC: Duke University Press.

Caban, P. (1999). *Constructing a colonial people: Puerto Rico and the United States 1898–1932.* Boulder, CO: Westview Press.

Creef, E. T. (2004). *Imaging Japanese America: The visual construction of citizenship, nation, and the body.* New York: New York University Press.

D'Souza, D. (1998). *Illiberal education: The politics of race and sex on campus.* New York: Free Press.

Daniels, R. (2002). *Coming to America: A history of immigration and ethnicity in American life* (2d ed.). New York: Perennial.

Ellison, R. (1995). Invisible man. New York: Vintage Press.

Freud, S., & Einstein, A. (1932). "Why War?" Letters commissioned by the League of Nations, translated by the Chicago Psychoanalytic Society.

Gabaccia, D. (2002). *Immigration and American diversity: A social and cultural history* (Problems in American History). Malden, MA: Blackwell.

Glazer, N. (1997). *We are all multiculturalists now.* Cambridge, MA: Harvard University Press.

Hamilton, C. V. (1973). *The black experience in American politics.* New York: Putnam.

Hatamiya, L. T. (1993). *Japanese Americans and the passage of the Civil Liberties Act of 1988.* Palo Alto, CA: Stanford University Press.

Healy, P. (2004, November 29). Long Island clash on immigrants is gaining political force. *New York Times.*

Higham, J. (1988). *Strangers in the land: Patterns of American nativism, 1860*–1925 (2d ed.). New Brunswick, NJ: Rutgers University Press.

Hirsch, E. (1990). *Urban revolt: Ethnic politics in the nineteenth century Chicago labor movement.* Berkeley: University of California Press.

Hollinger, D. A. (1996). *Postethnic America: Beyond multiculturalism.* New York: Basic Books.

Holt, M. I. (1992). *The orphan trains: Placing out in America.* Lincoln: University of Nebraska Press.

Honig, B. (2001). *Democracy and the foreigner.* Princeton, NJ: Princeton University Press.

Huntington, S. (2004). *Who are we: The challenges to America's national identity.* New York: Simon & Schuster.

Jentz, J. (1991, May). Class and politics in an emerging city: Chicago in the 1860s and 1870s. *Journal of Urban History, 17,* 227–263.

Jones, M. (2004, March–April). The new Yankees. *Mother Jones.*

Katznelson, I. (1981). *City trenches: Urban politics and the patterning of class in the United States.* New York: Pantheon Books.

Kristiva, J. (1991). *Strangers to ourselves.* New York: Columbia University Press.

Kymlicka, W. (1996). *Multicultural citizenship: A liberal theory of minority rights.* New York: Oxford University Press.

Lee, E. (2003). *At America's gates: Chinese immigration during the exclusion era, 1882–1943.* Chapel Hill: University of North Carolina Press.

Mouffe, C. (1993). *The return of the political.* London: Verso.

Murphy, P. (1979). *World War I and the origins of civil liberties in the United States.* New York: W.W. Norton.

Nelli, H. (1970). *Italians in Chicago, 1880–1930: A study in ethnic mobility.* New York: Oxford University Press.

O'Connor, S. (2001). Orphan trains: The story of Charles Loring Brace and the children he saved. New York: Houghton Mifflin.

Okin, S. M., Cohen, J., Howard, M., & Nussbaum, M. C. (1999). *Is multiculturalism bad for women?* Princeton, NJ: Princeton University Press.

Ordove, N. (2003). *American eugenics: Race, queer anatomy, and the science of nationalism.* Minneapolis: University of Minnesota Press.

Pernick, M. (1996). *The black stork: Eugenics and the death of "defective" babies in American medicine and motion pictures since 1915.* New York: Oxford University Press.

Ravitch, D. (2003). *The language police: How pressure groups restrict what students learn.* New York: Alfred A. Knopf.

Rosaldo, R. (1993). *Truth and culture: The remaking of social analysis.* Boston: Beacon Press.

Rosen, C. (2004). *Preaching eugenics: Religious leaders and the American eugenics movement.* New York: Oxford University Press.

Schlesinger, A. M. (1998). *The disuniting of America: Reflections on a multicultural society* (rev. ed.). New York: W.W. Norton.

Selden, S. (1999). *Inheriting shame: The story of eugenics and racism in America.* New York: Teachers College Press.

Stern, A. M. (1999, February). Buildings, boundaries, and blood: Medicalization and nation-building on the U.S.-Mexico border, 1910–1930. *Hispanic American Historical Review, 79*(1), 41–81.

Taylor, C. (1994). *Multiculturalism: Examining the politics of recognition.* Princeton, NJ: Princeton University Press.

Torres, C. A. (1998). *Democracy, education, and multiculturalism: Dilemmas of citizenship in a global world.* London: Rowman & Littlefield.

Torres, R., & Vazquez, F. (2002). *Latino/a thought: Culture, politics, and society.* London: Rowman & Littlefield.

Tuttle, Jr., W. M. (1993). *Daddy's gone to war: The second world war in the lives of America's children.* New York: Oxford University Press.

Wood, P. (2002). *Diversity: The invention of a concept.* New York: Encounter Books.

Young, I. M. (2000). Structure, difference, and Hispanic/Latino claims of justice. In J. Gracia & P. De Greiff (Eds.), *Hispanics/Latinos in the United States* (pp. 147–166). New York: Routledge.

Zaibert, L., & Millan-Zaibert, E. (2000). Universalism, particularism, and group rights: The case of Hispanics. In J. Gracia & P. De Greiff (Eds.), *Hispanics/Latinos in the United States* (pp. 167–180). New York: Routledge.

PART IV

ACCESS TO HEALTH AND SOCIAL SERVICES IN A DIVERSE SOCIETY

CHAPTER 11

DIVERSITY OR DISPARITY
IN HEALTH SERVICES

Edward F. Lawlor

INTRODUCTION

A national research, policy, and program effort is underway to reduce racial and ethnic health disparities. This effort was stimulated in large part by a series of influential Institute of Medicine (IOM) reports, the commitment thereto of the Secretary of the Department of Health and Human Services (HHS) and the Surgeon General, and the embrace of this national priority by the president (Institute of Medicine, 2001; Smedley, Stith, & Nelson, 2002). Explicit legislation, such as the Minority Health and Health Disparities Research and Education Act of 2000, focuses data, research, resources, and service development on racial and ethnic disparities in health. The federal government has implemented programmatic initiatives to address health disparities for cancer, diabetes, HIV/AIDS, and infant mortality. Within HHS, this initiative is centered in the Office of Minority Health, but is carried out through the individual institutes and agencies (the Agency for Health Care Quality, the Centers for Disease Control and Prevention, the National Cancer Institute, the Centers for Medicare & Medicaid Services, and others). Numerous programs, offices, and dedicated funding streams reinforce the emphasis on reducing racial and ethnic disparities in particular disease categories and services.

Various health care foundations, including the Robert Wood Johnson Foundation, the Commonwealth Foundation, and the Missouri Foundation for Health, have made health disparities a central priority for grants and programs. Indeed, racial and ethnic health disparities have become a major axis of research and health policy development, and now often are the basis on which data and evidence are presented, categorical programs are structured, and performance of the system is evaluated.

Disparities of all types in health care have been extensively documented in the literature; one might conclude that an entire public health and academic industry has grown up around the exercise of measuring, reporting, and understanding the etiology of various health and health care disparities. A short list of documented, significant racial and ethnic disparities related to health includes heart disease, numerous cancer sites, adverse birth outcomes (for example, low birth weight and infant mortality), communicable and sexually transmitted diseases (including West Nile virus), injuries (for example, bicycle accidents), rates and consequences of violence, alcohol and substance abuse, asthma and respiratory conditions, mental illness (for example, schizophrenia), and arthritis. These, as well as others, all involve differences in access to, utilization of, and quality of health services.

The most visible and manifest reported disparities are in the domain of health outcomes, particularly racial differences in mortality and life expectancy. The twofold difference between black and white infant mortality rates, for example, has been the subject of enormous investigation, commentary, and public health intervention. What makes this and other disparities so compelling is that they have stubbornly persisted, despite more than two decades of local, state, and federal resource commitment. Most troubling is the persistence of the racial disparity in mortality rates of African American males: The black–white gap has not changed since 1960 and has actually widened for men aged 35 years and over. Satcher and colleagues estimated that the gap between white and African American mortality rates overall accounts for 83,000 excess deaths per year (Satcher et al., 2005).

Life expectancy differences by race and ethnicity illustrate disparity in its most dramatic form. Life expectancy for the American Indian/Alaskan Native population, for example, is six years below that of the U.S. population as a whole. Infant mortality for the American Indian/Alaskan Native population is the second highest among all racial and ethnic groups. Deaths of children and youths stand at twice the national rate, and the suicide rate for youths 14 to 24 years of age is also twice the national rate. Death rates from injuries are especially high: In this population, the mortality rate for children from motor vehicle-related causes is four times the national rate. Almost one-quarter of American Indian and Alaskan Native men die before the age of 34. The five leading causes of death in this population are heart disease, cancer, accidents and unintentional injuries, diabetes, and cerebrovascular disease.

Even when observed rates of disease do not on their face suggest overt racial and ethnic disparities, more subtle underlying etiology reveals complicated patterns of disadvantage and inequity. Breast cancer, for example, exhibits higher base prevalence for white women, but higher mortality and later stage of diagnosis for African American women. More is being learned about the genetic bases of breast cancer, and the newest research suggests that African American women are more likely to have a genetic predisposition toward more aggressive forms of the disease. Thus, the evidence of later stage of diagnosis entails a third tier of research and concern about disparities: the wide differentials in insurance coverage, access to care, and quality of care.

One of the ironies of the current policy environment is that concern about and attention to racial and ethnic health disparities are being heightened at precisely the same time that the most important existing policy instruments for handling the problems are being dismantled. Erosion of Medicaid and state child health insurance programs (SCHIP) covering low-income beneficiaries, especially children, is one of the most significant threats to progress in addressing disparities in access to medical services. Consider the rates of Medicaid eligibility in one St. Louis zip code: More than half of the community is eligible for Medicaid coverage. Nevertheless, a Missouri budget proposal would eliminate 90,000 eligible beneficiaries from the program, as well as whole categories of coverage. Such legislation is potentially as significant a negative in the cause of redressing racial and ethnic disparities as elimination of any program that happens to carry a label of "minority health."

Missouri's proposed reduction of medical coverage underscores how policies that are not racially motivated nonetheless disproportionately affect diverse racial and ethnic groups, and can translate into greater health disparities. In an increasingly diverse society, traditional conceptualizations of racial and economic disparities lose explanatory power and policy impact when removed from the context of the communities in which those disparities arise. The intricate way in which social and economic determinants interact with race and ethnicity at the community level often render simple categories of race, ethnicity, and illness a poor basis for targeting interventions.

This chapter advances a "nondisparities" approach to understanding and addressing health disparities. The first part of the chapter discusses various social, behavioral, and theoretical underpinnings for an understanding of observed health disparities. The analytic and programmatic limitations of the racial and ethnic disparities paradigm are further highlighted through an examination of heart disease, the leading cause of death for all racial groups and the most costly diagnosis in the health care system. Although current approaches to health disparities lead to disease- and group-specific interventions, the alternate approach envisioned here proposes a community- or place-specific approach in which a constellation of health and social conditions is addressed within a particular geographic context. This chapter argues that organizing research, policymaking, and intervention by place, without initial disease or group focus, could stimulate more innovative approaches to addressing the underlying conditions and health behavior that ultimately give rise to disparities.

THEORY AND FRAMEWORKS FOR UNDERSTANDING DISPARITIES

Although disparities and their reduction has become almost a mantra of health services policy, the term "disparity" itself is subject to varying definitions and interpretations. The 2010 goals set by the Centers for Disease Control and Prevention (CDC) treat all differences in health status as evidence of disparities. The National Academy of Sciences report (Smedley et al., 2002) defined disparities in more analytic terms, as differences that remained after patients' preferences and needs were taken into account. For epidemiologists and health services researchers, disparities are a more complicated construct: the product of individual characteristics, behaviors, choices, social and economic circumstances, the environment, and the health system.

The pioneering framework for understanding variations in health services use was developed by Ronald Andersen at the University of Chicago in a series of studies beginning in the late 1960s (Andersen, 1968, 1995). Andersen's so-called behavioral model attributed inequities in health services use to predisposing, enabling, and need factors. This framework has provided the basis for a long line of empirical studies of access to and use of health care, including studies that have attempted to isolate the particular contribution of race and ethnicity after controlling for other relevant factors. The central insight of this work is that not all disparities represent inequities; in the parlance of this paper, some disparities do indeed represent diversity in health services demand, whereas some represent more problematic shortfalls or barriers to appropriate care and outcomes.

The literature on measurement and determinants of health disparities now recognizes a complex mix of biological, social, economic, medical, and environmental determinants—and the underlying epidemiology and social science reflected in the literature has become much more sophisticated in recent years. In addition to better understanding of this broad array of influences (in effect, a cocktail of determinants for almost any health outcome), there is also recognition that these influences accumulate over the life course of an individual. Health status also reflects fundamental historical influences, such as patterns of immigration, even at the neighborhood level. As communities and the United States become more multicultural—an important theme of this book—the simple prism of racial and ethnic disparities with regard to particular health conditions will become less analytically meaningful. It is well known, for example, that the health status of and challenges for new immigrants are profoundly different from those of their second- or third-generation counterparts, even when they all live in the same community and are categorized by the same nominal ethnicity.

Andersen's framework was enormously useful for conceptualizing and standardizing empirical studies of health care utilization. It did not, however, provide a strong theoretical foundation for understanding the sources of this variation. Several other bodies of social science, briefly touched on here, provide additional behavioral and theoretical underpinnings for understanding the sources of observable racial and ethnic differences.

Rational Choice
Although not well recognized or accepted in much of the public health literature, a powerful body of economic theory and evidence provides a partial explanation of observed differences in health status, use of services, and outcomes across population groups, including ethnic minority population groups. A set of insights about health behavior comes out of the work of Michael Grossman and others, who formulated a model of the "production" of health, largely based on the human capital tradition (Grossman, 1972). In this model, individuals and others invest in health, expecting a positive rate of return as a result of increased health-related human capital. This model considers

medicine, and a variety of other factors, to be an input into health. An important implication of this work is that returns to medical and other investments in improving the "stock" of health in any individual are powerfully conditioned by educational status and other characteristics.

Genetics and Immutable Factors

Although Andersen recognized the importance of predisposing factors in health status and outcomes, the significance of genetic predispositions was not fully appreciated before advances made in the human genome project. Even now, the connections of genetic factors, their interactions with environment and treatment, and race and ethnicity are only beginning to be understood. In diseases such as breast cancer, the interactions are believed to be powerful, but are only weakly comprehended. As the power of genetic information and knowledge of environmental and genetic interactions advance, a new armamentarium of treatments and approaches will undoubtedly follow.

Health Behavior

A broad theoretical and empirical literature traces differences in motivations, interpretation, and cognitive processing of risks. The traditional health belief model asserts that a person's health-related behavior depends on the person's perception of the severity of a potential illness, the person's susceptibility to that illness, the benefits of taking a preventative action, and the barriers to taking that action. A critical element of this theory is the idea that assessment of self-efficacy, or a person's confidence in his or her ability to successfully perform an action, is a key motivator for changes in behavior. A large body of related social science theory—including social learning theory, the theory of reasoned action, and social cognition—has been put forward to explain behaviorally the differences in health, as well as the likely efficacy of particular public health or medical interventions.

Socioeconomic Status and Social Class

The significance of class in explanations of disparities has been recognized and argued largely by European observers of U.S. health disparities. Clearly, all of the factors of socioeconomic status and social class—education, income and wealth, and related access to material resources—have powerful independent effects on health and interact in significant ways with race and ethnicity. Certain health outcomes, such as deaths due to violence, have overwhelming and tight relationships to education and community social and economic status. Certain health behaviors, such as nutrition and exercise, have strong socioeconomic gradients.

Although virtually no analyst of health disparities would dispute the underlying significance of race and ethnicity in health disparities, there is some controversy about the relative magnitudes and causal linkages in this web of relationships. For example,

Kawachi and colleagues (2005) argued, in effect, that race in the United States begets class standing (access to education, jobs, etc.) in the scheme of social stratification, and it is largely the consequences of this class standing that produce such large disparities in health outcomes (Kawachi, Daniels, & Robinson). These researchers believe that the systematic avoidance of class (including the lack of data collection and analysis by key socioeconomic variables) leads to a misunderstanding of the codeterminants of race and class in generating health outcomes, and, more importantly, leads to an ideological and political construction that effectively leaves key stakeholders out of the project to address health disparities.

Culture and Immigration

As other chapters in this book discuss, immigration and resettlement of diverse populations are having dramatic effects on the social and cultural makeup of the United States. These effects are even more pronounced in certain destinations such as Florida, Texas, and southern California. In health care, the implications for epidemiology, health status, and health services are only dimly appreciated at this point (Betancourt, Green, & Carrillo, 2002; Brach & Fraser, 2000). Discussions of health policy and service delivery have yet to take into account the within-group diversity of ethnic groups, much less nuances such as an individual's degree of acculturation or assimilation. Policy and practice are still relatively unsophisticated with respect to culture, with little customization in approach made according to knowledge, beliefs, and practices. These differences can profoundly affect the utilization of health care services, including (among others) prenatal care and screening tests for conditions and behaviors that can affect pregnancy outcomes.

The primary response to awareness of diversity has been the federal initiative to create more "culturally competent services," namely, the program for Culturally and Linguistically Appropriate Standards (CLAS) for health provider settings. In practice, this has meant initiatives (some of which are implemented and enforced) to promote publication and translation of materials to overcome language barriers in hospitals and clinics.

Discrimination

The pathways by which discrimination affects health outcomes include residential segregation and concentration; income, wealth, and access to health resources; and the potential biosocial and psychosocial consequences of stress and other byproducts of discrimination. Williams has argued, for example, that the profound and long-term consequences of racial discrimination and residential segregation warrant a massive economic investment in infrastructure, economic development, and social supports; this would yield important byproducts in improved health, but its underlying motivation would be reparation for past injustice (Williams & Collins, 2004).

Community, Environment, and Social Environment

The relationship of the surrounding social ecology and physical environment to variations in health status has been a long-standing preoccupation of those in the public health field. It is well understood that many racial and ethnic variations arise from or are strongly influenced by determinants in the social environment. Rates of asthma in children, for example, are strongly influenced by housing conditions and environmental exposure. The highest prevalence of active asthma is among Puerto Rican children. Poor interior air quality (for example, high levels of dust and particulates) and bad exterior air quality (for example, high levels of emissions from chemical sources, pesticides, and automobiles) are known to trigger increased incidence of acute asthma. These sources map to higher rates for groups that are exposed, a measurement that has its own racial, ethnic, and socioeconomic gradient. The environments of many public housing projects, for example, have long been known to expose children to many of the factors—both interior and exterior—associated with elevated rates of asthma.

Access and Insurance Coverage

To the degree that access to medical resources influences health status, significant differences in health insurance coverage, reimbursement, and the consequent access to providers (such as doctors, hospitals, allied health professionals) and supplies (such as prescription drugs and durable medical equipment) get reproduced along racial and ethnic lines. In the Hispanic population, for example, 34.3 percent lack insurance. It is not surprising that this lack of coverage has been shown to be the most cogent explanation for the number of Hispanics who lack a regular source of care (consistently about 30 percent across studies) (Lillie-Blanton & Hoffman, 2005).

Supply

Increasing awareness of variations in health resources and their quality (even when holding insurance coverage constant) is one of the great contributions of the modern health services literature. The best illustrations come from services available to Medicare beneficiaries, where in theory there is some standardization (and relative generosity) in coverage and payment policy. Still, Wennberg's work has demonstrated fourfold differences in availability of hospital beds, physician supply, and other health resources by geographical area (Wennberg & Gittelsohn, 1973). In important ways, these supply-side differences map to observed differences in use among racial and ethnic groups, even in the Medicare population where presumably some of the coverage inequities have been leveled (Baicker, Amitabh, Skinner, & Wennberg, 2004).

Quality

Understanding of quality differences in medical and health services, and their ultimate effect on health status, is a less developed area of health services research. Some of the indicators of lower quality are indirect. African Americans, for example, have lower rates of availability of numerous forms of health services believed to be clinically effective: mammograms, immunizations, prenatal care, diabetic screening, inpatient specialty and intensive care, cardiovascular procedures, kidney and bone marrow transplants, drug therapies for HIV, antidepressants, orthopedic procedures, and aggressive treatment for prostate cancer, to name just a few of the disparities.[1]

It is useful to bundle together these various strands of biological science, social science, and public health and ask how well the race/ethnicity paradigm works for understanding, and more important, intervening in, observed health disparities. The next section examines disparities in the case of heart disease.

THE CASE OF HEART DISEASE

A useful case example for understanding the complexities of the racial and ethnic disparities "paradigm" is deaths resulting from heart disease in various racial/ethnic/geographic communities. Heart disease is worth examining because it is the leading cause of death for all racial and ethnic groups, and is the most costly diagnosis in the health system. It also illustrates prototypical racial differences, as well as historical deviations for black people and white people. Death rates for black people are roughly 30 percent higher than for white people, although as recently as 1960 they were equivalent. Over recent history, death rates for white people have dropped precipitously—more than half since 1960—but this progress has not been proportionately shared by African Americans over this period.

This story is also not uniform by race: Studies of coronary heart disease in Appalachia, for example, have demonstrated trends and levels of heart disease among white men in contrast to the usual differentials, highlighting the importance of geographical, economic, and possibly occupational factors in these outcomes ("Coronary Heart Disease," 1998). The levels and variations in heart disease have sources in genetic predisposition; behaviors; environmental and occupational factors such as stress, social class, and economic class; and access and quality of medical care, in addition to other factors.

More important, differences in death rates due to heart disease vary tremendously from place to place, and within and across racial and ethnic groups. Figure 11-1 provides age-adjusted rates per 100,000 population of deaths resulting from cardiovascular disease for American Indians in a rural and impoverished county in South Dakota; African Americans in the city of St. Louis; Hispanics in Miami-Dade County; and white people in rural Missouri. These populations and place combinations were not selected because they were statistical anomalies, but because they reflect urban, rural, and wealth variations within and across racial and ethnic groups.

The other fallacy in simply looking at differences in heart disease rates is that the underlying etiology of heart disease is interrelated with numerous other diseases and conditions that also affect health status, social functioning, medical costs, and mortal-

FIGURE 11-1. HEART DISEASE MORTALITY BY RACE, ETHNICITY, PLACE

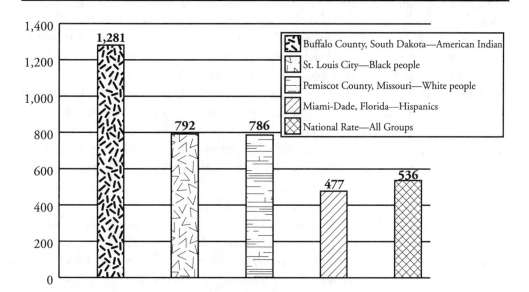

ity. Diet and nutrition, smoking, excessive alcohol use, exercise, stress, and adequate medical care (such as management of cholesterol and hypertension) are all implicated in a variety of other conditions ranging from stroke and cerebrovascular conditions to certain cancers. The social side of health status is also in the background of observed rates and differences in mortality for heart disease: new and interesting evidence has been published on the role of social networks, social and emotional support, and marital status in onset and survival of cardiovascular disease (reviewed in Berkman & Glass, 2000).

High death rates from heart disease, as with many major health conditions that account for significant mortality and morbidity, have no single explanation running through race or ethnicity, yet there is clearly a complex web of factors that interact with race, ethnicity, and culture. From a policy and interventions perspective, the idea is to use high rates of heart disease as one of several related targets for improvement, and to use the investigation of underlying etiology in a community context as the framework for understanding the roles of race, ethnicity, and other factors.

THE PITFALLS OF DISPARITY-BASED POLICY
The emphasis on racial and ethnic disparities as the entry point for addressing disturbing variations in health care access, health status, and health outcomes has much to commend it. The history and sociology of racial and ethnic discrimination and inequities undoubtedly have their counterparts and sequelae in health status and utilization of

health services. Just as redlining has had long-term consequences for access to housing, integration, and equity, so too do profound differences in insurance coverage, resource allocation to health services, and quality of care have long legacies (Oliver & Shapiro, 1995). One can think of the elimination of health disparities as one of the most significant remaining projects of civil rights and human rights redress in the United States. David Barton Smith, for example, argued that after the early gains from Medicare implementation and civil rights enforcement in the middle to late 1960s, a lack of accountability, enforcement, and political will meant that health services equity was never achieved. "The federal effort failed in a full degree of integration and accountability. These more demanding tasks met more resistance as the civil rights groundswell subsided after 1966. They remain the key parts of the unfinished federal civil rights agenda" (Smith, 2005, p. 323).

Second, the case for eliminating racial disparities is broadly understandable and politically compelling. Presentations of the black–white differentials in infant mortality, or rates of certain cancers, are understandable by the public at large, and serve as a call to arms by political and executive leadership. The diversity agenda is embraced by leaders as ideologically diverse as William Frist and Edward Kennedy, with Frist asserting, for example, that "I, and many other health professionals, find the disparities in U.S. health care unacceptable. They are an affront to the U.S. promise of equal opportunity for all" (Frist, 2005, p. 445; Kennedy, 2005).

Along with this broad political acceptance have come approaches to disparity reduction that are incremental, often symbolic, and extremely modest in funding and resource commitments. Programs such as "Take a Loved One to the Doctor Day," celebrated as one of the government's initiatives to address disparities, fall far short of addressing the profound social, economic, and health circumstances that ultimately produce reduced life expectancy and high rates of disease and disability in our communities.

A NONDISPARITIES APPROACH TO HEALTH DISPARITIES

The biggest shortcoming of the racial and ethnic disparities approach to national health status and health services utilization differences is that it provides, at best, a weak basis for policy and program intervention. First, almost any condition or disease of concern has a complex underlying epidemiology, and a simple race- or ethnicity-based strategy is difficult to reconcile with the larger social and economic determinants that transcend race. The subtlety here is that most of these social and economic determinants interact in important ways with race and ethnicity; nevertheless, race or ethnicity often provides a poor basis for targeting the intervention.

In an increasingly diverse society—one of the principal focuses of this book—the traditional categories of racial and economic disparity are less meaningful analytically, politically, and programmatically. Increasingly, we need to think of context and intervention in multicultural terms, especially in urban areas. In St. Louis, for example, more than two-thirds of refugees settling in the city recently have been Bosnian; this creates specific new challenges of social support, community integration, and even health delivery in particular neighborhoods. Given the phenomenon of the diverse society, data, policy, and interventions will have to be increasingly cognizant of and sophisticated about access and cultural competence—qualities of health care delivery that are hard to address at abstract macro levels.

Second, the disparities approach, from its foundation in data collection to its reification in administrative offices and funding streams, advantages certain disease or health condition categories, and treats them for policy purposes in partial terms. The National Cancer Institute, for example, collects and presents cancer data by site, organizes research and interventions in gender/diagnosis/treatment profiles, and has little interaction with other initiatives that target closely related behaviors, health services, and social conditions. Health policy experts and health services researchers have long lamented this "body-part medicine," and it is no less apparent and problematic in the disparities agenda.

Third, in its conceptualization and implementation, the disparities agenda is largely a top-down, national and state organized agenda, as opposed to a bottom-up, community, place-based agenda. The accountability for the disparities approach agenda is instructive: Congress has mandated a National Healthcare Disparities Report, and versions of state-level disparities reports are proliferating (see, for example, Moy, Dayton, & Clancy, 2005; Trivedi, Gibbs, Nslah-Jefferson, Ayanlan, & Prothrow-Stith, 2005). This approach produces a kind of geographic aggregation bias: As a statistical matter, we miss key underlying statistical variation in small areas. It also masks crucial epidemiological insights about the key social and environmental mechanisms that generate the disparities in the first place. This is an epidemiological lesson that goes back to the identification of John Snow's pump as the source of cholera in London, but is still lost in the aggregate, top-down approach to disparities reduction in the national initiative.

Formulation of an alternative to this disparities agenda begins by flipping the exercise over and asking the general question of what health and social outcomes lead to premature mortality, morbidity, and limitations in social functioning in particular (small) geographical contexts. Further, we should ask this question not in medical, or even conventional public health, terms; that tack inevitably leads to ignoring behavioral, institutional, social, and environmental sources and strategies. Too often the standard disparities and medical paradigms lead to diagnoses of underlying etiology that are too proximate, and do not take into account the broader life course and ecological determinants that are the major sources of variation. Of course, this latter, alternate approach involves difficult, more fundamental questions of social structure, poverty, and discrimination, but it also offers the potential for developing systematic strategies that could make observable difference in outcomes over the long term, and with disproportionate benefit to racial and ethnic minorities.

What would the elements of such a strategy look like?

Detailed, micro targeting of neighborhoods and rural areas, and development of place-based strategies for intervention. Instead of targeting particular categories of disease or mortality, the goal would be to conduct detailed and robust analyses of the social and health status of defined geographical areas. We now have tremendous research and sophisticated analytic capabilities for conducting this type of analysis, but precious few empirical examples in practice.[2] Ironically, many of the data exist for this initial diagnostic exercise, but they are rarely presented and studied intensively at this level or for this unit of analysis. There is a long tradition of cities, municipalities, county and state health departments, associations, and research organizations presenting epidemiological and social data by condition (for example, asthma rates, elevated lead levels, and so forth.), but rarely is there a comprehensive, targeted, and community-level workup of a particular neighborhood or rural county that cuts across social, health behavior, environmental, and service categories and goes into great analytic depth.

Every community will present different profiles of behavior, socioeconomic status, social networks and organization, health resources, and health outcomes (Williams, Neighbors, & Jackson, 2003). In terms of resource allocation, it might only be feasible and efficient to target the urban and rural areas with the highest levels of excess mortality (or other broad indicators) as candidates for intensive community strategy. For example, Table 11-1 illustrates a broad spectrum of data for one zip code in St. Louis, representing a place with about 11,000 residents and regarded as an area, it is safe to say, that demonstrates large health disparities. Virtually all of these social indicators are significantly higher than citywide rates, and they are often multiples of national rates. The health outcomes are situated in a context of dramatic economic and social change, including a depopulation rate of 30 percent during the 1990s.

This collection of data reveals how complex and interconnected the poor health status and outcomes at the community level are, beginning with an average life expectancy of only 65 years. The physical environment is characterized by poor housing stock (with high lead levels) and large numbers of vacant parcels, created by the rapid depopulation of this area. The social environment is characterized by high rates of poverty, unemployment, and crime. Rates of teenage pregnancy and births to mothers who do not have a high school education are high. Numerous health outcomes are disturbing: rates of heart disease, diabetes, and cancer, to name a few. Rates of hospitalization and avoidable hospitalizations are high. From a health policy perspective, the penetration of Medicaid coverage is both striking (51 percent overall and 80 percent of all births) and potentially important if new forms of capturing health financing for community health are to be considered (see discussion later in this chapter).

If one accepts the idea that place is a worthy organizing principle for understanding and addressing health disparities, it begs the question of what definition of boundaries and community make sense as a unit of analysis and action. The issues of community

TABLE 11-1. SOCIAL AND HEALTH INDICATORS FOR A NORTH ST. LOUIS NEIGHBORHOOD

Indicator	63106 Zip Code	St. Louis City	National
% population change 1990–2000	–30.4	–12.2	13.2
% young children (<5)	10.7	6.7	6.8
% older persons (>65)	13.0	13.7	12.4
Fertility rate per thousand	96.2	65.3	56.3
% African American	94.8	51.2	12.2
Average household income	$18,615	$37,455	$56,675
% below poverty	52.7	24.3	12.4
% female-headed household	41.6	12.8	7.0
% with high school diploma/GED	55.1	71.5	81.1
Unemployment rate	25.1	11.0	5.8
Crimes against persons per 1,000	40.0	NA	NA
Vacant lots per square mile	1,010	NA	NA
Hospital admission rates per 1,000	237.3	136.8	116.3
Avoidable hospitalizations per 1,000	36.1	27.2	NA
ER visits per 1,000	739	445.8	394
% eligible for Medicaid	51.4	24.2	NA
% without prenatal care, first trimester	23.8	18.3	16.3
% low birth weight (<5.5 lbs.)	12.4	11.6	7.6
Infant mortality per 1,000	13.8	12.8	7.0
% out-of-wedlock births	91.5	66.1	34.0
Teen abortions per 1,000 live births	346.9	188.5	NA
% births to Medicaid insured	80.0	59.3	NA
% birth mothers smoke	16.1	15.8	12.1
% birth mothers without high school	40.1	32.0	21.4
HIV rates per 100,000 population	34.1	34.8	9.1
% syphilis	37.2	7.4	2.2
% lead poisoning rates	28.9	31.1	2.2
Asthma admissions per 1,000	8.3	NA	NA
Foodborne illness rate per 100,000 population	69.5	46.6	NA
Nonmotor accident mortality per 100,000 population	42.2	38.1	18.3
Homicide rates per 100,000 population	45.6	31.5	5.9
Suicide rates per 1000,000 population	15.5	12.6	10.4
Overall mortality rates per 100,000 population	1,440.5	1,175.7	863
Heart disease mortality per 100,000 population	438.4	375	258.9
Cancer mortality per 100,000 population	263.2	239.1	198.6
Cardiovascular mortality per 100,000 population	100.5	75.4	60.4
COPD mortality per 100,000 population	56.6	43.7	44.4
Diabetes mortality per 100,000 population	57.9	40.8	24.8
Life expectancy (in years)	65.4	71.4	76.9

definition and conception are much deeper than can be addressed here, but the short answer is that some combination of administrative geography, political and cultural consideration, and health care market realities would have to drive the decision; no solution will be completely perfect.

Relentless focus on etiology and multiple social determinants of health outcomes. At this micro geographical level, the goal would be to understand how particular circumstances or health behaviors generate long-term health outcomes. Nationally, we are beginning to grapple with the relationship of diet, exercise, obesity, diabetes, and heart disease. Obviously, successful interventions will require policy and program reach-down into early childhood, engagement of families and schools, cultural competence and savvy, and potentially new forms of public education and regulation.

At the community level, a complete accounting would clarify the relative risks of diet, stress, tobacco use, medical care, occupational exposure, and the like; not only risks of heart disease, but also risks for a whole host of other related conditions and sources, such as diabetes and stroke. A complete accounting would generate enormous variation in the primary threats and feasible interventions from place to place; lead exposure, respiratory ailments, child abuse or neglect, cancer, and other conditions would have very different relative weights from community to community, and from rural area to rural area. This kind of diagnostic effort at the community level could lead to innovative and productive efforts to address the social ecology of health status, such as renewed attention to marketing of tobacco and alcohol at the community level, or intensive efforts to address the availability and quality of food in low-income neighborhoods (Morland, Wing, & Diez Roux, 2002; Morland, Wing, Roux, & Poole, 2002).

Capitalization on community resources, networks, and institutions. The lessons from modern sociology and community development about the potential efficacy of community mobilization and resources are significant, yet they have only sporadically been translated into organized community interventions for health improvement (see James, Schulz, & van Olphen, 2001). Some of the REACH 2010 models have this character, but they are typically organized around a narrow disease entity and connect to only a limited set of community institutions or community-based organizations. A progressive community-based strategy would identify and engage primary institutions, such as schools and churches, as well as tackle broader conditions such as housing and safety. It would lend itself to a life-course (and even multigenerational) approach, as opposed to a cross-sectional approach (Smith, 2003). For example, it is hard to systematically address the causes and consequences of elevated lead levels in communities without a schools-and-housing arm to the effort; nevertheless, a lead abatement program operates in many cities as its own discrete regulatory and enforcement enterprise.

Innovation in financing, governance, institutions, and organization of health services at the community level. The extraordinary fragmentation of health care financing, much less broader public health and social service financing, militates against intensive community-based strategies that would ultimately address disparities. Flows of health dollars are divided among categorical grant and contract programs in public health agencies (for example, STD versus HIV funding streams); hospital, physician, and outpatient reimbursement in Medicaid and Medicare; and safety net providers who receive a complex bundle of federal, state, county, and other funding. No mechanisms exist to pool, tax, or direct these flows systematically toward conditions or strategies of high need/high impact. Virtually no governance exists in urban areas or rural regions with the overall authority and command over resources to invest significantly in community-based strategies. It is hard to imagine significant progress in addressing disparities in places without reform—or at least demonstration of reform—in financing arrangements.

What would be needed is the creation of new forms of health financing districts, analogous to the districts that have been created for many other collective purposes (water, safety, community economic development, transportation, etc.), with significant investment capital. This kind of municipal reform is a daunting political undertaking, but without this scale, focus of funding, and governance, significant community-level improvements in overall health status are unlikely. The private analogy is to the kind of focus and innovation underlying the early prepaid health models, in which the incentives and resources for systemic and preventative health investments fundamentally shifted.

Historically, innovations in financing, from regional all-payer systems to the bundling of Medicaid and other public sources, have been used to fund particular regional or programmatic initiatives directed at access and community health. Currently, the ramping-up of safety net providers is cast as a place-based approach to basic and primary health care services. No examples exist, however, that bundle substantial categorical public health dollars, Medicaid provider resources, some uncompensated-care dollars from catchment-area hospitals, state or county assistance, Medicare reimbursement, and other sources to systematically address observed health challenges in a defined community.

CONCLUSIONS

The health disparities approach has been effective in changing the national consciousness about health outcomes for numerous racial and ethnic minority groups. The demonstration of order-of-magnitude differences for African Americans, American Indians/Alaskan Natives, Hispanics, and other groups provides both a serious critique of our current health and public health systems, and an indictment of our larger approach to social welfare and equality.

The disparities agenda has produced interesting and potentially effective interventions, some significant research funding, and new data collection, especially at the national and state levels. Programmatically, the disparities agenda has spawned some innovative models, such as some of the REACH 2010 projects, but in other respects it has reified the traditional ways of conceptualizing and tackling deep problems of health status and utilization of services.

A recommended alternative is the design and implementation of an approach to research, policy, and programs that is both bounded by geography and informed by the specific epidemiology, culture, behavior, social ecology, and community resources and institutions at play in that geographic area. Organizing the approach to disparities by place, without an initial disease focus, could stimulate more innovative approaches to addressing the underlying conditions and health behavior that eventually give rise to disparities. Imagine an alternative to REACH 2010—actually more like the son or daughter of REACH 2010—that creates a health developmental district, defined simply by the overall poor health and social outcomes of a place, and that creates a long-term strategy for addressing the interconnected social and behavioral determinants of those outcomes. The district initiative would: tackle multiple and interconnected health conditions; work on building such dimensions of community health as social capital, collective efficacy, and social networks; customize the approach to the social, cultural, and environmental circumstances of the community; and marshal public and private resources and institutions on a scale and with sufficient flexibility to make meaningful inroads into health outcomes.

The underlying etiology, behavioral explanations, and social and environmental determinants of health outcomes are extraordinarily complex, and require much more substantial investment than any of the current approaches now supplies. Current approaches envision tackling these disparities one disease or one racial/ethnic group at a time. A recommended alternative is intensive intervention and management of the constellation of health and social conditions that map to disparities—one community at a time. Such an alternative approach might, for example, target improving life expectancy beyond age 65 in areas such as North St. Louis City, and include all of the underlying work that would have to be done on the social and health determinants of that outcome. This requires a scale of investment and commitment to policy and program that is outside the scope of current thinking about health disparities. To change our approach and effectiveness, perhaps we must first change our thinking.

END NOTES

1. An extended accounting of the evidence is contained in Fiscella, Franks, Gold, & Clancy, 2000.
2. For an excellent overview of methods and issues in neighborhood health assessment, see Kawachi & Berkman, 2003.

REFERENCES

Andersen, R. M. (1968). *A behavioral model of families' use of health services.* Chicago: University of Chicago, Center for Health Administration Studies.

Andersen, R. M. (1995). Revisiting the behavioral model and access to health care: Does it matter? *Journal of Health and Social Behavior, 36,* 1–10.

Baicker, K., Amitabh, C., Skinner, J. & Wennberg, J. (2004). Who you are and where you live: How race and geography affect the treatment of Medicare beneficiaries [Electronic version]. *Health Affairs, 23*(variations suppl.), 33–44.

Berkman, L. F., & Glass, T. (2000). Social integration, social networks, social support, and health. In L. F. Berkman & I. Kawachi (Eds.), *Social epidemiology* (pp. 137–173). New York: Oxford University Press.

Betancourt, J. R., Green, A. R., & Carrillo, J. E. (2002). *Cultural competence in health care: Emerging frameworks and practical approaches.* New York: Commonwealth Fund.

Brach, C., & Fraser, I. (2000, November). Can cultural competency reduce racial and ethnic disparities? A review and conceptual model. *Medical Care Research and Review, 57,* 181–217.

Coronary heart disease mortality trends among whites and blacks: Appalachia and the United States, 1980–1993. (1998, November 27). *Mortality and Morbidity Weekly Report, 47,* 1005–1008, 1015.

Fiscella, K., Franks, P., Gold, M. R., & Clancy, C. M. (2000, May 17). Inequality in quality: Addressing socioeconomic, racial, and ethnic disparities in health care. *JAMA, 283,* 2579–2584.

Frist, W. H. (2005, March/April). Overcoming disparities in U.S. health care. *Health Affairs, 24,* 445–451.

Grossman, M. (1972). *The demand for health: A theoretical and empirical investigation.* New York: Columbia University Press.

Institute of Medicine. (2001). *Coverage matters: Insurance and health care.* Washington, DC: National Academies Press.

James, S. A., Schulz, A. J., & van Olphen, J. (2001). Social capital, poverty, and community health: An exploration of linkages. In S. Saegert, J. P. Thompson, & M. R. Warren (Eds.), *Social capital in poor communities* (pp. 165–188). New York: Russell Sage Foundation.

Kawachi, I., & Berkman, L. F. (Eds.). (2003). *Neighborhoods and health.* New York: Oxford University Press.

Kawachi, I., Daniels, N., & Robinson, D. (2005). Health disparities by race and class: Why both matter. *Health Affairs, 24,* 343–352.

Kennedy, E. M. (2005). The role of the federal government in eliminating health disparities. *Health Affairs, 24,* 452–458.

Lillie-Blanton, M., & Hoffman, C. (2005). The role of health insurance coverage in reducing racial/ethnic disparities in health care. *Health Affairs, 24,* 398–408.

Morland, K., Wing, S., & Diez Roux, A. (2002). The contextual effect of local food environment on residents' diets: The atherosclerosis risk in communities study. *American Journal of Public Health, 92,* 1761–1767.

Morland, K., Wing, S., Roux, A., & Poole, C. (2002). Neighborhood characteristics associated with the location of food stores and food service places. *American Journal of Preventative Medicine, 22,* 23–29.

Moy, E., Dayton, E., & Clancy, C. (2005, March/April). Compiling the evidence: The National Health Care Disparities Reports. Health Affairs, 24, 376–387.

Oliver, M., & Shapiro, T. (1995). *Black wealth/White wealth: A new perspective on racial inequality.* New York: Routledge.

Satcher, D., Fryer, G. E., Jr., McCann, J., Troutman, A., Woolf, S. H., Rust, G., et al. (2005). What if we were equal? A comparison of the black–white mortality gap in 1960 and 2000. *Health Affairs, 24,* 459–464.

Smedley, B. D., Stith, A.Y., & Nelson, A. R. (2002). *Unequal treatment: Confronting racial and ethnic disparities in health care.* Washington, DC: National Academies Press.

Smith, D. B. (2005). Racial and ethnic health disparities and the unfinished civil rights agenda. *Health Affairs, 24,* 323.

Smith, G. D. (Ed.) (2003). *Health inequalities: Lifecourse approaches.* Bristol, England: Policy Approaches.

Trivedi, A. N., Gibbs, B., Nslah-Jefferson, L., Ayanlan, J. Z., & Prothrow-Stith, D. (2005). Creating a minority health policy report card. *Health Affairs, 24,* 388–396.

Wennberg, J., & Gittelsohn, A. (1973). Small area variations in health care delivery. *Science, 182,* 1102–1108.

Williams, D. R., & Collins, C. (2004). Reparations: A viable strategy to address the enigma of African American health. *American Behavioral Scientist, 47,* 977–1000.

Williams, D. R., Neighbors, H. W., & Jackson, J. S. (2003). Racial/ethnic discrimination and health: Findings from community studies. *American Journal of Public Health, 93,* 200–208.

CHAPTER 12

SOCIAL WORK PRACTICE DIVERSITIES: CLIENTS, SOCIAL WORKERS, AND THEORIES ABOUT THEIR PARTNERSHIPS FOR CONSTRUCTIVE CHANGE*

Katherine Tyson McCrea

You, who gave me my first name, you,
Pawnee, Apache, Seneca, you
Cherokee Nation, who rested with me, then
Forced on bloody feet,
Left me to the employment of
Other seekers—desperate for gain,
Starving for gold.
You, the Turk, the Arab, the Swede,
The German, the Eskimo, the Scot,
The Italian, the Hungarian, the Pole,
You the Ashanti, the Yoruba, the Kru, bought
Sold, stolen, arriving on a nightmare
Praying for a dream.
Here, root yourselves beside me . . .
Lift up your faces, you have a piercing need
For this bright morning dawning for you.
History, despite its wrenching pain,
Cannot be unlived, but if faced
With courage, need not be lived again.
Lift up your eyes
Upon this day breaking for you.
Give birth again
To the dream.
—*Excerpted from Maya Angelou, "On the Pulse of the Morning" (1993)*
Reprinted with permission from Random House, Inc. ©1993

INTRODUCTION

Maya Angelou's eloquent poem "On the Pulse of the Morning" (1993) describes the historical injustices that continue to permeate contemporary United States society, and evokes the combination of suffering and hope that causes every client to seek out a social worker for care. Social services promise clients and their communities the possibility to "give birth again to the dream" of living lives of dignity and competence. Professor Cafferty has often said that because social work is applied, it is possible to rigorously study the link between theory and practice, potentially yielding both better theories and better practice. Cafferty and Chestang's (1976) landmark work identifies respect for diversity as the standard for the future if social work is to live up to its mission.

In the context of a society that is being transformed every day by the increasing diversity of its citizenry, this chapter focuses on a specific aspect of social services: the theoretical guidelines currently available for planning the partnerships that social workers and clients co-create. More specifically, this chapter considers the features of practice models that can help social workers enhance their clients' power and dignity, and make the client-worker partnership more responsive to an increasingly diverse client population confronted by continuing injustices.

DEFINITIONS

Culture and Diversity

With reference to social services, the term diversity most often means differences in culture, so we begin with a definition of culture derived from Cafferty and Chestang's (1976) seminal work: "Because it encompasses all human creations—tools, institutions, customs, beliefs, and so on—culture can be regarded as the sum total of man's external environment and his psychological predisposition toward that environment" (Chestang, 1976, p. 69). To speak about culture in this way presupposes in turn a viewpoint about people and the origins of a person's identity.

A moment's reflection reveals that an individual is part of many diverse communities (or reference groups, per Wimsatt, 1990–1991); among them are family; neighborhood; state and country of origin and residence; religious institution; place of employment; school; people of similar sexual orientation; people of similar health status; and peers in age, income, race, and cultural heritage. All these groups influence one's identity. Thus, one is never a solitary "I," but—as is recognized by many languages from Korean to Zulu—always a self in relation to some partner. In such a complex society, our identities themselves are diverse or many-layered. The values and responsibilities of one's partnerships may differ profoundly, because in some relationships one has more power than in others (McIntosh, 1988; Wyche, 2001). Fortunately, developments in social work codes of ethics set standards for how social workers handle the power they wield in relating with clients and each other (Mattison, 2000; Reamer, 1991; Strom-Gottfried, 2000).

202

Each person's interconnectedness with various groups has even more meaning in the light of contemporary human development research, which demonstrates the profound impact of relationships on human beings; even in utero, from the moment they become conscious, humans listen for the sounds of their parents' voices (Trevarthan & Aitken, 2001). For human beings, who will die if deprived of a respectful, loving caregiving partnership (Spitz, 1945), the quality of relationships is as important as food and water. Though many species help and care for each other and their young to some extent, humans have the most sustained period of dependency, caregiving responsibility, and ongoing interactive communication. Humans, who are hard-wired to focus on relational communication, have a greater variety of facial expressions than any other creature, and are the only species that has sexual intercourse—makes love—face-to-face. In the course of attaching meaning to their experiences and shaping patterns of relationships, humans create cultures that organize their interactions in ways that may be common across cultures (for example, all babies smile at their caregivers and all caregivers use baby talk, including deaf parents who baby-talk in sign language [Petitto & Marentette, 1991]), or unique to a specific culture (patterns of sleeping, diaper-changing, play, and so forth; Small, 1998).

Given the profound impact of relationships on identity, the term cultural also refers to the meanings of human relationships that represent, for any one individual, that person's most cherished experiences of intimacy, which in turn form the bedrock of identity (Aponte & Johnson, 2000; Wimsatt, 2002). Therefore, the challenge for any social worker seeking to care for someone from a different culture is not just to understand the language or customs of that culture, but to find a way to understand the entire worldview and experience of inner identity that constitute that person and her or his experiences of caring and being cared for.

Appreciating diversity includes recognizing diversities within a cultural group. As Ho, Rasheed, and Rasheed (2003) have pointed out, trying to identify character traits and values shared by members of social groups has the disadvantage of encouraging stereotyping (see also Kay & Jost, 2003; Lewontin, 2000). Avoiding stereotyping while recognizing similarities and differences between and among the multiple layers of socio-cultural groups requires analytic sophistication that social workers (and other social and behavioral scientists) are only beginning to develop (Lewontin, 2000). For example, in discussing the interaction between socioeconomic and multicultural status, LaFramboise and colleagues (1998) pointed out that "the role of minority group members' economic resources has been relatively unexplored in acculturation studies, prohibiting conclusions about the role of socioeconomic status in second-culture acquisition" (p. 130).

Considerations of diversity lead inevitably to considerations of equality and justice. Injustices can be understood as differences in access to resources, influence over and control of the policies that influence people, and the respect and honor accorded to one's personhood; injustices often are rooted in historically conditioned processes of exclusion based on differences in appearance, values, or access to resources. This state of social conflict (or oppression, in Freire's, 1970, terms) throws each member of an oppressed group into a struggle to maintain her or his survival, along with dignity and integrity in relation to that person's own culture and the dominant culture (Chestang, 1976). Maintenance of dignity and integrity may, all too often, come at the cost of an individual's physical well-being and even survival (Chestang). Nurturing human sustenance and dignity in the face of historical and present trauma is a primary task of contemporary social work practice in a context of diversity and injustice (Daly, Jennings, Beckett, & Leashore, 2000; Ho, Rasheed, & Rasheed, 2003).

Discussions of diversity also invariably include the topic of values. Typically the term "values" is used in at least two different ways, referring both to:

1. chosen standards used to guide one's choices (for example, the values of the social work profession), and

2. fundamental beliefs and traditions that are common within a cultural group. (For example, although white, Anglo-Saxon Protestant culture in the United States heavily values independence, a strong community orientation is a fundamental value of many diverse groups, including Asian, First Nations, Hispanic, and African American peoples.)

The value of advancing social justice is both appealing to most people and very difficult to actualize. Following Aquinas and Locke, one can speculate that humans have a natural sense of justice as being an equitable social order that can be discerned through the use of reason. In support of such a view, research demonstrates that the great apes also have notions of justice: baby chimpanzees can recognize when the distribution of banana rewards in their group is unfair. Humans also evaluate fairness and will even use their sense of justice to attenuate egocentric biases (Leung, Tong, & Ho, 2004).

When human communities are exclusionary, fear and anger result, creating destructive patterns of relating that distort community members' beliefs about justice and erode individuals' self-esteem (Kay & Jost, 2003). Although the consequences of injustice in communities vary considerably, social exclusion and marginalization clearly hamper the developmental processes of individuals, groups (Colquitt, 2004), and society as a whole. For example, the systematic disenfranchisement of African Americans by the criminal justice system negatively influences the lives of those outside the African American community, because it affects how all individuals experience their membership in the community of U.S. citizens; it also affects the ways in which tax dollars are spent (for example, large amounts to maintain prisons) and the outcomes of elections (when significant proportions of the population cannot vote), and hence legislation and judicial decision making. The toxic effects of social exclusion and marginalization can be seen in classrooms, which not only teach academic lessons, but also impart important lessons on citizenship. A child with cerebral palsy who is mainstreamed into a classroom that lacks adequate resources to care for her influences every child's experience of herself or himself as a citizen in society. The other children will be, at the least, sad and frightened for their classmate, and will wonder what help will be available for them if fate consigns them to a wheelchair.

The Caregiving Partnership

Any consideration of social services in the context of diversity rests on a definition of the key elements of social service. Social workers steeped in the tradition of Mary Richmond (Richmond, 1922), Charlotte Towle (Towle, 1936), and Helen Harris Perlman (1979) will not be surprised by findings from the past 30 years of social work practice, including both clinical social work and psychotherapy, consistently indicating that the most important variable in bringing about constructive client change is the quality of the client-worker relationship (Marziali, 1991). After interviewing, compiling, and reviewing data from the most effective social services all across the United States, the noted social program analyst Lisbeth Schorr (1997) concluded, "Successful programs operate in settings that encourage practitioners to build strong relationships based on mutual trust and respect . . . . It is the quality of these relationships that most profoundly differentiates effective from ineffective programs and institutions" (p. 10).

Accordingly, the focus here is on the relationships, called here caregiving partnerships, that exist between clients and social workers in the many modalities (individual, family, group) and contexts of social work today, including mental health, child welfare, medical social work, and school social work. Because social workers offer their clients a caregiving partnership in the context of community and national priorities and policies, a look at influential macro factors is an important foundation.

FACTORS INFLUENCING THE CAREGIVING PARTNERSHIP
Implications of the Global Community: Global Social Work Practice

Social work practice has changed profoundly in response to events that foster international interdependence. Some have been tragic, such as the Bhopal disaster at the Union Carbide plant in India and the al-Quaeda terrorists' destruction of the World Trade Center. Some have been joyous expressions of freedom, such as the fall of the Berlin Wall and the self-liberation of countries formerly under the yoke of the Soviet Union. Still other changes in the global community, such as the Internet, can serve either remediating or destructive purposes.

One complicating consequence of the rise of a global community is that, as citizens of the world, social workers in the United States are also involved in a wider set of communities. Although some communities in the United States are more impoverished than many in other developed countries (Sen, 1999a, 1999b), people in many countries believe that the opportunities afforded by U.S. civil society are an ideal toward which to strive. In a global context, the struggle for democracy becomes clearer—that is, democracy as defined by Jane Addams, who said that in a democracy every citizen has equal influence in shaping the policies that govern her or him (1990).

In the effort to work toward better democracies, social workers in a global community can learn from others who define social trauma and develop innovative services in radically different national contexts. For instance, some citizens in former Soviet-bloc countries became experts at identifying the effects of mind control and brainwashing. Social workers who understand these forms of group pathology are better equipped to help clients in groups where there is scapegoating or punishment for differences of appearance, behavior, resources, or belief (Walsh, 2001). Social workers in Kaunas, Lithuania, have developed a "Generation House" in which senior citizens live with single parents who have children; while the parents are at work, the senior citizens care for the children, creating the gift of an extended family where previously there was none. A powerful and universal human motive to bring about a society in which people can experience free minds and the capacity for self-determination becomes apparent when one considers the movements for freedom that have arisen despite massive and often murderous oppression, as in the former Soviet-bloc countries, South Africa under apartheid, or the United States under the Jim Crow laws (Schell, 2003).

Client Needs and Priorities within the United States
Within the borders of the United States, the massive wave of immigration that has occurred in the last 40 years has profoundly influenced both the country and the social sciences. Increasingly, a person is not of one culture, but multicultural; it is also more and more likely that a person is not a resident or citizen of one country only, but transnational (Baker, Bean, Latapi, & Weintraub, 1998). When dealing with transnational or multicultural clients, it is no longer feasible or desirable for social workers to conceptualize adaptation to U.S. society and culture as the primary goal, as would have been the case 40 years ago. Findings from cross-cultural analyses indicate that if social workers set a goal of assimilation to U.S. social values, they may actually do harm to their clients (Portes & Rumbaut, 2001). Many "discontents" are associated with assimilation, including, for examples, higher infant mortality and breast cancer mortality rates for Asian and Mexican immigrants.

Transnational comparisons also considerably temper overconfidence about the benefits of life in the United States. Though openness to immigrants in this country may be more salutary than in many European and Scandinavian countries, immigrants are also more exposed to violence in the United States, in comparison with other developed countries. Examples are the higher incidence of homicides in this country, compared to Japan, and the prevalence of practices associated with violence, such as the high rate of corporal punishment of children (Straus, 1991), compared with Scandinavian countries in which corporal punishment of children is illegal. The United States ranks alongside China and Iran as one of the four nations in the world with the highest number of executions of its citizens (Policy Almanac, 2006a). The higher rates of violence in the United States indicate that social services providers need to address the familial and societal causes of violence, and further mean that social workers are at risk of becoming victims of violence. Accordingly, a priority for the future is risk reduction for social workers and their clients (Dunkel, Ageson, & Ralph, 2000).

Many social work clients in the United States are subject to another form of violence—what Farmer (2003) called "structural violence," which occurs when socioeconomic stressors—ranging from exposure to environmental toxins to lack of adequate health care—aggravate poor clients' morbidity and mortality (Adler et al., 2002). The United States continues to have one of the highest infant mortality rates of any developed country. Although nearly all racial and ethnic groups in the United States showed improvement in infant mortality from 1995 to 2002, major disparities according to race and ethnicity still exist. For instance, in 2002, infant mortality rates ranged from 3.0 per 1,000 live births for Chinese American mothers to 13.8 for African American mothers (Centers for Disease Control and Prevention, 2004). Health care resources for children appear to have improved over the last 20 years: "Children now have better coverage and access to care than adults . . . , [so] addressing the health care problems of adults could be the next major challenge facing state and local policymakers" (Zuckerman, as cited in Brown & Leibovitz, 1999). Moreover, national figures mask extensive variation in uninsurance rates across states—which in turn are driven largely by differences in the extent of private coverage. Some states are likely to have a harder time closing their gaps in health care coverage than others. For instance, in Massachusetts, Michigan, Minnesota, and Wisconsin, only 5 percent to 6 percent of children are uninsured, whereas in Mississippi and Texas 19 percent to 21 percent of children are uninsured (Zuckerman, cited in Brown & Leibovitz, 1999). Inequalities in health care resources have profound implications; among them is that social workers encounter clients who are at risk of serious disability or death because they do not have adequate health care. Furthermore, many clients who can benefit from the care of social workers do not have the resources to obtain it.

Unfortunately, the past few decades have only increased the disparities between wealthy and impoverished people in the United States. Although welfare reform helped some escape the dependency of poverty, welfare-to-work programs have not yet brought about the long-term improvements in quality of life that many clients need (Anderson, Halter, & Gryzlak, 2004; Taylor & Barush, 2004). Even when they are no longer statistically registered as welfare recipients, social workers' clients can be "stuck at such low wages that their living standards are unchanged . . . . [T]hese are the forgotten Americans, who are noticed and counted as they leave welfare, but who disappear from the nation's radar as they struggle in their working lives" (Shipler, 2004, p. 4). The brutality of social inequalities in the United States is exacerbated by the fact that so many citizens could change the circumstances of their fellow citizens, but do not. As Shipler (2004) noted:

After all our economic achievements, the gap between rich and poor has only widened, with a median net worth of $833,600 among the top 10 percent and just $7,900 for the bottom 20 percent. Life expectancy in the United States is lower, and infant mortality higher, than in Japan, Hong Kong, Israel, Canada, and all the major nations of Western Europe. (p. 6)

A crucial consequence of poverty is that it erodes clients' freedom of choice. As Shipler (2004) pointed out:

The poor have less control than the affluent over their private decisions, less insulation from the cold machinery of government, less agility to navigate around the pitfalls of a frenetic world driven by technology and competition. Their personal mistakes have larger consequences, and their personal achievements yield smaller returns. (p. 7)

For decades, we have understood that juvenile delinquency is caused as much by deprivation of adequate opportunities and resources as it is by intrafamilial problems. Similarly, crime rates in the United States originate in part from violations of social justice: witness the father who, having recently immigrated from Guatemala, steals a fan to keep his young children cool in the midwestern summer heat; or the teenager who is so scared and angry about being caught in a "sweep" and falsely arrested that he punches a police officer. Although homicide, robbery, rape, and assault have all dropped sharply since the highs recorded in the early 1990s, substance abuse has declined less sharply, and drug-related arrests have actually increased steadily, reaching record highs over the past few years. The number of people under some form of correctional supervision has also reached new heights. In 1996, more than 5.5 million Americans (about 2 percent of the total population) were in prison, jail, on probation or parole (Policy Almanac, 2006b).

Institutionalized racism in the criminal justice and correctional systems is so widespread that the United States was cited by Human Rights Watch as violating fundamental human rights. In response to this crisis in justice, social workers need to develop models of practice that respond to such clients' needs; this area has been termed "forensic social work" (for example, Brennan, Gedrich, Jacoby, Tardy, & Tyson, 1986; Sternbach, 2000). Such practice models emphasize the development of an alliance with clients who are involuntarily ordered to receive services and are angry with the social workers as well as the entire situation.

The criminal justice system is just one institution in which racism remains corrosive. Discrimination in education, housing, and employment continues to create and exacerbate disparities between racial subgroups. For example, in the past decade poverty rates declined, the proportion of children living in two-parent families rose, and low-income families had fewer concerns about affording food than before (Zedlewski, 2000; Moore & Vandivere, 2000). Nevertheless, data from the National Survey of America's Families show:

> four widening gaps between white people and black people or white people and Hispanics and three narrowing gaps. The disparity in employment rates between black people and white people (among parents and low-income adults) has decreased, but disparities in housing hardship and the likelihood of being low income have increased. Disparities in child poverty and rates of single-parent families between white people and Hispanics have decreased, but disparities in health status and health insurance among higher-income children have increased. (Stavetig & Wigton, 1999)

As West (2001) wrote so eloquently:

> Race is the most explosive issue in American life precisely because it forces us to confront the tragic facts of poverty and paranoia, despair and mistrust . . . . [A] candid examination of race matters takes us to the core of the crisis of American democracy. And the degree to which race matters in the plight and predicament of fellow citizens is a crucial measure of whether we can keep alive the best of this democratic experiment we call America. (pp. 155–156)

Cumulating the impact of ethnicity, race, and socioeconomic status, it becomes apparent that the most vulnerable group of individuals is those who suffer multiple disadvantages (Foster & Furstenberg, 1999; Taylor & Barush, 2004). Disadvantages compound each other in complex, interactive ways (Sen, 1999a, 1999b): For instance, individuals in poverty are more likely to suffer physical health disorders (Farmer, 2003) and have higher rates of mental disorders than those who are not economically disadvantaged (Buckner & Bassuk, 1997; Zima, Wells, Benjamin, & Duan, 1996). Research findings indicate that the most severely disadvantaged experience the most obstacles to participating in social services, ranging from Temporary Assistance for Needy Families (Cherlin, Bogen, Quane, & Burton, 2002; Taylor & Barush, 2004), to Head Start (Foster, 2002), to mental health services (Rosenheck, 2000). Increasingly, there is documentation of a population that is multiply disadvantaged and whose disadvantages impede these individuals' access to and connection with the very social services that might prevent a spiral into severe physical or mental disorder and complete social alienation.

A 1997 study of homeless and poor urban youths found rates of diagnosed mental disorder as high as 32 percent, and also revealed that 65 to 80 percent of these youths did not receive mental health care (Buckner & Bassuk, 1997). A study of homeless mothers found that although 72 percent suffered from psychological distress, mental disorder, or substance abuse, only 15 percent received any kind of treatment. Moreover, their children showed signs of the behavior disorders that are precursors to adult mental disorder (Zima, Wells, Benjamin, & Duan, 1996). The plight of these people is variously conceptualized as an accumulation of risk (Orovwuje, 2001), or an interactive effect between multiple sources of disadvantage (Sen, 1999a). Multiply-disadvantaged individuals are at high risk for futures as inmates of the criminal justice system, patients in the back wards of state mental hospitals, or permanent dependency on public welfare while living in the most impoverished areas of the United States (Blankertz, Cnaan, & Freedman, 1993; Taylor & Barush, 2004; Woodward, Williams, Nursten, & Badger, 1999).

Although in the past multiply-disadvantaged people who did not use social services often were labeled "untreatable" or "resistant," increasingly it is recognized that the problem is social exclusion: "Social exclusion is the process by which multi-dimensionally disadvantaged individuals are prohibited from obtaining formal helping services. Although not a policy per se, many community helpers and organizations inadvertently contribute to erecting barriers" that discourage multiply-disadvantaged individuals from using services (Hilbert & Krishnan, 2000). A study of rural impoverished individuals with mental disorders concluded that

> few individuals sought professional help and significant others did not encourage them to seek treatment. The implication of these results for investigators and service providers is that motivating individuals to seek mental health services is a complex process; more attention must be devoted to the development of culturally relevant methods for facilitating help seeking. (Fox, Blank, Berman, & Rovnyak, 1999; see also Curtis, 2003)

Social exclusion occurs in many ways: agency policies that do not include help with transportation to appointments, definitions of clients' problems that do not match clients' perceived needs, protocols that clients experience as humiliating, or service providers' lack of understanding of the clients' language and values. A client from one of my first years as a practitioner comes to mind: an elderly gentleman, with a Native American father and an African American mother, who said that he had made his living primarily by being a thief. At age 65, he had stopped his criminal activity, but was suffering from glaucoma and other diseases of aging without even the minimal resources to which he would have been entitled had he been employed. Alarmed by his condition, I began flipping through my Rolodex (for younger readers, this was a manual device for storing addresses) and telling him how he could obtain those resources. He stopped me and said, "Young lady, I don't want you to tell me about those things, I just want you to listen to me."

I learned a great deal from him at that moment and throughout the course of our social work partnership. He told me about growing up in the South under the Jim Crow laws;

how he had sought an education and found himself repeatedly neglected and rejected; the discrimination he had experienced in the workplace; how he had managed to create and maintain sustaining relationships with friends and lovers. In the course of the next year, while telling me his story on a regular basis, he did obtain the resources he needed, but he did so without my advice or explicit encouragement. He taught me that clients who are oppressed by poverty and discrimination need two elements of intervention from social workers: First, knowledge about resources and encouragement in obtaining them; second, the restoration of dignity that can be brought about only when social workers accord their clients the same power to regulate the agenda of the session, and the same right to be listened to, that would be given to a client rich in resources and health. This client taught me that with the restoration of dignity, clients will seek for themselves what they are entitled to, and will do a great deal more for themselves and their loved ones than social workers can foresee.

Providing social services for multiply-disadvantaged clients is a profound challenge. From a macro system perspective, public education and advocacy are major priorities. From the micro system perspective that is the focus of this chapter, however, social workers can expect to encounter clients who are understandably angry or depressed. Some clients may perceive themselves as responding to society-wide injustices, but others may have such a deep need for the security afforded by believing in a just world (Hafer & Begue, 2005) that their frustration gets channeled against themselves or family members. In his comprehensive study of the working poor, Shipler (2004) found that his informants

> rarely are . . . infuriated by their conditions, and when their anger surfaces, it is often misdirected against their spouses, their children, or their co-workers. They do not usually blame their bosses, their government, their country, or the hierarchy of wealth, as they reasonably could. They often blame themselves. (p. x)

Because the erosion of freedom of choice also erodes self-esteem, as Shipler's findings imply, practice models should focus on empowerment and self-determination, while recognizing the therapeutic benefit of problem-solving and resource-providing models (Ewalt & Mokuau, 1995; Gutierrez, Parsons, & Cox, 1998; Ho, Rasheed, & Rasheed, 2003; Pinderhughes, 1989; Saleebey, 2002). Not too long ago, a student shared her concern about a client who had been discussed in a mental health center team meeting. The client, an elderly African American man, had been complaining about racism's effect on his life and his current efforts to obtain a job and health care. The treatment team labeled him "paranoid," whereupon the student exclaimed, "The things he was complaining about are true, though; he was being treated unfairly!" This example demonstrates markers of oppressive processes that workers should be alert for: most notably, when the worker does not focus on the client's motive to experience

211

dignity in an unjust society, and when the worker has a dismissive attitude toward the client's worldview. In addition, this example illustrates how theoretical concepts can be misused to replicate oppressive social processes (here, the term "paranoia"). This leads us to consider whether contemporary practice models can adequately respond to the many challenges confronting social service providers today.

DEVELOPING PRACTICE MODELS TO SERVE VALUES OF SOCIAL JUSTICE AND RESPECT FOR DIVERSITY

Reconceptualizing Fundamental Assumptions

In her pathfinding study of effective social service programs, Schorr (1997) emphasized that effective practitioners have a sound knowledge of practice theories, and are willing to reconsider their tenets and actively modify their theories in order to foster more collaborative relationships with clients. Emphasizing this finding, Wilson (1997) said that developing practice theories and using theory-based approaches to evaluation of services leads to both better social services and advances the development of sound practice knowledge. Certainly, as Guntrip (1975) wrote, theories do not heal people; people heal people. Nevertheless, every social worker is a practice theorist, to some degree, because every practitioner draws on her or his own assumptions and beliefs about how best to plan partnerships with clients. A practice theory is a tool to guide practitioners. Thus, with the aim of honing our tools, the following conceptual framework is offered as a way to examine and improve the responsiveness of practice theories to social justice and diversity concerns.

In the tradition of the post-Kuhnian philosophy of science, it is impossible for science to be value-free; optimally, social scientists reflectively choose the values that their scientific activities express (Tyson, 1995). Following Bhaskar (1989), practice theorists can strive to develop models that have an emancipatory impact. An important way in which social work practice theorists advance social justice is by understanding human beings' experience of the values of social justice, studying processes of exclusion and marginalization, and examining how fairness and democratic ideals can be nurtured in individuals and groups.

A review of 30 practice models revealed that the great majority of practice theorists did not specifically address the question of whether their practice models could be applied to populations other than those treated by the practice theorist (for example, to clients of diverse ages, sexual orientation, or health status, or with different racial, ethnic, or socioeconomic backgrounds). Thus, a major priority for the future is to undertake research about the applicability of practice models to diverse populations. Fortunately, in the past 20 years models of social work practice have been developed to respond to the increasing cultural diversity of clients, and to multiply-disadvantaged clients in particular. Social workers now have models for offering partnerships that empower clients who are faced with socioeconomic oppression, including empowerment models

212

(Gutierrez, Parsons, & Cox, 1998), culturally sensitive practice models (Lum, 2000; Pinderhughes, 1989), and models specifically for the most oppressed clients (such as the strengths perspective applied to severely mentally ill clients [Saleebey, 2002]).

A practice theory or model can be defined as a logically coherent combination of concepts, principles, and assumptions that provide guidance to a social worker in deciding how to relate with a client so as to bring about constructive change. As with all scientific theories (Bhaskar, 1989; Kuhn, 1970; Wimsatt, 1987), the validity and usefulness of many, but not all, of the components of a practice model will be supported by evidence at the time the social worker uses the model. Today there are more than 30 different theories of social work practice, among them aboriginal theory, communications theory, solution-focused therapy, the strengths perspective, existential social work, feminist theory, hypnosis, meditation, narrative theory, transpersonal theory, self psychology, object relations theory, ego psychology, ecological systems theory, strategic and structural family therapy models, ethnic-sensitive practice, empowerment practice, behaviorism, and cognitive behaviorism (Brandell, 1997; Goldstein, 1995; Ho, Rasheed, & Rasheed, 2003; Lum, 2000; Meyer, 1996; Turner, 1996). Some of these practice theories appear to be specific interventions that might seem usable in the context of many other theories—hypnosis is an example. However, hypnosis entails a theory of the unconscious as a force for change that is quite different from a behaviorist's assumptions about behavior change. Therefore, when importing interventions from a different model, a social worker needs to consider whether those interventions and the model from which they spring are consistent with the worker's core ideas.

Analyzing and Comparing Practice Theories
The following conceptual categories can be used to compare aspects of practice theories, to evaluate which aspects of theories can be synthesized and which are incompatible, and to reflectively update theories to be more responsive to the diverse values and priorities of clients and social workers. There are three primary components of theories: (1) assumptions, which are fundamental beliefs and values; (2) principles, which are causal assertions and explanations; and (3) concepts, which are the building blocks of principles and refer to specific aspects of the realities under study. Many of the analytic categories outlined in this chapter have been discussed elsewhere (Tyson, 1995), so the following focuses on categories that have not been previously discussed or that specifically address the values of social justice and respect for diversity.

Assumptions
- What is the reality under study? (Ontology refers to the aspect of reality that the scientist chooses to study, such as subjective experience, behavior, or family relationship patterns)
- How can one know that reality? (Epistemology; for example, free association, structured interview, or observation of family interactions)

- What view of consciousness and unconsciousness is assumed? (for example, Milton Erickson's view of the unconscious as a force for constructive change; Erickson & Haley, 1967; or Freud's [1953–1974] view of inherently conflicted instinctual drives)
- What is the nature of the community assumed in this theory, and how exclusive or inclusive is that community with regard to accepting differences in clients and in workers?

A social worker's ontology defines her or his beliefs about human nature; the epistemology concerns how one human being seeks to know another. The extent to which a practice theorist's assumptions allow for diverse understandings of human nature (including culturally specific spiritual traditions; Sermabeikian, 1994) influences the extent to which a practice theorist will be able to work with the many worldviews presented by an increasingly diverse client population. For instance, First Nations peoples often found that social workers were resistant to including their spirituality in the healing process. One practice model describes how stereotypes can be (unintentionally) imported into the client-worker partnership in the form of cultural transference and countertransference (Shorter-Gooden & Jackson, 2000).

All social work practice models imply a community as a resource, and also assume values about community life, such as degrees of exclusivity and inclusiveness. Social work practice in the United States is probably unique in the global context, in that practice with individuals and small family groups is so common; in most other countries, social work has a deep base in community action and work with larger kinship groups. Surely it is not a coincidence that many United States-based social work practice theories leave out the role of the community. This just reflects the U.S. sociocultural context: what Putnam famously called the "erosion of community" in the United States (2000). At the same time, people of color and many immigrant peoples retain strong traditions of community life that are deeply supportive and healing for their members; such models of community support have the potential to be salutary for other members of U.S. society who have been deprived of supportive communities.

Principles

- What is the mechanism of therapeutic change? (for example, Kohut's "transmuting internalization," Kernberg's ego regulation of the good/bad object split; Consolini, 1999)
- What is the optimal way to define (contract about) the purpose of the client-worker relationship?
- What causes of the problem do the social worker and client aim to remedy?
- How is the effectiveness of the treatment evaluated?
- How is the accuracy of the worker's interventions determined?
- What is the optimal worker response to worker mistakes?

- Who determines the termination of treatment, and what standards are used to do so?
- How do practitioners learn to apply this theory?

An important question raised by a focus on how theories can be applied across cultures is the extent to which principles can be developed that transcend cultural differences. In other words, given that a practice theorist's language and practice context are fairly culture-specific, can practice principles be developed that are universal, based on the aspects of human nature that are common across cultures? Our context includes increasingly diverse clients and even global comparisons, so data can be gathered naturally; hence, the future of global and culturally competent practice may yield answers.

With that question left open, practitioners in the trenches often are in the position of revising theoretical principles so as to better address their clients' diverse values and contexts (Nobles & Sciarra, 2000). In one study, practitioners sought to make a practice model more relevant to a population different from the one with which the model was developed. The practitioners had to modify the practice model considerably: specifically, the process of engagement, the scheduling and location of treatment sessions, the degree to which practitioners facilitated access to other social services and resources, and the approach to termination (Grote, Bledsoe, Swartz, & Frank, 2004).

Different cultural groups hold different beliefs about how healing occurs. They may follow a communitarian way, as in a Native American "healing circle"; or may subscribe to the upper-middle-class U.S. concept that an individual psychotherapeutic relationship is the best way to bring about psychological change. Positing that members of other cultural groups must, to get the "best" help, completely change their natural healing processes replicates the oppressive processes that pervade United States history. In sum, cross-cultural practice entails far more than translation: It requires that the social worker understand the concept of healing in the client's community and build a therapeutic plan with the client that resonates harmoniously with that community's beliefs.

Practice theories have defined goals as well as methods for evaluating whether those goals are being accomplished. The goals may be behavioral, such as the elimination of a phobic response, and be measured by counting the frequency of approach and avoidant behaviors. The goal may be a modification in an internal experience, such as alleviation of chronic self-blame, which would be measured by some form of self-report.

Closely linked to definition of the treatment goal is definition of the termination process. Most practitioners try to determine termination in response to clients' needs. Some clients want and benefit most from extended treatment in residential care; others seek short-term outpatient services (Grote, Bledsoe, Swartz, & Frank, 2004). A psychotherapeutic relationship that lasts several years can help severely traumatized children achieve and maintain normal development; one 10-year-old child emphatically expressed his wish to continue treatment, saying, "This is the beginning of life" (Tyson, 2005). Unfortunately, policies that enforce premature termination subject such clients to the recurrent trauma of severing helpful relationships. An example is the policy that a child welfare counseling agency reluctantly enforced, requiring the agency to limit mental health care for abused and neglected young state wards to six months. Workers and children alike complained passionately that that was not enough time to respond adequately to the developmental needs of these severely traumatized children.

Another important aspect of the termination process, relevant to social justice concerns, is that treatment without an explicit, achievable termination process can deepen clients' sense of isolation from "normal" society, thereby compromising the therapeutic aims of fostering hope and the client's self-recognition of developmental progress and therefore iatrogenically causing regression. Treatment models that continue indefinitely can, by implication, underscore clients' perceptions that the therapist believes the client is defective and that getting better is an unreachable goal. (This is an ironic and often unforeseen consequence, because treatment approaches that avoid termination often do so with a stated rationale of therapist availability.)

Although most practice theories address, to some degree, the first seven principles noted at the beginning of this subsection, the eighth principle—how the practice model can be taught and learned—remains a formidable challenge for all the mental health professions. Codes of ethics regard it as imperative that a practitioner participate in ongoing education and consultation, to assure quality practice. Nonetheless, development of theories about providing sound supervision and consultation, as well as empirical (in the sense of publicly accountable and reliable) processes for evaluating whether practitioners have learned to competently apply a practice model, remain one of the field's foremost priorities for the future (Falvey, 2002).

Concepts
- How is the partnership between worker and client defined?
- What does the social worker do?
- What does the client do?
- What constitutes psychopathology (or dysfunction or maladaptation)?
- What is normalcy?
- How are positive and negative treatment outcomes defined and measured?
- How does this theory define and address diversity?
- How does this theory define and address justice and injustice?

Because practice theories are based on linguistic structures, which in turn are culture-based, practice theorists invariably confront the problem of cultural bias in the process of theory development. For example, some theoretical terms do not translate readily into other languages. In English, the word "I" refers to a solitary self and is often used to refer to an individual's subjective experience of her or his most personal identity. In stark contrast, the term "I" does not exist in the Korean language; in Korean, every "I" denotes the individual in some form of relationship. Such a difference cannot be resolved through mere translation, because the term "I" entails deeply embedded understandings of how an individual is involved with others and the role of one's relationships in the definition and development of oneself. Differences in culturally based linguistic structures have a profound effect on how theories are conveyed, evaluated, and adopted across cultures. Therefore, an important priority for the future is to consider how we can handle this in the context of an increasingly multilingual, global social work profession. For instance, students in Hong Kong may learn practice theories in English, and practice in Chinese: what is happening to the theory and the practice in the process of translation? Perhaps even more importantly, what is happening to the students' experience of their own capacity to evaluate and develop theories that are relevant to their context and their language?

FEATURES OF PRACTICE MODELS EFFECTIVE WITH DIVERSE POPULATIONS: FOSTERING CLIENT SELF-DETERMINATION

To identify common elements that can be used to build practice models for the future, one can draw from practice models developed for partnerships with diverse populations that focus on advancing social justice (Ewalt & Mokuau, 1995; Gutierrez, Parsons, & Cox, 1998; Ho, Rasheed, & Rasheed, 2003; Lum, 2000; Norton,1978; Pinderhughes, 1989; Saleebey, 2002), as well as Schorr's (1997) findings about elements of practice that have been found to be effective. Such elements include:

- a nonhierarchical, respectful, partnership relationship in which clients' expressed purposes form the basis of the contract and plan.
- development of both client autonomy and client connectedness with a nurturing community that supports the client's cultural heritage and values. All close relationships have the potential to be healing for those who have been traumatized (Solomon & Siegel, 2003).
- an understanding of the client's experience of stigma, discrimination, inequality, and lack of resources, and the client's psychological adaptation to those stressors.
- assistance to the client with mourning historical trauma (Ho, Rasheed, & Rasheed, 2003).
- practitioner willingness to be uncertain and to modify practice principles to respond to clients' unique developmental needs (see Everett & Nelson, 1992; Grote, Bledsoe, Swartz, & Frank, 2004; Nobles & Sciarra, 2000).
- a focus on client dignity and self-determination, which has the effect of "helping clients take greater control over their lives" (Schorr, 1997, p. 13).

In concert with the revolution in the understanding of consciousness resulting from contemporary brain science (Baars, Banks, & Newman, 2003; Edelman, 2004; Sperry, 1993), the overarching goal of contemporary and future models of practice is less likely to be predetermined behavior change, and more likely to be helping clients to fulfill their natural motives for competence, self-worth, truth, and justice. Given the findings about how multiple disadvantages cumulate and constrain clients' freedom of choice, focusing on self-determination seems most important. Self-determination need not be understood in terms of culturally limited individualistic values; instead, it can reflect a concept of self more akin to that used in the Korean language, in which the self is always in relationship. For instance, "self-determination for cultures from the Pacific region is characterized by relationships of collective affiliation rather than individualism" (Ewalt & Mokuau, 1995, p. 170). The importance of this emphasis was foreshadowed by Chestang (1976) when he wrote that the social exclusion that results from discrimination

> results in two alternatives for the individual. He can succumb to the erosive denials of his humanity, or he can, as Merton has indicated, perform adaptive maneuvers to preserve his integrity. In the case of the black person interacting with the wider society, to choose the first alternative is to elect an empty physical survival while surrendering the dignity that is the essence of humanity. To choose the second, when one considers the cost, whether in the output of psychological energy or in the threat, under some circumstances, to physical survival, indicates the power of the impulse towards being—the inner push toward self-realization. (p. 70)

Self-determination can be synonymous with self-realization. It can include several components. For instance, people's health is compromised when they are pressured to accept acculturation. Thus, clients confronted with multiple cultural values can be supported in determining for themselves which values to adopt. LaFramboise and colleagues (1998) conceptualized an "alternation model" for multicultural clients, in which clients choose the cultural values that promise to give them the most dignity and freedom in their particular context.

Given the considerable research, documentation, and literature available about the value of developing client strengths, the empowerment models for the future are based on such an emphasis. At the same time, a conceptualization of goals and impediments to reaching those goals is needed, and for that one can draw from Amartya Sen's Nobel Prize-winning work in welfare economics. He reconceptualized social development based on the freedom of individual agency, or choice (Sen, 1999a, 1999b), a focus that echoes the social work profession's long-standing value of self-determination—both as a goal of treatment and as a value against which to measure specific casework interventions. While recognizing the importance of improving material resources for people who are experiencing economic disadvantage, Sen emphasized that the aim of social develop-ment is to expand human beings' freedom to live the kinds of lives that people have reason to value (1999a). He defined five distinct types of freedom, all of which focus on human choice: "(1) political freedoms, (2) economic facilities, (3) social opportunities, (4) transparency guarantees, and (5) protective security" (1999a, p. 10). The last two concepts of freedom are very relevant for social workers who seek to establish nurturing communities. By "transparency guarantees," Sen (1999a) means the need for openness that people can expect: the freedom to deal with one another under guarantees of disclosure and lucidity. When that trust is seriously violated, the lives of many people—both direct parties and third parties—may be adversely affected by the lack of openness . . . . These guarantees have a clear instrumental role in preventing corruption, financial irresponsibility and underhand dealings. (p. 40)

By "protective security," Sen means citizens' need for social, economic, and medical safety nets, which are lacking in many countries as well as in many communities in the United States. Sen's concept of unfreedom includes the recognition that threats to human sustenance are physically dangerous and psychologically shackling. His understanding of freedom offers a conceptual framework for understanding how the different layers of systems within which clients reside influence clients in the most intimate details of their lives: freedom of choice.

Empowerment models of the future can be significantly advanced by insights from research, if that research includes characteristics that are designed to foster, rather than obstruct, the constructive closeness between social workers and clients. Several practitioner-relevant approaches to research that have developed over the past decade offer practitioners scientifically valid ways of sharing their insights and learning from each other without compromising their values of supporting clients' self-determination and human rights (Hartman, 1990; Tyson, 1995; Witkin & Gottschalk, 1988). A consumer-focused empowerment approach to research offers unique advantages (Rapp, Shera, & Kisthart, 1993). Among the most important are that client feedback can bring to light iatrogenic practice processes that might otherwise be obscured by research that leaves out clients' perspectives or focuses only on outcomes. Also, social workers can share the fruits of their practice research with their clients (consumers). "If knowledge is power, then knowledge must be placed in the hands of those we seek to empower"; for example, through dissemination of research in client community gatherings and translation of results into laypeople's languages (Rapp, Shera, & Kisthart, 1993, p. 733). Finally, researchers can actively involve community members as participants in formulating problems, collecting data, and analyzing and disseminating findings, all with the goal of advancing their communities. This action-oriented and participant-focused approach to research offers the significant benefit of providing education and skills training to community members who are also participants in the research, and makes research a handmaiden of the empowerment process (Laws, Harper, & Marcus, 2003).

CONCLUSIONS

Many empirical studies document the powerful relationship between experiences of community and leadership and individuals' ideals of justice, self-esteem, and sense of empowerment. For example, when teammates' behavior consistently reflects natural ideals of justice, each individual team member's sense of justice is strengthened, as well as that of the team as a whole (Colquitt, 2004). When community leaders generously reward treatment and fairness toward community members, the self-esteem and sense of empowerment of the community members are powerfully strengthened (DeCremer, Van Knippenberg, Van Knippenberg, Mullenders, & Stinglhamber, 2005).

> If group authorities treat people with dignity, people infer that they are respected members within the group and that there is good reason to have pride in their group membership. If group authorities treat people rudely, people infer that they are not well-respected members within the group and that there is no valid reason to have pride in their group membership. (van Prooijen, van den Boss, & Wilke, 2004)

In other words, justice is more than a belief or an abstract ideal: People live and experience justice every day in their communities, and the quality of each individual's community influences the development of that person's sense of justice, how she or he treats others, and her or his most private experience of value and competence.

These findings have important implications for social workers. In fact, Schorr (1997) emphasized that if social service providers are to offer effective relationships, they need organizational community contexts that support the essential factors of those effective relationships: "Life-transforming relationships do not exist in a vacuum—they must be sustained by supportive institutions" (p. 10). The community of practitioners in which a social worker resides potentially has a profound effect on his or her practice and development as a social worker. Learning from others by example, benefiting from their support during hard times, and being inspired by others are among the most important functions a community can provide for social workers.

However, developing a nurturing community is challenging. It is easy for human communities to be exclusive. Chestang (1976) defined one of the characteristics of oppressive communities as "social inconsistency," a form of "social immorality" in which practices do not match words (p. 62). Throughout the history of the United States, and of many other countries, ranging from the totalitarian Soviet Union to Communist China to Nazi Germany, communities that espouse ideals of justice and claims to truth have acted quite differently, persecuting and excluding those who look different or hold different beliefs. Persecution occurs on the basis of differences in beliefs alone, even in psychotherapy "communities" such as Freud's psychoanalytic "Committee" (Sulloway, 1991); more often, differences in race, culture, and class become lightning rods for exclusion and persecution. Although exclusionary behavior opposes values of democracy and social justice, group members doing the excluding tend not to recognize their own inconsistency, because they project their own hostile motives onto those they persecute. Individuals who strive to bring about more justice and inclusiveness usually confront considerable opposition from others who fear inclusion of marginalized individuals or believe that inclusion would be harmful (for example, a cause of some significant loss). Creating nurturing communities is perhaps even more challenging in the United States, where increasingly people are different from each other in many ways, and the individual-oriented values of the mainstream culture can erode community values. Yet, if U.S. citizens are to rebuild community life, we need to "transcend our social and political and professional identities to connect with people unlike ourselves" (Putnam, 2000, p. 411).

To bring about a better society, it is as important to articulate the sought-for good as it is to identify the obstacles to accomplishment of that good. What does an empowering, inclusive community look like? Powerful examples of effective community formation can be found in various struggles for human freedom and dignity, from the civil rights movement, to the liberation of South Africa from apartheid, to the movements for freedom from the oppression of Soviet communism (Schell, 2003). Those movements are characterized by a community praxis that is broadly accepting of diversity of opinion, endorsing community values of inclusion and foregoing vindictiveness or rejection of others.

One significant aspect of Cafferty's work is its emphasis on social work's long-standing commitment to making society more just. When Cafferty authored *The Diverse Society* (1976), the United States was still recovering from the traumas of the Vietnam War and the intense racial conflict that was the legacy of the subjugation of people of color in the United States. Just eight years before the publication of *The Diverse Society*, leading social workers had found it necessary to walk out of the National Association of Social Workers' annual meeting, because of insensitivity to the needs of people of color and African American people in particular. In response, the National Association of Black Social Workers was formed; only six years later, in 1983, the National Association for Puerto Rican and Hispanic Social Workers was founded. Thus, one of the most important steps taken during that time was the formation of communities that could advocate for the dignity, values, and rights of their members and work toward a more democratic society. In the academic sector, that advocacy was embodied in *The Diverse Society*, which was groundbreaking in its reflective approach to the problems of social exclusion and social inconsistency and its proposal of the ideal of an inclusive community. It inspired social workers to live up to the democratic ideals that are the foundation of our profession, and set a standard that can continue to guide the community of social work practitioners and scholars as we seek to "give birth again to the dream."

END NOTE
* I am most appreciative of the thoughtful comments of Professors Harold Richman, Lissette Piedra, and David Engstrom on earlier versions of this chapter, and I am also grateful for the support, insight, and examples provided me so generously over the years by Professors Dolores Norton, Janice Rasheed, and Daniel Lee.

REFERENCES

Addams, J. (1990). *Twenty years at Hull House.* Urbana: University of Illinois Press. (Original work published 1910)

Adler, N. E., Boyce, T., Chesney, M. A., Cohen, S., Folman, S., Kahn, R. L., & Syme, S. L. (2002). Socioeconomic status and health: The challenge of the gradient. In J. Cacioppo, G. Berntson, R. Adolphs, C. Carter, R. Davison, M. McClintock, B. McEwen, M. Meaney, D. Schacter, E. Sternberg, S. Suomi, & S. Taylor (Eds.), *Foundations in social neuroscience* (pp. 1095–1110). Cambridge. MA: MIT Press.

Anderson, S., Halter, A., & Gryzlak, B. (2004). Difficulties after leaving TANF: Inner-city women talk about reasons for returning to welfare. *Social Work, 49,* 185–194.

Angelou, Maya. (1993). "On the pulse of the morning: The inaugural poem." New York: Random House. Retrieved March 23, 2006, from http://eserver.org/poetry/angelou.html

Aponte, J. F., & Johnson, L. R. (2000). The impact of culture on the intervention and treatment of ethnic populations. In J. F. Aponte & J. Wohl (Eds.), *Psychological intervention and cultural diversity* (2nd ed., pp. 18–39). Boston: Allyn & Bacon.

Baars, B., Banks, W., & Newman, J. (2003). *Essential sources in the scientific study of consciousness.* Cambridge, MA: MIT Press.

Baker, S. G., Bean, F., Latapi, A. E., & Weintraub, S. (1998). U.S. immigration policies and trends: The growing importance of immigration from Mexico. In M. M. Suarez-Orozco (Ed.), *Crossings: Mexican immigration in interdisciplinary perspectives* (pp. 79–112). Cambridge, MA: Harvard University Press.

Bhaskar, R. (1989). *Reclaiming reality: A critical introduction to contemporary philosophy.* London: Verso.

Blankertz, L. E., Cnaan, R. A., & Freedman, E. (1993). Childhood risk factors in dually diagnosed homeless adults. *Social Work, 38,* 587–596.

Brandell, J. (1997). *Theory and practice in clinical social work.* New York: Free Press.

Brennan, T., Gedrich, A., Jacoby, S., Tardy, M., & Tyson, K. (1986). Forensic social work: Practice and vision. *Social Casework, 67,* 340–350.

Brown, S., & Leibovitz, H. (1999). *National survey of family well-being exposes vulnerability and reveals strengths of low-income families.* Washington, DC: Urban Institute. Retrieved November 28, 2004, from http://www.urban.org

Buckner, J. C., & Bassuk, E. L. (1997). Mental disorders and service utilization among youths from homeless and low-income housed families. Journal of the American *Academy of Child and Adolescent Psychiatry, 36,* 890–900.

Cafferty, P.S.J., & Chestang, L. (Eds.). (1976). *The diverse society: Implications for social policy.* Silver Spring, MD: NASW Press.

Centers for Disease Control and Prevention. (2004, November). Infant mortality statistics from the 2002 period linked birth/infant death data set. NVSR 53(10), 30 pp. (PHS) 2005-1120. Retrieved November 28, 2004, from http://www.cdc.gov/nchs/pressroom/04facts/healthcare.html

Cherlin, A. J., Bogen, K., Quane, J. M., & Burton, L. (2002). Operating within the rules: Welfare recipients' experiences with sanctions and case closings. *Social Service Review, 39,* 387–405.

Chestang, L. (1976). The black experience. In P.S.J. Cafferty & L. Chestang (Eds.), *The diverse society: Implications for social policy* (pp. 59–74). Silver Spring, MD: NASW Press.

Colquitt, J. (2004). Does the justice of the one interact with the justice of the many? Reactions to procedural justice in teams. *Journal of Applied Psychology, 89,* 633–646.

Consolini, G. (1999). Kernberg vs. Kohut: A (case) study in contrasts. *Clinical Social Work Journal,* *27,* 71–86.

Curtis, C. (2003). Why special populations are not the target of family preservation services: A case for program reform. *Journal of Sociology and Social Welfare, 30,* 149–164.

Daly, A., Jennings, J., Beckett, J. O., & Leashore, B. (2000). Effective coping strategies of African Americans. *Social Work, 40,* 240–248.

DeCremer, D., Van Knippenberg, B., Van Knippenberg, D., Mullenders, D., & Stinglhamber, F. (2005). Rewarding leadership and fair procedures as determinants of self-esteem. *Journal of Applied Psychology, 90,* 3–12.

Dunkel, J., Ageson, A., & Ralph, C. (2000). Encountering violence in field work: A risk reduction model. *Journal of Teaching in Social Work, 20*(3/4), 5–15.

Edelman, G. (2004). *Wider than the sky: The phenomenal gift of consciousness.* New Haven, CT: Yale University Press.

Erickson, M., & Haley, J. (1967). *Advanced techniques of hypnosis and therapy: Selected techniques of Milton H. Erickson.* Boston: Allyn & Bacon.

Everett, B., & Nelson, A. (1992). We're not cases and you're not managers: An account of a client-professional partnership developed in response to the "borderline" diagnosis. *Psychosocial Rehabilitation Journal, 15*(4), 49–60.

Ewalt, P., & Mokuau, N. (1995). Self-determination from a Pacific perspective. *Social Work, 40,* 168–175.

Falvey, J. (with Bray, T.). (2002). *Managing clinical supervision: Ethical practice and legal risk management.* Pacific Grove, CA: Brooks/Cole.

Farmer, P. (2003). *Pathologies of power: Health, human rights, and the new war on the poor.* Berkeley: University of California Press.

Foster, E. M. (2002). Trends in multiple and overlapping disadvantages among Head Start enrollees. *Children and Youth Services Review, 24,* 933–954.

Foster, E. M., & Furstenberg, E. F. (1999). The most disadvantaged children: Trends over time. *Social Service Review, 7,* 560–578.

Fox, J. C., Blank, M., Berman, J., & Rovnyak, V. G. (1999). Mental disorders and help seeking in a rural impoverished population. *International Journal of Psychiatry in Medicine, 29,* 181–195.

Freire, P. (1970). *Pedagogy of the oppressed.* New York: Herder and Herder.

Freud, S. (1953–1974). J. Strachey (Ed., in collaboration with Anna Freud), *The standard edition of the complete psychological works of Sigmund Freud* (Vols. 1–24). London: Hogarth Press.

Goldstein, E. (1995). *Ego psychology and social work practice* (2nd ed.). New York: Free Press.

Grote, N. K., Bledsoe, S. E., Swartz, H. A., & Frank, E. (2004). Culturally relevant psychotherapy for perinatal depression in low-income ob-gyn patients. *Clinical Social Work Journal, 32,* 327–347.

Guntrip, H. (1975). My experience of analysis with Fairbairn and Winnicott: How complete a result does psycho-analytic therapy achieve? *International Review of Psychoanalysis, 2,* 145–156.

Gutierrez, L. M., Parsons, R. J., & Cox, E. O. (1998). *Empowerment in social work practice: A sourcebook.* Pacific Grove, CA: Brooks/Cole.

Hafer, C. L., & Begue, L. (2005). Experimental research on just-world theory: Problems, developments, and future challenges. *Psychological Bulletin, 131,* 128–167.

Hartman, A. (1990). Many ways of knowing [Editorial]. *Social Work, 35,* 3–4.

Hilbert, J. C., & Krishnan, S. P. (2000). Addressing barriers to community care of battered women in rural environments: Creating a policy of social inclusion. *Journal of Health and Social Policy, 12,* 41–52.

Ho, M. K., Rasheed, J. M., & Rasheed, M. N. (Eds.). (2003). Family therapy with ethnic minorities: Similarities and differences. In M. K. Ho, J. M. Rasheed, & M. N. Rasheed (Eds.), *Family therapy with ethnic minorities* (pp. 284–330). Thousand Oaks, CA: Sage Publications.

Kay, A. C., & Jost, J. T. (2003). Complementary justice: Effects of "poor but happy" and "poor but honest" stereotype exemplars on system justification and implicit activation of the justice motive. *Journal of Personality and Social Psychology, 85,* 823–837.

Kuhn, T. S. (1970). *The structure of scientific revolutions.* Chicago: University of Chicago Press.

LaFramboise, T., Coleman, H., & Gerton, J. (1998). Psychological impact of biculturalism: Evidence and theory. In P. B. Organista, K. Chung, & G. Marin (Eds.), *Readings in ethnic psychology* (pp. 123–155). New York: Routledge.

Laws, S., Harper, C., & Marcus, R. (2003). *Research for development: A practical guide.* London: Sage Publications.

Leung, K., Tong, K., & Ho, S. (2004). Effects of interactional justice on egocentric bias in resource allocation decisions. *Journal of Applied Psychology, 89,* 405–415.

Lewontin, R. (2000). *Human diversity.* New York: Scientific American Library, HPHLP.

Lum, D. (2000). *Social work practice and people of color: A process-stage approach* (4th ed.). Monterey, CA: Brooks/Cole.

Marziali, E. (1991). The power of therapeutic relationship. *American Journal of Orthopsychiatry, 61,* 383–391.

Mattison, M. (2000). Ethical decision-making: The person in the process. *Social Work, 45,* 201–212.

McIntosh, P. (1988). White privilege and male privilege: A personal account of coming to see correspondences through work in women's studies. *Race and Racism,* 94–105.

Meyer, C. (1996). *Assessment in social work practice.* New York: Columbia University Press.

Moore, K., & Vandivere, S. (2000). Children's family environment. In *Snapshots of America's families II: A view of the nation and 13 states from the National Survey of America's Families.* Retrieved November 28, 2004, from www.urban.org/ANF

Nobles, A. Y., & Sciarra, D. T. (2000). Cultural determinants in the treatment of Arab Americans: A primer for mainstream therapists. *American Journal of Orthopsychiatry, 70,* 182–191.

Norton, D. (1978). *The dual perspective.* New York: Council on Social Work Education.

Orovwuje, P. R. (2001). The business model and social work: A conundrum for social work practice. *Social Work in Health Care, 34*(1/2), 59–70.

Perlman, H. H. (1979). *Relationship, the heart of helping people.* Chicago: University of Chicago Press.

Petitto, L., & Marentette, P. (1991). Babbling in the manual mode: Evidence for the ontogeny of language. *Science, 251,* 1493–1496.

Pinderhughes, E. (1989). *Understanding race, ethnicity, and power: The key to efficacy in clinical practice.* New York: Free Press.

Policy Almanac. (2006a). Retrieved March 23, 2006, from http://www.policyalmanac.org/crime/death_penalty.shtml

Policy Almanac. (2006b). Retrieved March, 23, 2006, from http://www.policyalmanac.org/crime/index.shtml

Portes, A., & Rumbaut, R. G. (2001). *Legacies: The story of the immigrant second generation.* Berkeley: University of California Press.

Putnam, R. (2000). *Bowling alone: The collapse and revival of American community.* New York: Simon & Schuster.

Rapp, C., Shera, W., & Kisthart, W. (1993). Research strategies for consumer empowerment of people with severe mental illness. *Social Work, 38,* 727–735.

Reamer, F. (1991). AIDS, social work, and the duty to protect. *Social Work, 36,* 56–60.

Richmond, M. (1922). *What is social casework? An introductory description.* Philadelphia: Russell Sage Foundation (W. F. Fell Co., Printers).

Rosenheck, R. (2000). The delivery of mental health services in the 21st century: Bringing the community back in. *Community Mental Health Journal, 36*(1), 107–124.

Saleebey, D. (2002). *The strengths perspective in social work practice* (3rd ed.). Boston: Allyn & Bacon.

Schell, J. (2003). *The unconquerable world: Power, nonviolence and the will of the people.* New York: Henry Holt.

Schorr, L. B. (1997). *Common purpose: Strengthening families and neighborhoods to rebuild America.* New York: Anchor Books.

Sen, A. (1999a). *Development as freedom.* New York: Random House.

Sen, A. (1999b). The possibility of social choice. *American Economic Review, 89,* 349–378.

Sermabeikian, P. (1994). Our clients, ourselves: The spiritual perspective and social work practice. *Social Work, 39,* 178–183.

Shipler, David. (2004). *The working poor: Invisible in America.* New York: Alfred A. Knopf.

Shorter-Gooden, K., & Jackson, L. C. (2000). The interweaving of cultural and intrapsychic issues in the therapeutic relationship. In L. C. Jackson & B. Greene (Eds.), *Psychotherapy with African American women: Innovations in psychodynamic perspectives and practice* (pp. 15–32). New York: Guilford.

Small, M. (1998). *Our babies, our selves: How biology and culture shape the way we parent.* New York: Doubleday Anchor.

Solomon, M., & Siegel, D. (Eds.). (2003). *Healing trauma: Attachment, mind, body and brain.* New York: W.W. Norton.

Sperry, R. W. (1993). The impact and promise of the cognitive revolution. *American Psychologist, 48,* 878–885.

Spitz, R. (1945). Hospitalism: An inquiry into the genesis of psychiatric conditions in early childhood. *Psychoanalytic Study of the Child, 1,* 53–74.

Stavetig, S., & Wigton, A. (1999). *1999 snapshots of America's families II.* Washington, DC: Urban Institute. Retrieved November 28, 2004, from www.urban.org/ANF

Sternbach, J. (2000). Lessons learned about working with men: A prison memoir. *Social Work, 45,* 413–423.

Straus, M. (1991). Discipline and deviance: Physical punishment of children and violence and other crime in adulthood. *Social Problems, 38,* 133–154.

Strom-Gottfried, K. (2000). Ensuring ethical practice: An examination of NASW code violations, 1986–1997. *Social Work, 45,* 251–261.

Sulloway, F. (1991). Reassessing Freud's case histories: The social construction of psychoanalysis. *Isis, 82,* 245–275.

Taylor, M. J., & Barush, A. S. (2004). Personal, family, and multiple barriers of long-term welfare recipients. *Social Work, 49,* 175–183.

Towle, C. (1936). Factors in treatment. In *Proceedings of the National Conference on Social Work, 63rd Annual Session,* Atlantic City. Chicago: University of Chicago Press.

Trevarthan, C., & Aitken, K. J. (2001). Infant intersubjectivity: Research, theory, and clinical applications. *Journal of Child Psychology and Psychiatry, 42*(1), 3–48.

Turner, F. (1996). *Social work treatment* (4th ed.). New York: Free Press.

Tyson, K. (1995). *New foundations for scientific social and behavioral research: The heuristic paradigm.* Needham Heights, MA: Allyn & Bacon.

Tyson, K. (2005). *Developing self-determination from the child's perspective: Effective social services for traumatized children*. Invitational Lecture for International Social Work Conference, University of Lapland Department of Social Sciences, Rovaniemi, Finland.

van Prooijen, J., van den Boss, W., & Wilke, H. (2004). Group belongingness and procedural justice: Social inclusion and exclusion by peers affects the psychology of voice. *Journal of Personality and Social Psychology, 87*, 66–79.

Walsh, Y. (2001). Deconstructing "brainwashing" within cults as an aid to counseling psychologists. *Counselling Psychology Quarterly, 14*(2), 119–129.

West, C. (2001). *Race matters*. New York: Random House.

Wilson, W. J. (1997). Introduction. In L. B. Shorr (Ed.), *Common purpose: Strengthening families and neighborhoods to rebuild America* (pp. ix–xii). New York: Anchor Books.

Wimsatt, W. C. (1987). False models as means to truer theories. In M. H. Niteck & A. Hoffman (Eds.), *Neutral models in biology* (pp. 23–55). New York: Oxford University Press.

Wimsatt, W. C. (1990–1991). *Teaching notes*. Unpublished manuscript.

Wimsatt, W. (2002). Using false models to elaborate constraints on processes: Blending inheritance in organic and cultural evolution. *Philosophy of Science, 69*, S12–S24.

Witkin, S., & Gottschalk, S. (1988). Alternative criteria for theory evaluation. *Social Service Review, 62*, 211–224.

Woodward, M., Williams, P., Nursten, J., & Badger, D. (1999). The epidemiology of mentally disordered offending: A systematic review of studies, based on the general population, of criminality combined with psychiatric illness. *Journal of Epidemiology and Biostatistics, 4*(2), 101–113.

Wyche, K. F. (2001). Sociocultural issues in counseling for women of color. In R. Unger (Ed.), *Handbook of the psychology of women and gender* (pp. 330–340). New York: John Wiley & Sons.

Zedlewski, S. (2000). Family economic well-being. In *Snapshots of America's families II: A view of the nation and 13 states from the national survey of America's families*. Washington, DC: Urban Institute.

Zima, B. T., Wells, K. B., Benjamin, B., & Duan, N. (1996). Mental health problems among homeless mothers: Relationship to service use and child mental health problems. *Archives of General Psychiatry, 53*, 332–338.

INDEX

ABOUT THE EDITORS

DAVID W. ENGSTROM, PHD, MA, is associate professor of social work at San Diego State University. He received his MA in 1983 and his PhD in 1992 from the School of Social Service Administration, University of Chicago. Dr. Engstrom is author of *Presidential Decision Making Adrift: The Carter Administration and the Mariel Boatlift* and coauthor of *Hispanics in the United States*. His research interests focus on immigration policy and services to immigrants and refugees. Dr. Engstrom has written extensively on the plight of vulnerable immigrant populations, such as torture survivors, trafficked people, and people who have suffered from political violence. In addition, Dr. Engstrom has explored the role of bilingual social workers in service delivery.

LISSETTE M. PIEDRA, PHD, MSW, is assistant professor at the University of Illinois, Urbana-Champaign. She has served on the internal advisory board of the Center for Democracy in a Multiracial Society. Dr. Piedra received her MSW from Loyola University-Chicago and her PhD from the School of Social Service Administration, University of Chicago. Her research interests center on how race and ethnicity intersect with class to influence the development, delivery, and use of health and social services for vulnerable populations. Dr. Piedra is particularly interested in the way that language issues affect the delivery of health and social services and how the use of language interpreters alters the dyadic nature of helping relationships into triadic relationships. Her work has appeared in the *Journal for Immigrant and Refugee Services* and in the *Illinois Child Welfare* journal.

ABOUT THE AUTHORS

SARAH K. BRUCH, MPA, is a doctoral student in the Sociology Department at the University of Wisconsin–Madison. She received an MPA from the Evans School of Public Affairs at the University of Washington. Her research interests include the identification and understanding of the pathways through which inequalities are exacerbated or ameliorated. She is interested in investigating how social policies and structures within society work as stratification mechanisms, how they shape access to opportunities, and how they ameliorate or exacerbate existing social inequalities and alleviate poverty.

ANDREW M. GREELEY, PhD, MA, is professional lecturer as the University of Arizona and research associate at the Ogburn-Stouffer Center for the Study of Social Organization. Father Greeley is an ordained Catholic priest who holds an MA and PhD in sociology from the University of Chicago. A prolific writer, he has published 98 books, including the path-breaking *Ethnicity in the U.S.: A Preliminary Reconnaissance* and *Ethnic Drinking Subcultures*. A widely read and respected researcher, Father Greeley has published in major academic journals such as *American Journal of Sociology, Ethnicity, Scientific American*, and *Public Interest*. His social, political, and religious analyses have been featured in *The New York Times*, the *Atlantic Monthly*, and *Commonweal*.

ANNA HALEY-LOCK, PhD, MA, is assistant professor at the School of Social Work, University of Washington. She received her MA and PhD degrees from the School of Social Service Administration, University of Chicago. Dr. Haley-Lock's organizationally focused research examines how work is designed, rewarded, and experienced for those employed in human services and low-wage or low-skill jobs. She is particularly interested in how a range of employment benefits facilitates workers' professional and personal development and the well-being of their families and communities. Dr. Haley-Lock also considers the link between human resource management strategies and organizational performance, in the forms of effective workforce recruitment, retention, and diversity.

NORA L. ISHIBASHI, PhD, MSW, MA, is a psychotherapist and consultant who treats children and adults in private practice in Chicago. Dr. Ishibashi holds an MA in the anthropology of comparative cultures from Sophia University in Tokyo and an MSW from the Jane Addams College of Social Work, University of Illinois, Chicago. She received her doctorate from the School of Social Service Administration, University of Chicago. Dr. Ishibashi has extensive experience in school social work, as well as in the provision of consultation to social workers in diverse settings. She has taught seminars on clinical practice and parenting and has presented around the country on these topics. Her work on the treatment of multicultural adolescents has appeared in the *Journal of School Social Work*.

239

EDWARD F. LAWLOR, PHD, is the dean and William E. Gordon Professor at the George Warren Brown School of Social Work, Washington University, St. Louis. He received his PhD from the Florence Heller Graduate School for Advanced Studies in Social Welfare, Brandeis University in Massachusetts. Professor Lawlor has published widely on access to health care, policy analysis, health care reform, and aging. He is author of *Redesigning the Medicare Contract: Politics, Markets, and Agency* and founding editor of the *Public Policy and Aging Report.*

CHARLES HOWARD LIPPY, PHD, MDIV, is the LeRoy A. Martin Distinguished Professor of Religious Studies at the University of Tennessee at Chattanooga. Dr. Lippy has been a visiting professor at Emory University, Atlanta, and University of North Carolina at Chapel Hill and has taught at Clemson University for 18 years. He received his master's in divinity degree from the Union Theological Seminary and a PhD from Princeton University. Dr. Lippy has served as president of the Southeastern Region of the American Academy of Religion, and is the author or editor of 18 books, including *Pluralism Comes of Age: American Religion in the Twentieth Century.*

DAMIAN J. MARTINEZ, MA, holds a joint appointment in the School of Criminal Justice and the Department of Social Work at Rutgers University, Newark, New Jersey. He is a PhD candidate at the School of Social Service Administration at the University of Chicago. Mr. Martinez holds a BA in sociology from the University of California at Los Angeles (UCLA) and an MA in social service administration from the University of Chicago. His research interests include social work and corrections; former prisoner re-entry; Hispanics/Latinos in the criminal justice system; and the dynamics of, and support mechanisms involved in, released former prisoners' re-entry into families. Mr. Martinez's work has appeared in the *Journal of Ethnicity in Criminal Justice* and the *Columbia Human Rights Law Review.*

NORIKO ISHIBASHI MARTINEZ, MSW, teaches at the School of Social Work, Loyola University-Chicago; and is a school social worker in a program for at-risk adolescents in Evanston, Illinois. She is working toward her doctorate at the School of Social Service Administration at the University of Chicago. Ms. Martinez received her bachelor's degree from New York University in anthropology and linguistics, and her MSW from Loyola University-Chicago. She is interested in international social work, the impact of clients on clinicians, and the intersection of language, culture, and clinical decision making.

KATHERINE TYSON MCCREA, PHD, MDIV, is professor of social work at Loyola University-Chicago and is the founding editor-in-chief of the journal *Illinois Child Welfare.* She holds a BA and MDiv from Yale University and received her MA and PhD degrees from the School of Social Service Administration, University of Chicago. Dr. McCrea is the author of *New Foundations for Scientific Social and Behavior Research: The Heuristic Paradigm*. Most recently, her research has involved international collaborative work in the areas of social work education and the pursuit of social justice and community development, especially in economically deprived and socially traumatized communities.

GINA MIRANDA SAMUELS, PHD, MSSW, is an assistant professor at the School of Social Service Administration, University of Chicago. She holds a BS in social work from the University of Wisconsin-Oshkosh and an MSSW and PhD in social welfare from the University of Wisconsin–Madison. Her research is interpretive and broadly explores the processes of constructing social and personal identities in the context of foster care and adoption. Dr. Samuels's specific interests examine how structural factors (for example, race, foster care, or adoption placement) inform patterns of maintaining or seeking out biological and nonbiological family relationships and shape how sociocultural identities develop and function across the life course. She uses the extended case method to restructure identity theories and to inform child welfare practice and policy.

TERESA A. SULLIVAN, PHD, is provost and executive vice president for academic affairs at the University of Michigan, Ann Arbor, where she is also professor of sociology. Professor Sullivan received her PhD in sociology from the University of Chicago and was affiliated with the University of Texas from 1981 to 2006 as a member of the faculty and as executive vice president of the University of Texas system. As a labor force demographer, Dr. Sullivan's research interests are issues of economic marginality. She is coauthor of the award-winning book, *The Fragile Middle Class,* and coauthor of the leading textbook on the sociology of work, *The Social Organization of Work* (3d ed.).

MARIA DE LOS ANGELES TORRES is professor and director of Latin American and Latino Studies at the University of Illinois, Chicago. She received her PhD in political science from the University of Michigan, Ann Arbor. Dr. Torres served as executive director, Mayor's Advisory Committee on Latino Affairs, City of Chicago, from 1983 to 1987. She has authored two books: *The Lost Apple: Operation Pedro Pan, Cuban Children in the U.S. and the Promise of a Better Future,* and *In the Land of Mirrors: U.S. Cuban Exile Politics.* She is editor of an anthology, *By Heart/De Memoria: Cuban Women's Journeys in and out of Exile,* and coedited *Borderless Borders: Latinos, Latin America, and the Paradoxes of Interdependence.* Dr. Torres has published extensively on the political participation of Latinos and has been a regular contributor to *The Nation,* the *Washington Post,* and the *Chicago Tribune.*